THE SPIRIT IN THE CHURCH
and
THE WORLD

THE SPIRIT IN THE CHURCH AND THE WORLD

Bradford E. Hinze

Editor

THE ANNUAL PUBLICATION
OF THE COLLEGE THEOLOGY SOCIETY
2003
VOLUME 49

ORBIS BOOKS

Maryknoll, New York 10545

Library of Congress Cataloging-in-Publication Data

The Spirit in the church and the world / Bradford E. Hinze, editor.
    p. cm. — (The Annual publication of the College Theology Society ; 2003, v. 49)
Includes bibliographical references.
    ISBN 1-57075-528-0 (pbk.)
    1. Holy Spirit—Congresses.   2. Catholic Church—Doctrines—Congresses.   I. Hinze, Bradford E., 1954- II. Series.
    BT121.3.S64 2004
    231'.3—dc22
                    2004001439

In gratitude for the life of
Stephen P. Happel (1944-2003),
who served the People of God as presbyter and theologian
with extraordinary intelligence, wit, and warmth.

Contents

PART III
ADVANCING THE SPIRIT'S WORK OF COMMUNION AND JUSTICE

Acknowledgments

I would like to thank the Board of Directors of the College Theology Society Board for the invitation to serve as editor of this volume. Let me express my sincere thanks to Bernd Jochen Hilberath, Robert J. Schreiter, and Jamie T. Phelps for their plenary addresses at the convention. This volume also is indebted to all those who presented papers at the convention and who submitted essays for consideration. The essays included in this volume are but a fraction of the quality work submitted.

I owe a special debt of thanks to all of those who generously served as referees in the evaluation process and I am pleased that previous editors have listed the names of the referees as a witness and tribute to the standards of excellence and collective deliberation this project represents. They include Gerald Vigna (Alvernia College); Jane Russell (Belmont Abbey College); Bruce Morrill (Boston College); Dawn M. Nothwehr (Catholic Theological Union); William Loewe (Catholic University of America); Barbara Miller (Edgewood College); Mary Hines (Emmanuel College); Fred Norris (Emmanuel School of Religion); Elizabeth Dreyer (Fairfield University); John O'Donnell (Gregorian University); T. Howland Sanks (Jesuit School of Theology, Berkeley); Shannon Schrein (Lourdes College); James Fredericks and Michael P. Horan (Loyola Marymount); William French, Jon Nilson, and Susan Ross (Loyola University Chicago); special thanks to my colleagues at Marquette University—Michel Barnes, Deirdre Dempsey, Michael Duffey, Alexander Golitizin, Christine Firer Hinze, Thomas Hughson, Paul Misner, David Schultenover, Jame Schaefer, Carol Stockhausen, Wanda Zemler Cizewski; Barbara Finan (Ohio Dominican College); Eileen Daily (Saint Mary's Press); Paul Joseph Fitzgerald (Santa Clara University); Jeanette Rodriguez (Seattle University); Joseph Martos (Spalding University); Mark Fischer (St. John's Seminary, Los Angeles); Susan Wood (St. John's University, Collegeville); Ronald Modras, Julie Hanlon Rubio, and Daniel

Finucane (St. Louis University); Terrence Tilley, William Roberts, and Dennis Doyle (University of Dayton); Matthew Ashley (University of Notre Dame); Carol Dempsey (University of Portland); Michael Hollerich and Ted Ulrich (University of St. Thomas, St. Paul, Minnesota); Richard Gaillardetz (University of Toledo); Margaret Guider (Weston School of Theology); and James Redington (Woodstock Center, Georgetown).

Robert Masson deserves a special commendation for serving as local coordinator for the 2003 CTS convention held at Marquette University. Thanks also to the team of graduate students and staff members who helped. I am especially grateful for the expert editorial assistance of Pamela Shellberg, a doctoral student in biblical studies at Marquette University. Finally, it was a great pleasure to work with Susan Perry, editor at Orbis Books.

Introduction

Bradford E. Hinze

The 2003 College Theology Society convention was devoted to "Spirit, Church, and World." This collection of selected essays invites readers not only to reflect upon the identity and mission of the Spirit, but also to seek out the impulses of the Spirit of God in the harsh and magnificent realities of church and world. Precisely in the beauty and betrayal found in the church and the world, glorious and horrible, this search for the Spirit takes place. How is this Spirit present and active in the church and the world, making whole, healing, drawing into the fullness of life and joy? And how is this same Spirit nurturing life-giving relationships, freedom, and peace in the same church and world that mediate division, destruction, and death? In the very places in the church and world where the Spirit of God's glory has been both bestowed and besmirched, how are we to test and discern the spirits? And how are we, individually and collectively, to cooperate with the Spirit of life and holiness through the struggle of resistance and confrontation needed to promote fidelity and to foster life-giving change in both the church and world? These essays challenge the reader to search for the hard-to-find passageways that connect the Spirit, church, and world.

How are we to construe the relationship between the terms Spirit, church, and world? Kilian McDonnell addresses this issue in his recent book, *The Other Hand of God: The Holy Spirit as the Universal Touch and Goal.* He advises that a comprehensive theology of the Spirit must be "controlled by trinitarian norms and a trinitarian movement: God reaches through the Son in the Spirit to reconcile and transform, leading the church and the world in the Spirit through the Son back to the Father."[1] Stated differently, "pneumatology is the divine point of entry into the world and church as God reaches out to history—God's descent. In our ascent to God, the Spirit is the portal to the christological and trinitarian mystery. Within this 'place' of meeting—the very mediation of the mediator, the termination point of God's descent, and the point of departure for our ascent—we know the Spirit."[2] Through the Spirit, God reaches out in the world and church, and human beings are drawn and cooperate with the Spirit as they journey into the fullness of the divine life.

This movement of the Spirit of God's descent and the human ascent, or of God's acts of openness to and embracing the human, can be further specified in terms of communication, both the self-communication of God and human communication with God. Communication can provide a frame of reference for understanding each of the terms and finding patterns of relationship between them. Thus, it is possible to speak of the communicative action of the Spirit of God in the church and the world. This particular formulation served as the backdrop for the contributions of the keynote speakers, Bernd Jochen Hilberath, Robert J. Schreiter, and Jamie T. Phelps. In their careers each of these theologians has given special attention to the communicative action of God and the specific agency of the Spirit in the church and the world: in bonds of love and friendship, in places where destructive powers are confronted and liberation and justice advanced, where interpersonal and social wounds are touched and sometimes healed, where forgiveness is sought and sometimes given, and where reconciliation among those in conflict is promoted and sometimes realized.

In order to clarify what distinguishes the contributions in this collection of essays, it may be helpful to recall that the second half of the twentieth century brought a renewed interest among Roman Catholics, Orthodox, and Protestants in the doctrine of the Holy Spirit, alongside of a revival of trinitarian theology. We cannot help but think of the contributions of Catholic theologians Yves Congar and Heribert Mühlen, Orthodox theologians Vladimir Lossky and Nikos Nissiotis, Reformed theologian Jürgen Moltmann, and Lutheran theologian Wolfhart Pannenberg, to name a few. We see also signs of this retrieval of pneumatology in the documents of Vatican II, in John Paul II's 1986 encyclical on "The Holy Spirit in the Life of the Church and the World" (*Dominum et Vivificantem*), and in the Seventh Assembly of the World Council of Churches held in 1991 on the theme: "Come, Holy Spirit—Renew the Whole Creation." This veritable renaissance of pneumatology is associated with a retrieval of biblical and historical sources and theological traditions. Concomitantly there have been numerous constructive efforts by theologians and official church teaching bodies to affirm the traditional beliefs.

All told this period has been marked by burgeoning efforts to develop a pneumatology that redresses the limited attention to this doctrine over the course of Western Christian history. The array of traditional topics continues to be addressed: the Spirit's identity and mission within the fullness of the triune God as gift and bond of mutual love between the Parental Source and Son, the Spirit's role in the doctrine of grace and sanctification, and the Spirit's role in the foundation of the church and as the source of charisms, offices, and ministries. Fresh attention has been given to the relation of the identities and missions of the Spirit and the Word and Wisdom incarnate to one another and to the Primal Source in the biblical texts, in the immanent Trinity and in the economic Trinity; debates have been revisited about the epistemological and ontological ordering (*taxis*) of the Trinitarian persons, their relations, processions, missions, and the Eastern doctrine of Monopatrism and the Western doctrine of Filioque; and new attention has been given to the Spirit's role in the birth, baptism, ministry, death, and resurrection of Jesus, resulting in the ascendance of so-called Spirit christologies, as well as new studies of the Spirit's role in the life of Mary, the apostles and the disciples, and the presence of the Spirit in those individuals and communities and cultures beyond the borders of Jews and Christians. Finally, growing awareness of the depths and dimensions of the Spirit's presence and agency in the church and the world has been a key ingredient in the momentous rediscovery of the ecclesiological import of the doctrine of *koinonia* or *communio* of the Holy Spirit (2 Cor 13:13) among Catholics and in ecumenical circles especially since the mid-1980s.

In truth, however, this renewed interest in the Spirit is not only or primarily the work of scholars. It must likewise be attributed to the new stirrings of the Spirit and the new attentiveness and receptivity to experiences of the Spirit among the faithful in many sectors: in spirituality and liturgy, in the sense of vocation, apostolic ministries, and prophetic and healing witness in service and works for justice. One of the most dramatic events of the Spirit has been the growing influence of Pentecostal churches and charismatic experiences in churches and among local peoples and communities around the world.

Against this larger backdrop of spiritual awakening and scholarly attesting, what distinguishes the essays in this volume is the preponderance of interest in the practical implications of the doctrine of the Spirit for the church and the world. Certainly questions about the identity of the Spirit and the Spirit's role in spirituality and liturgical worship appear in these essays. But far more often the focus is on the activity of the Spirit in the mission of the church in the world, in apostolic mission, in evangelization, in creating communities of communion. Specifically, and above all, it is the activity of the Spirit in the promotion of justice and liberation, in the work of forgiveness and reconciliation in a world rife with conflict and division that is at stake. Both striking and saddening is the considerable concern these essays give to the activity of the Spirit in the groans and sighs too deep for words (Rom 8:22-26) as we confront scandals in the church, wars in Afghanistan and Iraq, armed conflicts and abusive situations around the world, and the ongoing effort to deal with excluded and maltreated others, including the endangered earth and cosmos. Learning to walk in the Spirit, we are taught here, is as much a school of lamentation as it is of resistance and hopeful action in the church and world.

The collection is divided according to three theological operations: naming the Sprit of God, narrating the action of the Spirit in a divided world and wounded church, and advancing the Spirit's work of communion and justice.

Naming the Spirit of God

The theological task of naming involves searching for those metaphors and concepts that disclose the identity of the Spirit of God. Three receive special attention here: the Spirit of God is communicator, fully divine, and grieving.

This section begins with the plenary address given by Bernd Jochen Hilberath, "Sender, Receiver, and Message: The Holy Spirit as the Communicator between God and the World." Drawing on his extensive work on the treatment of the Spirit in the scriptures and the history of doctrine, Hilberath focuses on naming the Spirit as the communicator. His aim is to overcome two extremes: the pneumatological deficit in Western theology long criticized by Eastern theologians; and, more recently, the Western tendency to invoke the Spirit as the solution to every problem in the church and the world without specifying any personal or ecclesial responsibilities. The challenge is to understand the identity and role of the Holy Spirit in the process of communication between God and the world. To name the Spirit the communicator requires understanding that "the Holy Spirit enables, accompanies, and accomplishes" communication. Hilberath investigates the vistas opened up by naming the Spirit as sender, receiver, and message, while vigilantly acknowledging the presence of finitude and sin that threatens to thwart every effort at communication. His effort to explore the Spirit in the act of communication is connected to his larger effort to advance a communicative theology that concentrates not only on the sender-message-receiver, but also on the impact of the global context and personal psychological dynamics, following the theories of psychologist Ruth C. Cohn.

Harold E. Ernst turns our attention to one of the most important moments in the ancient history of naming the Spirit as fully divine. Ernst's essay, "A Clearer Manifestation of the Spirit: Gregory Nazianzen on the Divinity of the Holy Spirit," offers a valuable analysis of Gregory's Oration 31. In this text Gregory explicitly advances the full divinity of the Holy Spirit beyond the key positions developed by Athanasius and Basil. Particularly striking in his rhetorical justification is the original precedent he provides for doctrinal development through inferences from scripture, as ratified by authentic Christian experience of the Spirit: "At the present time, the Spirit resides amongst us, giving us a clearer manifestation of the Spirit than before" (Oration 31.26). Beyond its important role in challenging his Eunomian and pneumatomachian opponents, the author believes that Gregory's argumentation may provide a fruitful paradigm for evaluating contemporary efforts to recognize the Spirit's ongoing activity in the church and the world.

Jane E. Linahan concentrates on what is surely one of the most provocative biblical metaphors, the description of the grieving Spirit of God in the letter to the Ephesians. Her essay, "The Grieving Spirit: The Holy Spirit as Bearer of the Suffering of the World in Moltmann's Pneumatology," explores what might be entailed in the grieving of the Holy Spirit by examining the development of the pneumatological dimension of the cross in the thought of Jürgen Moltmann. While Moltmann's earlier work depicts the Spirit merely as the "fruit" of the mutual passion of Father and Son, his subsequent work sees the Spirit in an increasingly central role in empowering, mediating, and bearing that passion. This deepening insight has implications for understanding the Spirit's role in bringing about the fullness of life for all creation. The Spirit is poured out in empowering the life, autonomy, and freedom of every creature; the Spirit is self-emptied in bearing the suffering of the world, "spending" itself to sustain and heal the world in its brokenness. The caution against grieving the Holy Spirit reminds us that violence against any part of God's creation impinges upon the One who holds it in life and loves it passionately.

Narrating the Action of the Spirit in a Divided World and Wounded Church

Theology identifies the Spirit of God not only by naming, but also by narrating the agency of the Spirit in the everyday dramas of the struggling church and suffering world. The essays in this section explore ways to narrate the agency of the Spirit of God in situations of conflict, in mission, in war, and in multicultural communities.

Robert J. Schreiter's plenary paper is devoted to the topic "Mediating Repentance, Forgiveness, and Reconciliation: What Is the Church's Role?" Schreiter was invited to reflect upon the communicative action of the church in situations of conflict, drawing upon his many years of research and writing on this topic. He introduces and frames his discussion with a litany of concrete narrative settings: first, the end of authoritarian regimes in Latin America, Central and Eastern Europe, and South Africa; second, civil wars in Africa, the Balkans, Sri Lanka, and Indonesia, where poverty and displacement of peoples are widespread; third, the efforts to come to terms with the past abuse of native peoples in the Americas, Australia, and South Asia; and fourth, the sexual abuse scandals in the Roman Catholic Church, of religious women in Africa and of minors by United States clergy, as well as in Europe and in Australia. Schreiter begins by discussing St. Paul's understanding of the church's mandate: "All this is from God, who reconciled us to himself through Christ, and has given us the ministry of reconciliation" (2 Cor 5:18). In keeping with this passage, Schreiter's essay accentuates the christological character of this ministry and underscores the need for the church to promote trustworthy communication. He delineates three aspects of this process of reconciliation: apology, repentance or reparation, and forgiveness. While the church is widely recognized as playing an important part in post-conflict situations, church leaders rarely receive the training to do so. Moreover, since reconciliation involves the healing of victims and the reconstruction of societies, more than a set of strategies and skills is needed; one needs a spirituality, a way of participating with God. Ultimately the church is called upon to reconnect people in keeping with the deepest Christian convictions about catholicity and communion that follow from the belief in the triune God. This last challenge stands as an invitation to the reader to think through how "the Spirit gives life" (2 Cor 3:4) after death-dealing conflict and the violent narrative of the lie, and how one may be led to "walk according to the Spirit" (Rom 8:4) on the path of conversion, forgiveness, and the mediation of new bonds of relationship.

Dennis Hamm invites readers to revisit the most important narration of the agency of the Spirit in the Christian scriptures, that found in Luke's gospel and the Acts of the Apostles. In "The Mission Has a Church: Spirit, World, and Church in Luke-Acts," Hamm explores Luke's portrayal of the mission of the Spirit-driven church in three ways. First, he considers the implications of two phrases in Gabriel's announcement (Lk 1:32-33) as a brief overview of Luke's narrative theology about the en-spirited church in the world. Second, he focuses on two passages that, though they are largely neglected in discussions about the role of the church in the world, can contribute powerfully to that conversation. They are Jesus' commissioning of servant-leaders at the Last Supper (22:24-30) and Luke's portrayal of the community at prayer (and its consequences for mission and community) in Acts 4:23-35. Finally, he suggests how these examples of narrative ecclesiology can contribute to our contemporary efforts to understand the Spirit-led mission of the church in our world today.

Elizabeth Groppe examines various ingredients in the recurrent stories of war in search of pneumatological resources in "The Spirit and the Church in a World at War: The Promise and Challenge of Nonviolent Action." Usually Christian ethics reflects upon war in terms of the teaching and example of Jesus Christ, but this essay develops a pneumatological perspective, evaluating warfare through some of the pneumatological principles articulated in the New Testament and in the writings of theologians Yves Congar and Jürgen Moltmann. This essay advances the argument that war is an obstruction to the presence and activity of the Spirit; it is contrary to the Spirit's work of conversion, truth, discipline and order, communion, and the renewal and sustenance of life. In contrast, the form of nonviolent action practiced by Mahatma Gandhi and Martin Luther King, Jr., offers a strong pneumatological basis and alternative method to confront tyranny. The mission of the Christian Church in a world where injustice has not yet been vanquished must include the education, training, and mobilization of persons of faith in the practice of nonviolent action.

Maria Teresa Morgan investigates the Pentecost narrative in search of resources for addressing the tensions and opportunities in multicultural contexts. Her essay, " 'Tongues as of Fire' : The Spirit as Paradigm for Ministry in a Multicultural Setting," contends that the images in the Pentecost narrative offer a foundational model for ministry in a multicultural church. Her reflection begins in an ecclesial setting in Miami Dade in South Florida where Creole, French, Portuguese, and Spanish are spoken alongside English. Ministers are forced to face the contentious issues raised in communities by the gifts of different languages and cultural diversity. Morgan builds her case by drawing on the patristic affirmation that Pentecost reverses the division of Babel and on the pneumatologies of Yves Congar and George Montague. The revelatory and religious dimensions of language, "the gift of tongues," are examined in light of three biblical episodes: the tower of Babel (Gn 11:1-9), the Exodus/Sinai event (Ex 19; Dt 4:36; 5:5, 23-31), and Pentecost (Acts 2:1-12). Morgan offers a fresh formulation of the classical claim that Pentecost offers a model that moves beyond the exclusivity evidenced at Babel to the inclusivity presented at Pentecost.

Advancing the Spirit's Work of Communion and Justice

The third set of essays features the church's role in advancing the Spirit's work of fostering right relations in the world. Each of the papers in this section gives special attention to the challenges of being in right relation and the connections needed to support practices that promote relational truth and life: in liberation for the sake of communion and communion committed to justice ministry, in a more Spirit-conscious justice-oriented community, in cosmic mutuality, in a catechesis that not only forms and socializes, but also radically transforms individuals and communities, and in an approach to evangelization that includes the promotion of justice.

The third plenary address by Jamie T. Phelps is entitled "Liberation for Communion: The Church's Justice Mission in an Unjust Society." The church's mission in an unjust society is to promote liberation for the sake of communion. Phelps emphasizes the importance of Jesus' proclamation of the kingdom of God and the church's call to advance the kingdom, but she also underscores the role of the Spirit in this process. Her essay addresses four questions: What are the destructive power dynamics in unjust personal and collective human encounters? Does God choose some and abandon others? What is the relationship between liberation and conversion for the oppressed and the oppressors? What are the important aspects of the concept of church as communion that bear upon the pursuit of justice? Central to Phelps's argument is the claim that ecclesial and social institutions must face their own racial-cultural diversity in order to realize concretely the processes of personal, interpersonal, and social liberation and communion, processes that require the cooperation of the power of the Holy Spirit. The Spirit empowers the church to realize ecclesial and social unity, which fulfills Jesus' mandate to be open to the coming kingdom or reign of God. "Situations of oppression and domination contradict this call to unity and communion. Processes of liberation that conform to the way of Christ are directed toward overcoming our personal and social sins and enable the emergence of ever widening communities of inclusion characterized by love and justice. These communities are maintained as grace-filled spaces of hope rooted in an interior change brought about by our participation in the sacramental life of the community" (p. 146).

In "Toward a Theology of Spirit that Builds Up the Just Community" Mary Elsbernd explores the importance of pneumatology for developing a justice-oriented community. She begins by examining the link between the Spirit and works of justice in the documents of Catholic social teaching from *Rerum Novarum* (1891) to *Centesimus Annus* (1991). This is followed by an analysis of the role of the Spirit in a survey concerning the motivations and ministries of over fifty justice practitioners in the Chicago area. She identifies four building blocks toward a theology of the Spirit that promotes work for justice. First, the indwelling Spirit shapes human desires and longings for justice and motivates action on behalf of justice. Second, the Spirit opens up an eschatological horizon, the dawn of a new creation, beyond the injustice in the present. Third, the Spirit creates an inclusive community of diverse persons who realize the trinitarian reality of commun-

ion in diversity. Fourth, the Spirit is a symbol of abundance and flourishing, not scarcity and deprivation. These four building blocks are
rooted in the scriptures and can be traced in Catholic social teaching
as well as in the lived experience of ministers of justice. Elsbernd
proposes that a theology of the Spirit based on these building blocks
will provide strong foundations for the formation of a community that
works for justice.

Dawn M. Nothwehr challenges readers to enlarge their vision of
the Spirit's activity in the world in her essay "The Ecological Spirit
and Cosmic Mutuality: Engaging the Work of Denis Edwards." This
essay examines Edwards's recent ecotheology of the Holy Spirit, which
denounces the abuse and destruction of the earth by human beings.
Her essay draws on Edwards's work in support of the thesis that "it is
possible to hold that there is a proper role for the Holy Spirit in the one
divine work of creation." Edwards's understanding of the role of the
Holy Spirit in creation deepens our consciousness of the significance
of the Holy Spirit for an adequate ecological theology and ethics.
Nothwehr argues that Edwards's ecotheology of the Holy Spirit provides a warrant for mutuality as a central norm for Catholic environmental ethics.

Gerald J. Beyer in "Evangelization and Social Justice in Poland
after 1989" analyzes the response of the Roman Catholic Church to
the recent turbulent period in Poland's history. He advances the claim
that Paul VI appropriately challenged local churches to apply the
church's social teaching to their specific contexts, and that this requires proposing policies that embody the values espoused by Catholic social teaching. With this in mind, Beyer argues that the institutional church, more specifically the Polish bishops' conference, has
not yet fully recognized the promotion of concrete structures and policies necessary for social justice as a constitutive dimension of the
preaching of the gospel (see 1971 Synod of Bishops, *Justitia in Mundo*).
Moreover, the church in Poland must do so in order to be faithful to its
mission of evangelization. Following Paul VI's *Evangelii Nuntiandi*,
Beyer's essay invites further reflection on how "the gentle action of
the Spirit" (no. 75) can result not only in the bold proclamation of the
gospel, but also the courageous promotion of justice.

In "Discipleship and the Logic of Transformative Catechesis" Robert Brancatelli offers a critique of the current state of catechesis in the
church and argues that its limitations result from its faulty philosophi-

cal foundation, which is inadequate for the purpose, objectives, and tasks of catechesis. Employing Rosemary Haughton's distinction between formation and transformation and the hermeneutical theory of Jürgen Habermas, Brancatelli offers an alternative theory of transformative catechesis based on "paradoxical logic." By way of illustration, he uses the Matthean story of the "rich young man," arguing that the way in which contemporary catechesis functions often leads to the kind of discipleship associated with the young man rather than the commitment demanded by Jesus. Rather than catechesis as formation, following a socialization model, the author advocates recognition of the transformative dimension of catechesis, which requires a radical change of the person and the community. Brancatelli elaborates this new type of catechesis in comparison with other contemporary forms of experiential catechesis. The author finds this kind of vision of catechesis intimated in the 1997 *General Directory for Catechesis*, which challenges the disciples of Jesus "to be poor, without money or knapsack; to know how to accept rejection and persecution; to place one's trust in the Father and in support of the Holy Spirit; to expect no other reward than the joy of working for the Kingdom" (no. 86). But how are we to support the work of the Holy Spirit in the process of catechesis? The author implies that this requires a life-long journey of ongoing conversion. Here the Spirit not only consoles, but also disturbs.

Notes

[1]Kilian McDonnell, *The Other Hand of God: The Holy Spirit as the Universal Touch and Goal* (Collegeville, Minn.: Liturgical Press, 2003), 207.

[2]McDonnell, *The Other Hand of God*, 216-17.

Part I

NAMING THE SPIRIT OF GOD

Sender, Receiver, and Message:
The Holy Spirit as the Communicator
between God and the World[*]

Bernd Jochen Hilberath

Up to the 1960s the Christian East could reproach the Western church for its forgetfulness of the Spirit. In both theory and praxis a strict Christomonism was operative, which was reflected in an over-emphasis on the institutional and hierarchical external side of the church. Since then the Holy Spirit has been in vogue. By the end of the twentieth century books and congresses drew up the first balance sheet of the rediscovery of the Holy Spirit.

This charismatic and pneumatological boom shows itself in movements of spiritual renewal as well as in official documents of the magisterium and theology. Yet now a real danger threatens from the other side: the Holy Spirit is overly stressed and can often be invoked as a panacea. This happens frequently, especially in ecumenical contexts. In such contexts, Christians often profess that unity is solely the gift of the Holy Spirit, which means that we can do nothing but pray for unity. Without questioning the validity of this belief, we must still ask whether that argument does not contradict itself. On the one hand, Christians stress that the division of the church of Jesus Christ into different confessional churches is scandalous, that it is a sin committed by human beings against the divine wish *ut unum sint*. On the other hand, other Christians maintain that the Holy Spirit alone is supposed to repair everything that human beings have destroyed. Would it not be much more adequate to say that all that human beings have destroyed by acting against the Holy Spirit has to be repaired by them

---

[*]Translation by Annemarie Mayer and Bradford Hinze.

with the help of the Holy Spirit? Or formulated more theo-logically or pneumato-logically: All the divisions that the Spirit of God has suffered by the sinful abuse of freedom, all the while respecting human freedom, the Spirit will restore to unity by engaging the freedom of human beings for the divine work of unity.

The work of the Spirit and the action of human beings should be understood in their interrelatedness. According to the logic of grace, this interrelatedness is of course asymmetrical. The Holy Spirit enables, accompanies, and accomplishes all that human beings do.

The title of my essay could likewise give the impression that the Holy Spirit would act in the place of human communication. It is quite common to see the Holy Spirit treated as a sort of medium and also as means of communication. But how can the Spirit be sender as well as receiver at the same time? And does the communication between God and the world consist in that?

Seen from the perspective of a theology of grace, the question is how the work of the Holy Spirit and the action of human beings are related. Here, indeed, another confessional difference could make itself felt, not the one between East and West, but that within Western Christianity. For instance, if we remember the early Karl Barth, then Reformed theology can theologically stress the action of the triune God so much that God alone is acting. God is then revealer (sender), revelation (message), and receiver of that very revelation.[1]

But pneumatology, of which a theology of grace is the reverse side, cannot be dissolved into a trinitarian theology; neither can it be reduced to a reflection of the inner life of the Trinity. The Spirit as the "*vinculum amoris*" also is the "*condilectus,*" the "co-beloved third," in whom God transcends God's self ecstatically toward the world.[2] The Spirit both joins and opens. Pneumatology is not a self-contained system, because the work of the Spirit does not take place in a self-contained area. Where human beings restrict themselves, as individuals and as groups, the Spirit breaks open the doors.[3] The Lord, risen by the power of the Spirit, enters through closed doors, breathes on his disciples and says, "Receive the Holy Spirit!" The affirmation follows, "If you forgive the sins of any, they are forgiven; if you retain the sins of any, they are retained." Therefore, sending and receiving the Spirit means empowerment. If the basic asymmetry in the human relationship with God or the divine relationship with humans is not abolished into a synergism, then we can say that human communication is at the same time and primarily communication of the Spirit.

Thus we have reached a first formulation of our topic: the Holy Spirit enables, accompanies, and accomplishes human communication. To put it more precisely, the Holy Spirit enables, accompanies, and accomplishes the human being as sender as well as receiver of communication, and the Holy Spirit enables, accompanies, and accomplishes the message itself. This indwelling of the Spirit has to be construed in such a way that we can say, according to the theological asymmetry, that the Holy Spirit *is* sender, receiver, and message. I would like to investigate the outcome if we consider the Holy Spirit in this way. What is the impact on one's understanding of the Holy Spirit, on the one hand, and on the conception of human communication on the other?

The model of communication as sender, message, receiver must certainly be expanded: communication is achieved through media; communication has a context, an environment in which it takes place; and communication is practiced in a certain spirit. Therefore, we will also take into account this expanded structure of communication and try to understand it pneumatologically. Step by step we will recognize the outline of a communicative theology,[4] which is indebted for some substantial inspirations to the Theme-Centered Interaction theory (TCI) developed by psychologist Ruth C. Cohn.[5]

The Holy Spirit as Sender

From a theological point of view the noblest human communication is *prayer*—when the human being turns to God and addresses God by giving thanks and praise and by petitioning and lamenting. This is an activity of a person who seeks God again and again, even though this God sometimes seems totally remote and hidden. Thus human beings can forget to whom they should give thanks, to whom they should give praise for the fact that they exist. People can become petitioners if they are at their wits' end or completely at a loss and perhaps would like to implore God as *Deus ex machina*. As a result, they may forget that they can lament in God's presence and even accuse God. Because this happens again and again people need the assistance of the Spirit. But can they use the Spirit like a "stopgap," as a *Deus ex machina*?

"It is no longer I who live, but Christ who lives in me" (Gal 2:20).

Does St. Paul have a split personality? No. Paul has had the experience that he is a new human being since he joined the followers of the new way, the new doctrine; more precisely, since Christ came to meet him and threw him out of his usual way of life. Paul is totally clear-headed, his eyes have been opened, he knows what he is doing, and he does not refrain from claiming authority. But he distinguishes between divine and human authority, between the authority of the Lord and his own. That means it is no longer I, in my self-centeredness,[6] who am the measure of things, but rather it is my relationship to Jesus Christ that is the orientation of my life. All I can accomplish, insofar as it is relevant for my life and my salvation, I can accomplish only within this orientation. Since as a human being I do evil again and again, which I do not want to do, I need the vigilance, the orientation, and the assistance of the Spirit. Even in this orientation I am still "on the way," insofar as I am full of joy and at the same time still exposed to troubles and dangers.

How close the indwelling of the Spirit is in relation to the human person, without dissolving the human ego, can easily be seen from the fact that the Spirit is not only found in the fruits of the Spirit that pertain to the sunny side of life. Patience and perseverance are also fruits of the Spirit. "And not only creation, but we ourselves, who have the first fruits of the Spirit, groan inwardly as we wait for adoption as sons and daughters, the redemption of our bodies" (Rom 8:23). Here, however, the Spirit does not remain outside, but dwells within us: "Likewise the Spirit helps us in our weakness; for we do not know how to pray as we ought, but the Spirit himself intercedes for us with sighs too deep for words" (Rom 8:26). Not only when we groan and complain, not only in the prayer of petition, but in all our praying the Spirit is the inspirer, the communicator: "God is spirit, and those who worship him must worship in spirit and truth" (Jn 4:24).

It seems obvious that to speak to God, which is to pray, is only possible in and through the Spirit. Does this apply also to other speech acts of the human sender? The highest form of communication between humans is mutual *self-revelation*, the mutual self-opening to one another. Expressing one's self is an act of self-revelation. Does the Spirit have a decisive function here too?

Already the person presented as praying in the Old Testament knew that God knew his innermost self better than he himself. Modern psychoanalysis made available to us a process to recognize ourselves, particularly our past, and for the first time to understand ourselves better and perhaps to accept ourselves too. At the same time, however, it also heightens our sense of how difficult it is for us to really comprehend ourselves. Despite the insights of modern psychology, can we say that opening oneself to the other, openly finding and pronouncing the correct words—being authentic in communication—has become any easier for us?

Theologically we characterize the Holy Spirit as the Spirit of the Father and the Son, the one who joins in *communio* and *communicatio* and, indeed, links those who open themselves to each other. As the co-beloved third, the Spirit is at the same time the bond of love between Father and Son. In the Spirit the ecstatic self-transcendence of God toward the other, the one different from God's self, personalizes itself. That which God opens up, God also embraces. In the Spirit of creation the Creator embraces creation. In the Spirit of life God welcomes creation into the circle of life. Here the Spirit does not force itself onto creation, but gives room and freedom. For the sake of freedom God refrains from freedom. However, God does not stay in the background because God is afraid of losing the character of divinity. That is exactly what the Spirit stands for—that God can transcend God's self toward the non-divine, without ceasing to be God. Precisely the same thing distinguishes spiritual human beings: they can transcend themselves toward the other, without being overcome by fear of ending up the loser.[7]

In this way it is the Holy Spirit that enables the human sender to send authentically and to be open to others. Yet at the same time one's own boundaries are to be respected and we ought to consider what we can expect from others. Ruth Cohn calls this "selective authenticity."

Among the things that the sender can communicate to the receiver, the most important seems to be *what enables* life, supports life, and makes life worth living. "I am here. . . . I will accompany you. . . . You can count on me. . . . I'll be with you through thick and thin." As human beings we depend on such promises. What gives us the strength, the courage to make such promises? The psychoanalyst Hanna Wolff once said, "No therapist can give to a client what they do not have themselves."[8] My own experience with therapists is that they need an orientation for themselves that points beyond themselves, or they must be able to offer such an orientation to their clients. For uncovering the truth of the past does not in itself open any future. Hanna Wolff added,

"Jesus did it." Indeed, Jesus depends completely on God in his life and opens himself toward God. Thus he can render himself completely to others, can open himself up to them, and can enable them to transcend themselves.

Gabriel Marcel said, "To say I love you means: You shall not die."[9] But how are we to take strength from this? Who of us can take on this responsibility? Do we not come to depend on someone else if we say "I love you"? Frequently, presumably unconsciously, we lay this burden on the other, and it is all right that this often happens unconsciously. This prevents us from abusing our care for others as a substitute for our relationship with God. However, in order to achieve this relationship with the human other, we must completely rely on the total otherness that is the Spirit of God.

The Spirit frees us to be ourselves, makes us capable of having a relationship with God as well as a relationship with our fellow human beings that furthers life. Any communication that wants to create, sustain, or support life lives off the resources of the life-creating Spirit of God, at least unconsciously. This spiritual life, this spiritual communication is no exception to our communicative relationships. Here, rather, our basic attitude toward communication is at stake. Ultimately, every single piece of objective information wants to serve the shaping of life.

The Holy Spirit as Receiver

No one is only a sender, but rather also a receiver. In its fundamental meaning this has already become indirectly obvious. Only because we receive communicative energy from the Spirit, can we send messages. That is the asymmetry: people send as senders who beforehand have received and must receive again and again.

This is also true for inter-human relations. Nobody can exist only as a sender, "on the air" so to speak, and stay alive; his battery and his stock of information would be exhausted sooner or later. And everyone who receives at the same time sends out a message, even if he does not say anything. To accept tacitly is itself a signal. What does this have to do with the Holy Spirit of God? All that was said in the first part from the perspective of the sender is also true from the perspective of the receiver.

The fact that human persons in their relationships with God remain primarily receivers does not need any justification; this is already part of the realization of the abiding asymmetry in the relationship between God and human beings. The Holy Spirit enables the human addressee to receive the self-revelation of God. This is what grace means: on the one hand, God gives God's free, unearned attention to the human being and, on the other hand, God must enable the finite person to receive God's attention. The sender must even provide the receiver with an antenna, because God and the human person are not on the same wavelength. Here, despite all the problems of the so-called *gratia increata* and *gratia creata*, lies the very center of truth.

More important is the recollection that can or rather must become temporarily a prophetic admonition: abiding in the truth of the self-revelation of God and the perfection of faith are made possible only by God, through the Spirit, through grace. The human person can never be in total possession of God's revelation. It is always necessary to "stay on-line" in life. We cannot print out God's revelation and then possess it in black and white.

Is this also true for inter-human communication? How could we live in our information-based society without anything printed in black and white? We cannot avoid this. However, we can survive only if these resources are relegated to their limited instrumental function and directed to the service of life, the good life of all. Paper can be destroyed, hard disks can fail, and PCs can break down. This can often be annoying; it can even be threatening. However, human life ends only if relationships among us are destroyed, if memories break down, and if care is refused. When human communication fails, life freezes, . . . perhaps to death.

"What do you have that you did not receive?" (1 Cor 4:7). This marks the receiver's attitude, the one who does not abuse the sender and his or her message, but respects and accepts them in their intrinsic value. Since every receiver is always also a sender, these two functions of the human communicator should mutually orient and correct themselves. I can refuse to receive the message because the message is not accurate or the sender seems suspicious. I can also refuse to accept the message because I do not want to get involved with the sender or the message. The more Spirit-filled the sender and the message, the more Spirit-filled will the receiver have to be in both willingness and attitude. I am free to decide. This is exactly why I have to ask myself whether I will open myself up to the message of the other, and perhaps under certain circumstances even rely on it. Many communication processes in the church and in the world fail and are not life-supporting because the receivers always already think they know what the sender wants to tell them, if indeed they even accept the person as someone who has something to say.

Hans-Georg Gadamer considered the relationship between the reader and the text as analogous to the relationship of a human being to his/her fellow human being.[10] Here he distinguishes among three attitudes.

First, I treat a text and/or a human being like an object. I ask them for information, which serves my interests, and use them for my purposes.

Second, I treat a text and/or a human being in such a way that I grant them their own opinion, but I always know beforehand what the other wants to tell me. This can mean that I subject their message exclusively to a hermeneutics of suspicion or a hermeneutics of genesis: "You cannot but argue in this way, because you are: German, Jew, Protestant, Catholic, priest, layman and so on and so forth." Related to texts and related indirectly to their senders: "I do not read an encyclical letter anymore, one already knows what it says; I do not read theological literature, theologians only confuse people (which based on my own experience is rarely true) or miss the point in talking about life (which can indeed be a danger)."

Third, only on the third level do I grant some intrinsic value to the text and/or the other, even to such an extent that I do not question the text or the other first, but let them question me. I do not reduce the other to a mere responder to my questions, but let myself be questioned by the words and replies of the other.

This attitude of a receiver requires the same power of self-transcendence and self-relativization as is required of the sender. Being able to switch over to reception without succumbing to fear presupposes the attitude of a spiritual human being.

The Holy Spirit as Message

Even if it is obvious to what extent the Holy Spirit is sender in the human sender and is receiver in the human receiver, it nevertheless can be difficult to understand why the Spirit is also a message. Is the Spirit not by nature a force, so to speak, that enables, that stays permanently in the background, "the Unknown beyond the word," in the words of Hans Urs von Balthasar?[11]

We have seen that the importance of the Holy Spirit becomes all the more evident when we have to deal with life-supporting communication between senders and receivers. From there we can recognize the extent to which the Spirit is part of all our communications—even in the Spirit's absence or when the Spirit is perhaps replaced by the demons of miscommunication. Can we conclude that the highest form of communication would be the exchange of the Spirit's self?

- "Receive the Holy Spirit!" (Jn 20:22)
- "He gave up his spirit" (Jn 19:30)
- "Your Holy Spirit come upon us and cleanse us" (used in some ancient text versions of Luke 11:2 instead of "Your kingdom come")
- He will give "good things" (Mt 7:11)
- And to the disciples, who can ask the Father for everything: "If you then, who are evil, know how to give good gifts to your children, how much more will your Father in heaven give good things to those who ask him!" And according to a parallel in Luke 11:13, these good things are "the Holy Spirit" ("If you then, who are evil, know how to give good gifts to your children, how much more will the heavenly Father give the Holy Spirit to those who ask him!").

We can conclude that the Holy Spirit embodies the message that the divine sender gives to us human receivers. This is not meant to compete with the gift of the Son, whom the Father gives to us as his word and sacrifice for us that we might live. We remain rather in the Holy Spirit, in the realm of the Father and the Son; we remain in the one whose words are "Spirit and life" (Jn 6:63). Therefore Paul can say, "The Lord is Spirit" (2 Cor 3:17).

Here it becomes very evident that revelation is not the communication of truths but communication of the truth; that the process of revelation is not primarily a cognitive process but rather a personal process that includes the whole human being. The *ruach*, this *pneuma*, by which God at the beginning forms living human beings out of clay is given to us as the Spirit of new life.

In the processes of teaching and learning at our theological schools we have long realized that teaching and learning have to be integrated processes. Theological training does not aim at turning students into small theological dictionaries, but aims at providing them with the competence to think, analyze, and judge theologically as well as to develop ways of action. It is a question of competence and of attitude. This is the most important element that we can provide in a process of mutual mediation, in which those who teach also learn.[12]

In this experience I see an analogy that can show us why the greatest good in communication between God and human beings can be called Holy Spirit. I think this is also true for inter-human communication.

The Spirit of Communication Creates Room and Needs Room

Earlier I pointed out that the model of sender-message-receiver would have to be expanded. This is true because we must consider that communication always takes place in a specific environment, an environment that influences it all the more effectively the more it is neglected. As the Theme-Centered Interaction theory of Ruth Cohn states: "The globe devours those who disregard it."[13] This statement comprises an indicative as well as an imperative. Thus, all communication is carried out in a field of communication, in an area or a structure. These factors influence communication; they can enable it or even prevent it. The imperative that results is the following: We must form communication in such a way that all conversation partners are taken seriously as subjects and that the perspective on the topic is opened up and not obstructed. What has been formulated here as a more or less Kantian imperative of communication, recent theology has often understood in connection to Jürgen Habermas as an ideal community of communication.[14]

First of all, I think it is important in general that the "globe," that is, the global condition of communication, is taken into account. The problems of communication, characteristic of the Roman Catholic Church, and to which there are certain parallels in our secular societies, sometimes tempt us to keep the circle of the community of communication very small. Individuals, families, small groups, spiritual communities, sometimes even parishes concentrate on themselves, their internal relationships, the intact world of the internal life. This is to some extent understandable and necessary for surviving in this current global church but it is only half of the idea of *communio*. Just as no Christian community lives by its own account, but rather by all that the triune God did and is still doing for it, so too does no Christian community live for itself. Rather, it has a mission, a calling, a task. Just as the essence of Jesus Christ must be described as a "person for others," the church—which could be called "Christ existing as a community" (Bonhoeffer)—can be determined as "existing for others." The *missio* appertains to the *communio*.[15] This is not only a consequence of self-existence, but also the fulfillment of it.

In transcending ourselves how can we take the globe into account? How can we change its structures? How can we change the structures that work to prevent our making such modifications? Here we have to distinguish between the senses of power: power, on the one hand, that can exert and sanction force, and power, on the other hand, that is powerless in the sense of the system but that unfolds power as "proof of the Spirit and of power." The asymmetry of the first power constellation is balanced by the asymmetry of the second, if not again and again partially overcome. The spirit of power, the spirituality of power, is what matters!

In the theory of TCI, Ruth Cohn proposes certain axioms and postulates or rules that describe a corresponding attitude of the spirit.[16] This can be expressed anthropologically, not without some inspiration from religious, especially Jewish, sources. From a biblical perspective we may speak of some important elements of an anonymous pneumatology and doctrine of grace.

Cohn's Axioms

The first axiom formulates the dialectical interconnection of independence and relatedness in human beings, a thought that plays a major role in the theologies of the Trinity of the last decades. In a particular way the Holy Spirit embodies this interconnection. The Spirit remains entirely with the Spirit's self even when joining together with the Father and the Son as *vinculum amoris* and keeping together the human beings as *communio* "so that they all may be one." Communication as self-relatedness by means of and in relationship with others requires an attitude, a spirituality that is freed from being fixed on fear for oneself and that overcomes the fear of contact with others.

The second axiom, the so-called "ethical" one, reads in its brief version: respect above all every thing living and its growth. A sign of successful communication is that life is respected and supported. Successful communication does not necessarily have to lead to a result that can be publicly presented or to a consensus or to an objective agreement on something. Communication fulfills the criterion that this axiom states even where it recognizes differences, tolerates dissent, and "unsuccessfully" breaks up, for, thereby, it does justice to the actual state of the life process. Yet the dynamics of life, the growth potential of the living certainly demand that we do not content ourselves with such apparently unsuccessful results of communication processes.

The third "pragmatic-political" axiom reads: "Free decision happens within formative internal and external boundaries. Extension of these boundaries is possible. . . . Consciousness of our universal interdependence is the basis of more humane responsibility." Basically, this third axiom transcends the second one. It moves beyond mere individual ethics or ethics limited to one small group to include the communicative community of humankind. At the same time, it is clear that the ethics of communication cannot be limited to describing individual attitudes. Expanding the areas of communication, without running blindly against fortified boundaries, belongs to the process of communication. This takes place through the Spirit-inspired, and to that extent intelligent, overcoming or relocation of the boundaries of communication.

Cohn's Postulates

Besides these three axioms the Theme-Centered Interaction theory postulates two "existential demands of existence," two elementary rules of communication. Cohn's first rule of communication states: "*Be your own chairperson.*" Pay attention to yourself, your interior, your present situation, and your environment. Then decide when and how you want to play a part in communication. Ecclesial communication in particular must avoid the two extremes of compulsive extroversion and the refusal to communicate. The only way communication can be authentic is if self-determined authenticity is present. This will always remain selective in that the manner in which he or she will take part is left to the decision of the sender. This decision has to consider, of course, the receiver, the character of the message, and the globe; in this sense, the sender's autonomy is a relative autonomy. Let's take an example. A papal encyclical letter can contain as much of personal faith experience and spirituality as the sender, the pope, wants to include. He has to consider what the receivers can receive and what is appropriate to the message that is to be communicated. For example, can the pope's personal theology concerning the Eucharist, which must be respected as such, support the receivers' theology and practice of the Eucharist? Is it also an appropriate message? Since the receivers are very different from each other, an extremely differentiated form of message is demanded. Does an "encyclical to the whole world" not come up against limiting factors? What can be mediated by a "catechism of the Catholic Church," a so-called world catechism?[17]

The second rule of communication or existential postulate of existence states: "*Disturbance and passionate involvements take precedence.*" This might mean that every participant in communication can interrupt the communication processes through a disturbance and therefore can ultimately dominate. In fact, however, the rule wants to draw attention to the fact that there can be disturbances in a communication process if a participant cannot follow the process because he or she is neglected, emotionally blocked, or fixated.

This rule points to the complicated relationship between the level of the object and the level of relationship. In the communication of faith the "object" is also at stake. This means that it is not the relationships between people that are the issue, but rather the fact that God becomes alive in our midst and that human relationships take shape accordingly. Shaping our relationships in a way appropriate to God is the "object" of faith, which should be reflected by theology and ought to be facilitated by magisterial rules of communication. In communication in the church as well as in society, these two levels are frequently confused. It is dangerous if we allegedly act on the object, when in fact, however, we act on the level of relationship. This confusion can indeed harden into structures. For example, there is no debate on statements in an encyclical letter. Instead the question is posed, are you for or against the pope? Since the Roman magisterium has lost much credibility since *Humanae vitae*, some, on the one hand, no longer expect anything at all from papal writings. Others accept everything coming from Rome. To them, obedience is more important than an insight into the subject matter (the object). If theologians do not make the same statements as the magisterium, they are blamed for making the faithful uncertain. This may apply for some; others, in turn, cannot be made uncertain. Still others struggle to come to terms with the arguments.

Whoever thinks that he or she already knows the truth, whether representative of the magisterium, theologian, or member of the community, becomes in the long run incapable of communication. Since it is the Spirit who initiates us into all truth and deepens our faith in the life of the church, the truth of the *communio* and the *communicatio* with God cannot be found in our interior life but rather must be experienced in community. God is a communicative being. God's self is given to us in God's *logos*. In God's Spirit, we are held in the communication of truth. Thus, the Holy Spirit is associated in a special manner with truth and therefore called "Spirit of truth." Only a spiritual human being can participate in this living process of communication. Spiritual human beings authentically open themselves to others and communicate the life-supporting truth with them. At the same time, they give all that is living a chance to grow, working together with others to extend the limits of our communication and cooperate in institutional structures that promote communication and the *communio* of life.

Notes

[1] One of the prominent critics is Wolfhart Pannenberg; see, for example, *Theology and the Philosophy of Science* (Philadelphia: Westminister Press, 1976), 265-276 (Karl Barth and the Positivity of Revelation); idem, *"Die Subjektivität Gottes und die Trinitätslehre,"* in *Grundfragen systematischer Theologie*, vol. 2 (Göttingen:Vandenhoeck & Ruprecht, 1980), 96-111; see also Jürgen Moltmann, *The Trinity and the Kingdom* (San Francisco: Harper & Row, 1981), 139-144; Eberhard Jüngel, *God's Being in Becoming*, trans. John Webster (Edinburgh: T & T Clark, 2001); idem, *God as the Mystery of the World* (Grand Rapids, Mich.: Eerdmans, 1983), passim.

[2] Bernd Jochen Hilberath, *Die Problematik des trinitätstheologischen Personbegriffs in Rückfrage von Karl Rahner zu Tertullians, Adversus Praxean*, Innsbrucker Theologische Studien, no. 17 (Innsbruck: Tyrolia Verlag, 1986).

[3] Bernd Jochen Hilberath, "Identity through Self-Transcendence: The Holy Spirit and the Fellowship of Free Persons," in *Advents of the Spirit: An Introduction to the Current Study of Pneumatology*, ed. Bradford E. Hinze and D. Lyle Dabney (Milwaukee, Wis.: Marquette University Press, 2001), 265-294.

[4] Matthias Scharer and Bernd Jochen Hilberath, *Kommunikative Theologie: Eine Grundlegung* (Mainz: Matthias-Grünewald-Verlag, 2002, [2]2003) (an English translation is in progress).

[5]See her main work *Von der Psychoanalyse zur themenzentrierten Interaktion* (Stuttgart: Klett-Cotta, 1975; [13]1997).

[6]For the function of this term, see John Hick, *An Interpretation of Religion: Human Responses to the Transcendent* (New Haven: Yale University Press, 1989).

[7]Bernd Jochen Hilberath, *Pneumatologie* (Düsseldorf: Patmos Verlag, 1994); idem, "Der Heilige Geist–ein Privileg der Kirche?" in *Das Judentum–eine bleibende Herausforderung christlicher Identität*, ed. W. Groß (Mainz: Matthias-Grünewald-Verlag, 2001), 174-183.

[8]Hanna Wolff, *Jesus als Psychotherapeut* (Stuttgart: Radius-Verlag 1978, [10]2001), 11-13; see also Bernd Jochen Hilberath, *Heiliger Geist–heilender Geist* (Mainz: Matthias-Grünewald-Verlag,1988), 11-37.

[9]See Gabriel Marcel, *Das ontologische Geheimnis* (Stuttgart: P. Reclam 1961), 79.

[10]See his major work *Truth and Method* (New York: Crossroad, [1]1960, [5]1991).

[11]Hans Urs von Balthasar, "The Unknown Lying beyond the Word," in *Explorations in Theology, III: Creator Spirit* (San Francisco: Ignatius Press, 1993), 105-116.

[12]See Monika Scheidler, Bernd Jochen Hilberath, and Johannes Wildt, eds., *Theologie lehren. Hochschuldidaktik und Reformdera Theologie* (Quaestiones Disputatae, 197) (Freiburg im Breslau: Herder, 2002).

[13]Paul Matzdorf and Ruth C. Cohn, "Das Konzept der Themenzentrierten Interaktion," in *TZI: Pädagogisch-therapeutische Gruppenarbeit nach Ruth C. Cohn*, ed. Cornelia Löhmer and Rüdiger Standhardt (Stuttgart: Klett-Cotta, 1992), 73.

[14]Jürgen Habermas, *Theorie der Gesellschaft oder Sozialtechnologie* (Frankfurt am Main: Suhrkamp, 1971); for Habermas's relevance for theology see Edmund Arens, ed., *Habermas und die Theologie* (Düsseldorf: Patmos, [2]1989).

[15]Ottmar Fuchs, "Die Communio der Kirche," in *Communio–Ideal oder Zerrbild von Kommunikation*, ed. Bernd Jochen Hilberath (Quaestiones Disputatae, 176), (Freiburg im Breslau: Herder, 1999), 209-234.

[16]See Scharer and Hilberath, *Kommunikative Theologie*, Chap. 6, III.

[17]See Bernd Jochen Hilberath, "Zum Verhältnis von Ortskirchen und Weltkirche nach dem II. Vatikanum" in *Was ist heute noch katholisch?* ed. Albert Franz (Quaestiones Disputatae, 192) (Freiburg im Breslau: Herder, 2001), 36-49.

A Clearer Manifestation of the Spirit: Gregory Nazianzen on the Divinity of the Holy Spirit

Harold E. Ernst

Gregory of Nazianzus is sometimes credited with having "invented" the doctrine of the Trinity, for having provided the first full expression of what was to become classical trinitarian language and categories. A constitutive element in this foundational statement of trinitarian thought was Gregory's explicit insistence on the full divinity of the Holy Spirit, a step beyond the pneumatological positions of Athanasius and Basil. Given its seminal position in the evolution of trinitarian reflection, Gregory's original pneumatology is of obvious historical interest. What theological arguments regarding the person and work of the Holy Spirit were coincident with the first explicit insistence on the Spirit's full divinity? How does Gregory characterize the proper role and function of the Spirit among us? The project of this essay, however, is to examine a more limited question. What justification does Gregory provide for his important advancement in explicitly declaring the full divinity of the Holy Spirit? The argumentation Gregory employs, in addition to its clear importance in its historical context, may also provide a resource for contemporary theological reflection on the Spirit's continuing role in the church and the world. While this further investigation is only gestured at in what follows, my hope is that this project will provide the basis for considering the extent to which Gregory's approach might serve as a fruitful paradigm for enabling (and critiquing) contemporary attempts to recognize the Spirit's role in broader realms of human endeavor.[1]

Gregory's fullest exposition of his pneumatology occurs in Oration 31, the last of the five great Theological Orations, preached at the

Church of the Anastasia in Constantinople during 380.[2] It is on the basis of these orations on the inner life of God that Gregory was later described as "The Theologian"; even today they are "a central part of the basic theological curriculum in Eastern Orthodox schools of theology."[3] But while all five of these orations are remarkable for their elaboration of Christian trinitarian doctrine in high rhetorical style, the last stands out for its bold originality. While the preceding orations elegantly recast (not without innovation) already extant arguments against neo-Arianism, Oration 31 takes a more aggressive stand against Eunomian and pneumatomachian positions than did Gregory's predecessors. An examination of select segments of this oration will serve to outline Gregory's justification for this advancement.

The theological opponents Gregory seeks to answer here are those who, regarding the Holy Spirit, challenge him by asking, "Where did you get this strange, unscriptural 'God' you are bringing in?"[4] Gregory acknowledges that some posing this question are "people already fairly sound so far as the Son is concerned."[5] These are the pneumatomachians, otherwise orthodox Christians denying the divinity of the Spirit. But the same challenge is also raised by the Eunomians, whom Gregory mocks as doubly contentious regarding the Spirit's divinity on account of having already been routed in their neo-Arian denial of the Son's divinity. These "men exhausted by discussions of the Son are more eager to take on the Spirit—they must have something to blaspheme or life would be unlivable."[6] Not so explicitly indicated here, but also implicitly addressed, are those members of Gregory's own Nicene-orthodoxy party who (perhaps in imitation of Basil's approach) are reluctant to make the bold assertions Gregory will propose. Gregory chides these for having adopted "a sort of halfway (or should I say 'a thoroughly pitiful'?) position" about the Spirit's status, in which "they offer him neither worship nor disrespect."[7]

What is common to the objection of all these groups, however, is the absence of any explicit scriptural affirmation of the Spirit's divinity. "Yes, some people, very eager to defend the letter, are angry with us for introducing a God, the Holy Spirit, who is a stranger and an intruder."[8] But Gregory rejects this "love for the letter" as a "cloak for irreligion," and notes that his opponents are "afraid where no fear is."[9] He is ready to proclaim what he takes to be authentic Christian experience of the Trinity: "We receive the Son's light from the Father's light in the light of the Spirit."[10] In a passage that suggests not only a contrast with his direct opponents but also a definitive rejection of Basil's verbal "economy" with regard to the Spirit, Gregory declares: "*we* shall preach what we know. We shall climb a lofty mountain and shout it out, if we are not given a hearing below. We shall extol the Spirit; we shall not be afraid. If we do have fear, it will be of silence not of preaching."[11] Gregory will go on to state as explicitly as possible what Basil and others would not, that the Holy Spirit is fully divine and *homoousion*. "Is the Spirit God? Certainly. Is he consubstantial? Yes, if he is God."[12]

It is these explicit and public assertions of the Spirit's full divinity and consubstantiality that mark Gregory's momentous step beyond Basil's diplomatic and reserved preference for artfully ambiguous language that would better maintain church unity.[13] Concerned to preserve the somewhat fragile agreement that had been more or less achieved concerning the proper interpretation of the Nicene Creed, Basil seemed unwilling to propose what might appear to some as a new and unsubstantiated doctrine. So how does Gregory justify these claims, neither explicitly witnessed in scripture nor affirmed by the Council of Nicaea? He begins by pointing to the *revelatory experience* of Christian believers. The Spirit in question is not a "smuggled-in alien" but rather "something disclosed in the consciousness of men past and present."[14] Gregory grants that "the Biblical text does not very clearly or very often call him 'God,' "[15] but he will not allow that the divinity of the Spirit is not attested to in scripture, or that the concept can rightly be regarded as "unbiblical." For there are those who have "read the Holy Scriptures not in a frivolous, cursory way, but with penetration so that they saw inside the written text to its inner meaning. They were found fit to perceive the hidden loveliness; they were illuminated by the light of knowledge."[16] Gregory's basic justification for his claim that the Spirit is God is his assertion that some Christian believers (himself included) have experienced, in penetrating to the inner meaning of scriptural language, an authentic revelation of the Spirit's divinity. For Gregory, the place where the Christian first experiences the Spirit is in biblical interpretation in the church.[17]

Gregory does not, however, simply stop at this assertion of subjective experience as if it were a datum not subject even to criteria of plausibility. Rather, he proceeds to defend its consistency with a more sophisticated interpretation of scripture by "a brief disquisition on things and names, with special reference to Biblical usage."[18] The hermeneutical construct Gregory introduces here consists of four categories or possible states for the relationship between the reality of things and their being named in the biblical texts. "Some things mentioned in the Bible are not factual; some factual things are not mentioned; some nonfactual things receive no mention there; some things are both factual and mentioned."[19] Gregory produces illustrative examples for each of these four pairings.

The last two categories are certainly uncontroversial, because each exhibits a positive correlation between the reality of a thing and its being named in Scripture. The fourth category (factual and named things) includes all realities that are named as such, while the third category (nonfactual and unnamed things) includes false and unmentioned propositions such as "a sphere has four corners."[20] The first and second categories are potentially more troublesome, because each posits a possible separation between the truth of reality and the truth of scripture, but Gregory thinks examples are easily obtained to make these also nonthreatening. The first category (nonfactual but named things) includes all the many anthropomorphisms in biblical language, such as references to God's anger. This need not suggest that the Bible is unreliable, however, but merely that "we have used names derived from human experience and applied them, so far as we could, to aspects of God."[21] For the second category (factual but unnamed things), Gregory calls upon those most beloved Eunomian ascriptions to God, ingenerate and unoriginate. The fact that neither of these terms ("the wall of defense you trusted in"[22]) appears in scripture does not *ipso facto* make the concepts they represent "unscriptural," or deny their truth in reality. "Is it not plain that these terms are derived from passages that imply, without actually mentioning them?"[23]

Gregory concludes by chastising his opponents for their too literal devotion to scripture, an interpretive error that limits their perception of the inner meaning of the biblical texts. "There really is a great deal of diversity inherent in names and things, so why are you so dreadfully servile to the letter, . . . following the syllables while you let the realities go?"[24] And surely, Gregory suggests, it is the *meaning* communicated by the words of the revelatory texts that is important, and not simply the words themselves. It is this analysis that is at the heart of Gregory's willingness to set aside Basilian "economy," a reticence about using unscriptural language for the sake of accommodation and

communal peace. "If I hit upon something meant, though not mentioned, or not stated in clear terms, by Scripture, I should not be put
off by your quibbling charge about names—I should give expression
to the meaning. This is how we shall make our stand against people
whose views are only half right!"[25]

Thus Gregory has not only allowed for the possibility that the divinity of the Holy Spirit is among those realities that are simply not
expressly named in scripture, but he has also established that the ultimate norm for Christian belief is not the words themselves but the
meaning properly inferred from them. But before making his case for
how the divinity of the Spirit might be inferred as the legitimate meaning of the biblical witness, Gregory thinks he must first address one
additional question from his more contentious opponents. "I shall go
on now to take the argument a short stage further back and explain to
you (experts though you are supposed to be) the reason for all this
concealment."[26] That is, he will address the question of how such a
crucial topic as the Spirit's divinity could reasonably fall into the second of his categories (factual but unnamed things) instead of the fourth
(factual and named things). What *reason* could explain God's not having revealed the divinity of the Spirit expressly and clearly?

Gregory begins his answer by noting that the old and the new cov-
enants constitute "two remarkable transformations of the human way
of life in the course of the world's history."[27] For all their differences,
with the first representing the transition from idols to Law and the
second the transition from Law to Gospel, they have at least one fea-
ture in common. "They were not suddenly changed, even at the first
moment the changes were put in hand. We need to know why. It was
so that we should be persuaded, not forced."[28] At issue here is his
understanding of the accommodative nature of the divine pedagogy,
such that God's full self-revelation only unfolds in stages over time,
in a manner suited to human receptivity and in accordance with human freedom. "It belongs to despotic power to use force; it is a mark
of God's reasonableness that the issue should be ours."[29] Gregory com-
pares God to a schoolmaster or doctor who yields for a time on some
matters in order to better ensure the ready acceptance of others. And
just as God's revelation unfolds in stages respecting the human condition, he hints that so too should the response of God's servant in proclaiming that revelation. Evidence Paul adjusting his teaching on the
question of circumcision: "His earlier conduct was an accommoda-

tion to circumstance; his later conduct belonged to the full truth."[30]

Gregory understands his own time as a critical third stage in God's progressive self-revelation, a progression in which "growth towards perfection comes through additions. In this way, the old covenant made clear proclamation of the Father, a less definite one of the Son. The new covenant made the Son manifest and gave us a glimpse of the Spirit's Godhead. *At the present time, the Spirit resides amongst us, giving us a clearer manifestation of himself than before.*"[31] It would not have been appropriate, Gregory argues, for the Spirit to be explicitly named as God when the community of faith had not yet been able to accommodate the awesome doctrine of the Word's incarnation. "It could mean men jeopardizing what did lie within their powers, as happens to those encumbered with a diet too strong for them or who gaze at sunlight with eyes as yet too feeble for it."[32] Thus Gregory thinks he *can* provide a reason for the Spirit's divinity being only gestured at rather than explicitly announced. Indeed, he does so by pointing to the divine reason, the Logos, Christ the Physician, who responds in a manner best befitting the condition of the patient.

The discernment of this divine reason, however, also places demands on those to whom this progressive revelation is given. "You see how light shines on us bit by bit, you see in the doctrine of God an order, which we had better observe, neither revealing it suddenly nor concealing it to the last. To reveal it suddenly would be clumsy, would shock outsiders. Ultimately to conceal it would be a denial of God, would make outsiders of our own people."[33] Gregory recognizes an obligation to respond to God's ordered self-disclosure in a correspondingly ordered way, according to the *taxis* of that revelation. Referring to Jesus' own words ("When the Spirit of truth comes, he will guide you into all the truth"[34]), Gregory says: "One of these truths I take to be the *Godhead* of the Spirit, which becomes clear at a later stage, when the knowledge is timely and capable of being taken in, when after our Savior's return to heaven, it is, because of that miracle, no longer an object of disbelief."[35]

Now all the elements of Gregory's justification for his insistence on declaring the Spirit's full divinity are in place. While he acknowledges that the scriptures contain no explicit claim to that effect, he denies absolutely that this condition requires regarding the concept as "unscriptural," and this in three ways. First, through his hermeneutical reflection on "things and names" in biblical usage, he has established that there can be realities that are not explicitly mentioned. Second, he has provided an explanation for the fittingness of this circumstance, through his consideration of the accommodative nature of God's pedagogy progressively disclosing divine truths in a manner consistent with a supremely rational order. Third, he will provide a "swarm of proof-texts"[36] that strongly imply the divinity of the Spirit as a personal agent acting as only God can act and bearing titles only God can bear.[37]

These rhetorical arguments, however, are necessary but not sufficient conditions for licensing Gregory's particular pneumatological advancement. After all, Basil would certainly have agreed in essence with each of them, and yet he stopped short of declaring the Spirit to be consubstantial with God, and this despite his sharing Gregory's sense of the soteriological imperative underlying such belief.[38] Gregory diverges from Basil with respect to the degree of confidence he has in the authority of experience, and in his particular judgment that the "fullness of time" in the revelation of the Spirit's divinity has arrived. These are the two further ingredients required to justify throwing off the constraints of verbal economy.

The first is Gregory's *confidence* in placing ultimate normativity not in the letter of the biblical texts, nor even in the "spirit" of those texts as discerned through some secularized approach to interpretation, but rather in the Spirit of God who enables God's chosen to penetrate to their inner meaning of divine truth. This is Gregory's understanding of "David's prophetic vision: 'In your light we shall see light.' "[39] It is the revelatory experience of Christian believers that is decisively compelling in defining Christian doctrine, though the ultimate normativity accrues not to the recipients themselves but to the authority of the divine agent revealing. "They were found fit to perceive the hidden loveliness; they were illuminated by the light of knowledge."[40] And the divine agent referred to here is none other than the Holy Spirit revealing the Spirit's own self. Thus Gregory thinks he can answer his opponents' objection concerning the scriptural justification for his teaching: "for the divinity of the Holy Spirit the witness of Scripture must be supplemented by, or interpreted in the context of, the religious experience of the church and of the Christian individual."[41]

The second and final remaining ingredient is Gregory's *judgment* that the *taxis* of God's progressive revelation now demands proclaiming the truth of the Spirit's divinity. This is clearly a kind of "timing issue," then, a question of perception about which reasonable persons could (and did) disagree. As indicated above, Gregory allows that such a proclamation could occur both too early and too late. "To reveal it suddenly would be clumsy, would shock outsiders. Ultimately to conceal it would be a denial of God, would make outsiders of our own people."[42] But it is Gregory's judgment that in his time the orthodox Christian community has been granted a sufficiently "clearer manifestation"[43] of the Spirit to take the decisive step of proclaiming the Spirit's full divinity.[44] He has judged that "the time of reserve is over."[45] "This is the time: a new transition point in the seismic events that constitute the divine pattern of revelation in history. Gregory is the proclaimer. He does not say as much but he is undoubtedly implying that he, like Paul, is standing at the edge of the third seismic shaking."[46] Gregory takes Paul as his model of Christian ministry, and he interprets that ministry in prophetic terms.

The combination of these final two ingredients with his rhetorical argumentation regarding scripture comprises a potent formula for emboldening Gregory's resolve. His interest is in the salvific meaning of scripture, not a servile devotion to its words. His trust is in the God who reveals Godself as light from light in light, not merely to how God is finitely "named" in the Bible. And his vocation is to respond to the sapiential ordering of God's loving self-disclosure in a manner consistent with the form and dictates of that revelation itself. Thus Gregory views continued silence as more to be feared than controversial preaching.[47] Like Paul before him, who adjusted his Christian teaching concerning the then-controversial issue of circumcision, Gregory has determined that deference to the uncertainty of some must now yield to bold affirmation. "His earlier conduct was an accommodation to circumstance; his later conduct belonged to the full truth."[48]

Gregory's rhetorical method in expounding his pneumatological doctrine is itself instructive for its thorough basis in the economy of salvation and its robust reliance on scripture, liturgy, and doxological formulae. But its most striking element is the original precedent he provides for doctrinal development in the Christian tradition through inferences from scripture, which, while certainly going beyond the revealed texts, can never be regarded as "unbiblical." The step Gregory takes in pneumatology beyond the positions of Athanasius and even Basil is, importantly, empowered by the Spirit itself: "At the present time, the Spirit resides amongst us, giving us a clearer manifestation of himself than before."[49] Even allowing for its constitutive context in opposition to his Eunomian and pneumatomachian opponents, Gregory's pneumatology may provide a constructive model for contemporary efforts to discern the ongoing activity of the Spirit. Because the Spirit *continues* to reside among us, the Spirit may ever be giving us a clearer manifestation of the Spirit's work in the church and the world.

Notes

[1] Gregory's exposition, as will shortly become clear, also resonates with contemporary questions concerning legitimate doctrinal development and proper interpretation of scripture.

[2] In his grand survey of patristic pneumatology, H. B. Swete calls Gregory's Oration 31 the "greatest of all sermons on the doctrine of the Spirit." See *The Holy Spirit in the Ancient Church: A Study of Christian Teaching in the Age of the Fathers* (London: Macmillan, 1912), 420.

[3] John A. McGuckin, *Saint Gregory of Nazianzus: An Intellectual Biography* (Crestwood, N.Y.: St. Vladimir's Seminary Press, 2001), xxiv and 278.

[4] Frederick W. Norris, *Faith Gives Fullness to Reasoning: The Five Theological Orations of Gregory Nazianzen*, trans. Lionel Wickham and Frederick Williams (Leiden: E. J. Brill, 1991); Or. 31.1 (hereafter, Or. 31.1).

[5] Ibid.

[6] Or. 31.2.

[7] Or. 31.5.

[8] Or. 31.3. In his commentary on the text appearing in *Faith Gives Fullness to Reasoning*, Frederick Norris points to this passage as suggestive of an undeveloped wordplay on *letter* versus *spirit*—"What will the spirit of the text be without the Holy Spirit?" (see p. 185).

[9] Or. 31.3.

[10] Ibid.

[11] Ibid.

[12] Or. 31.10.

[13] Note that it was just this kind of artfully ambiguous language that found its way into the Creed of Constantinople in 381, over Gregory's most vehement objection.

[14] Or. 31.21.

[15] Ibid.

[16] Ibid.

[17] From Gregory's perspective, of course, this experience presupposes both the church's liturgical usage and its ascetical-mystical tradition.

[18] Or. 31.21.

[19] Or. 31.22.

[20]Or. 31.23.

[21]Or. 31.22.

[22]Or. 31.23.

[23]Ibid.

[24]Or. 31.24.

[25]Ibid.

[26]Ibid.

[27]Or. 31.25.

[28]Ibid.

[29]Ibid.

[30]Ibid.

[31]Or. 31.26, emphasis mine.

[32]Ibid.

[33]Or. 31.27.

[34]Jn 16:13 (NRSV).

[35]Or. 31.27.

[36]Or. 31.29.

[37]Particularly important among these, for Gregory, is the Spirit's activity as sanctifier bringing about our *theosis*, or deification, because only God can make a creature like God.

[38]For a concise statement of Gregory's sense of this soteriological imperative, see Or. 31.28. For Basil's typically more reserved position (though still in evident agreement), see chapter 23 of *St. Basil the Great on the Holy Spirit*, trans. David Anderson (Crestwood, N.Y.: St. Vladimir's Seminary Press, 2001), 85-86.

[39]Or. 31.3; Ps 36:9.

[40]Or. 31.21.

[41]R. P. C. Hanson, *The Search for the Christian Doctrine of God: The Arian Controversy, 318-381* (Edinburgh: T & T Clark, 1988), 783.

[42]Or. 31.27.

[43]Or. 31.26.

[44]An interesting (though likely irresolvable) question is to what extent this judgment was *in spite of* the evident disharmony between Gregory's orthodoxy and the pneumatomachian and Eunomian positions, or conversely, *precisely because of* that disharmony and his interest in overcoming it.

[45]John A. McGuckin, " 'Perceiving Light from Light in Light' (*Oration* 31.3): The Trinitarian Theology of Saint Gregory the Theologian," *Greek Orthodox Theological Review* 39 (1994): 20.

[46]McGuckin, *Saint Gregory of Nazianzus*, 308.

[47]Or. 31.3.

[48]Or. 31.25.

[49]Or. 31.26.

The Grieving Spirit:
The Holy Spirit as Bearer of the Suffering of the World in Moltmann's Pneumatology

Jane E. Linahan

"Therefore, putting away falsehood, let everyone speak the truth with his neighbor, for we are members one of another. . . . Let no evil talk come out of your mouths, but only such as is good for edifying, as fits the occasion, that it may impart grace to those who hear. And do not grieve the Holy Spirit of God, in whom you were sealed for the day of redemption. Let all bitterness and wrath and anger and clamor and slander be put away from you, with all malice, and be kind to one another, tenderhearted, forgiving one another, as God in Christ forgave you" (Ephesians 4:25, 29-32).[1]

For a systematic theologian deeply engaged with the question of God's relation to the world, this biblical passage evokes an intriguing line of inquiry: What might it mean for the Holy Spirit to grieve? What would grieving mean for the Holy Spirit? What happens to the Holy Spirit if and when that Spirit is grieved? Why is it a matter of such solemn importance not to grieve the Holy Spirit of God?

It might be objected that this line of questioning is presumptuous, first, because it appears to pry into the very mystery of God. Can we presume to have access to the inner "emotional life" (if there is such a thing!) of the Spirit, the One who has ever seemed most "hidden" and elusive to our theology? We are warned, with good reason, of the hazards of over-confident speculation about God's "inner" life. For example, in her masterful analysis of the doctrine of the Trinity, Catherine LaCugna argues persuasively that it is precisely such speculation, venturing beyond the bounds of what is self-revealed by God in the economy of salvation, that has led to theological mistakes in appropriating the true significance of the doctrine and, especially, its implications for Christian faith and life.[2] In awareness of the need for caution, then, this inquiry will attempt to draw from reflection upon the history of God's dealings with the world, and specifically the scriptural witness to that history, for possible insights into the grieving of the Spirit. I would add that I do not at all consider this an exercise in idle speculation because I believe it has urgent significance: the grieving of the Spirit encompasses our own, both that which has already been brought to pass and that which yet hangs over our heads. As I hope to show, we and our world, in the totality of our existence together, are enfolded in the Spirit's grief.

A second count of presumption concerns attributing the possibility of grieving to One who is divine and then daring to analyze that grief. How can an utterly transcendent God who "dwells in unapproachable light" (1 Tm 6:16) be vulnerable to such a mortal condition as grieving—for it is precisely our mortality that enmeshes us in grief? Divine impassibility, a corollary of the classical theistic definition of God's perfection, entailing that God cannot be capable of suffering or of being affected, has received overwhelming, though not unanimous, support in the Christian theological tradition.[3] But has this weight of tradition obscured valuable sensitivities about the necessary role of passivity and vulnerability in authentic relationship? Admittedly, to affirm that God could be subject to suffering seems to undermine God's radical otherness and to call into question something at the very heart of what we depend on God to be for us. How can we reconcile a suffering, vulnerable God with our need—and hope!—for an all-powerful, invincible protector and savior who will effect our definitive deliverance to unassailable blessedness? At the same time, the language of divine vulnerability—which we must make clear is metaphorical language—says something crucial for our understanding of the nature of God's love for and involvement in the world. Terence Fretheim, for example, argues that the images of divine suffering and vulnerability in the Hebrew Bible manifest the seriousness with which God takes human beings: God's relationship with humanity is real and has integrity because God allows human actions and responses to make a real difference to the relationship.[4] These images themselves may not be dismissed as "merely figurative" without undermining the integrity and coherence of God's dealings with humanity to which they give witness: "[D]oes God really mean what is said or not?"[5] The language of divine vulnerability speaks to us of God's openness to and respect for the dignity of the creature, a message that could mean the difference between life and death to a world imperiled by massive indifference and violence toward all forms of life, especially the weak and the different.

Here we will reflect upon one dimension of divine vulnerability, that of the Holy Spirit. Hence, to return to our initial question, what is the grieving of the Holy Spirit? In what might the grieving of the Spirit of God, which we are warned against causing, consist?

The Spirit and Grief?

The Christian theological and spiritual tradition customarily characterizes the Holy Spirit in positive and uplifting images, images of comfort and consolation. Especially since Augustine, the Spirit has been linked in a particular way with love: the Spirit is the *vinculum amoris*, the love with which Father and Son love each other and the gift of love mutually given by them to us: "God's love has been poured into our hearts through the Holy Spirit which has been given to us" (Rom 5:5).[6] The Creed of Constantinople calls the Holy Spirit the Giver of Life. In the Gospel of John, the Spirit is the Advocate (NAB) or Counselor (RSV) sent by the Father (14:16, 26) and by the Son (16:7). In the Hebrew Bible, the Spirit of Yahweh is "God's own power of creation, and the power of life which it communicate[s] to all created things." It is the power by which God led Israel out of slavery to freedom, and the power that enabled the prophets to speak God's word. The Spirit is thus God's creative energy, the vital energy of all living things, and the energy for salvation working through all those commissioned for service to God's saving plan.[7] The Spirit is the dynamism of God's creating, enlivening, sustaining, self-communicating, and saving love, and is thus intimately associated with all the activities by which God is known as God. The *Sequence* for the Feast of Pentecost, one of the most beautiful hymns in the Roman Catholic liturgy, is a comprehensive summary of this life-giving and saving work of the Spirit, even going so far as to attribute to the Spirit some characterizations more usually linked to the Father and Son: "Lord," "Light," "Rest," and "Father of the poor."[8] Theologically speaking, the Spirit makes the saving love of the triune God present, real, and effective in every possible circumstance of life in this world.

Against this background the notion of grieving the Spirit seems paradoxical. According to the *Oxford English Dictionary*, in older usage the English word grieve meant "to burden," "to do wrong or harm to," "to cause pain, anxiety, or vexation to"; in a narrower, more current sense it means "to affect with grief or deep sorrow." Grief, in turn, means "deep or violent sorrow, caused by loss or trouble; a keen or bitter feeling of regret for something lost, remorse for something done, or sorrow for mishap to oneself or others."[9] We usually think of grief in correlation with death: it is the overwhelming, life-altering, sometimes passionate, sometimes numbing sense of emptiness, sorrow, protest, and upheaval at the irretrievable loss of a loved one. Grieving is the filter through which we most commonly encounter death as it affects us personally. How astonishing to suggest a link between our experience of death and "the Lord and Giver of Life"!

Scriptural Clues

While some strands of our theological tradition may shy away from speaking of grief in connection with God, the Bible does not. When divine grieving is mentioned in the Hebrew Bible, it is in the context of the vicissitudes of relationship. The grieving of God and of the Spirit is an expression of divine *pathos*, which occurs at moments of crisis in the passionate, conflicted relationship between God and God's people. Psalm 78:40-41 says, "How often they rebelled against him in the wilderness and grieved him in the desert! They tested him again and again, and provoked the Holy One of Israel." The context of these verses is a turbulent narrative of the give and take between God's overwhelming favor and fierce anger in response to the people's fidelity or lack thereof, but the overarching theme is God's steadfast fidelity and compassion that persist in spite of everything.

Isaiah 63 is a recounting of praise for "the steadfast love of the LORD" (v. 7), speaking movingly of God's tender, loving solidarity and parent-like solicitude for the people in their suffering and need: "In all their affliction he was afflicted, and the angel of his presence saved them; in his love and in his pity he redeemed them; he lifted them up and carried them all the days of old" (v. 9). This is followed by a startling reversal: "But they rebelled and grieved his holy Spirit; therefore he turned to be their enemy, and himself fought against them"

(v. 10). But then the Lord "remembered the days of old" (v. 11), reminded by the prophet of the "yearning of thy heart and thy compassion" (v. 15), and that "Thou art our Father" (v. 16).

In Genesis 6:6, God experiences bitter regret upon seeing the great human wickedness on earth: "And the LORD was sorry that he had made man on the earth, and it grieved him to his heart." Fretheim, who sees the biblical images of divine grieving as expressions of the depth of God's self-investment in the relationship with the world, notes that this passage from Genesis indicates that divine grieving is not limited to God's relationship with Israel. "God's grieving goes back to the morning of the world. Grief has been characteristic of the history of God almost from the beginning of things."[10] The divine grieving passages in the Hebrew Bible highlight a sometimes painful, tempestuous, even heartbreaking, but never (by God) abandoned, relationship.

When the suggestion of divine grieving is introduced in the Second Testament, the context is, again, relationship. But now, as the Ephesians text makes clear, the focus is on the relationship of human beings to each other. This is, of course, grounded in the prior and primary relationship of God with human beings: "And do not grieve the Holy Spirit of God in whom you were sealed for the day of redemption" (4:30). But the point is very clear that relationship with God implies responsibilities for relationship with each other: "Put on the new nature, created after the likeness of God in true righteousness and holiness . . . for we are members one of another. . . . [A]nd be kind to one another, tenderhearted, forgiving one another, as God in Christ forgave you" (4:24, 25, 32). The implication proposed is profound: to diminish another human being, to act toward anyone with irreverence, malice, or violence is to "grieve the Holy Spirit of God." I believe that there is much more at stake here than a simplistic notion about making God "unhappy" by our sinning—a remnant of childhood's piety that could never be taken completely seriously in the context of the doctrine of divine impassibility. In order to get at the "much more" that is at stake, it is necessary to take the possibility of grieving the Holy Spirit of God with complete and utter seriousness.

Insights from Moltmann: A "Pneumatology of the Cross"

The work of Jürgen Moltmann provides a fruitful approach for exploring the question of the grieving of the Spirit. In *The Crucified*

God, published in German in 1973, Moltmann engaged the issue of divine suffering in a radical way, and his subsequent work has continued that line of questioning. Significantly, this has included an impressive development in his reflections on the Holy Spirit, specifically on the self-emptying of the Spirit. Tracing some of the lines of that development will yield important insights for our investigation. However, the unwavering backdrop against which to understand the *kenosis* of the Spirit is the Holy Spirit's fundamental role as the giver of life—life understood in the most holistic, all-encompassing sense.[11] The Spirit is God's power making possible both creation and new creation, bringing the cosmos into being and drawing it toward its eschatological transformation and fulfillment.[12] All of this is rooted in God's gracious turning toward us in love, in God's superabundant, overflowing, ecstatic generosity toward that which is Other, desiring that Other's fullness of life. The Holy Spirit issues forth out of God's profoundly generous love[13] and is poured forth in order to realize—make real—the gracious designs of that love.

A "Trinitarian" Interpretation of the Cross?

To understand how this pouring forth entails a true *kenosis* of the Spirit and includes within itself the potentiality for the grieving of the Spirit, it will be helpful first to explore Moltmann's interpretation of the cross, focusing especially on his theology of the surrender of the Son.[14] For Moltmann, the cry of Jesus from the cross, "My God, my God, why hast thou forsaken me?"(Mk 15:34), "stands at the centre of the Christian faith."[15] Christian theology stands or falls according to how it is able to speak of God in the light of this "open question concerning God" with which Jesus dies.[16] Jesus' death cry expresses a devastating experience of abandonment that strikes at the very heart of his relationship with the Father and hence of his understanding of God. "The One who knew himself to be the Son"—the One who had the insight into God's tender love that enabled him to say, "Abba, Father"—"is forsaken, rejected and cursed. And God is silent."[17] According to Moltmann, Jesus' death on a cross would have been understood by both Jesus himself and by its various witnesses (the disciples, the Jewish religious leaders, and the crowds) as death under God's curse, and thus as the very public repudiation by God of Jesus and all that he stood for, specifically his gospel of the reign of God with what it implied for understanding who God is. Thus Moltmann suggests that Jesus' cry is really a plea for God to be faithful to Godself, for God to *be* God, the One Jesus knows as Father. It could, then, even be interpreted to mean, "My God, why hast thou forsaken *thyself?*"[18] The core of the event of the cross is thus the contradiction between Jesus' experience of profound relationship with the Father and his experience of utter abandonment by God, the horrifying anomaly of God's self-repudiation (for what could be more horrifying than the possibility that God is not *God?*).

It is essential to this interpretation to make clear that the cross happens not because God wills or causes Jesus' suffering and death, but because the world rejects Jesus' gospel of the reign of God. Jesus' death is caused by human beings and is the consequence of his ministry lived out in fidelity to the Father. And precisely because God is God, the loving, merciful Father whom Jesus has proclaimed (Lk 6:36), this Father refuses to respond with coercion and force to the world's rejection of his own Son, but, rather, gives him up for us all (Rom 8:32).[19] The cross happens because God's kingdom is the kingdom of justice and mercy, to which all are freely invited, but which the world rejects in rejecting Jesus. God opens Godself to the world's response, which means that God identifies Godself with Jesus' experience of rejection. The Father is caught up in and personally affected by the Son's experience of godforsakenness. Precisely because the Father is the Father of the Son, that Father suffers through what happens to the Son. Says Moltmann, "The Son suffers his dying in this forsakenness. The Father suffers the death of the Son. He suffers it in the infinite pain of his love for the Son. The death of the Son therefore corresponds to the pain of the Father."[20] Because Father and Son are defined in their very being by their love for and relation to each other, their surrender of self and of each other upon the cross impinges upon their very identities and relationship. Speaking of Father and Son being affected in their very being, but in distinctive ways, brings the language of divine suffering into conjunction with trinitarian language: "To understand what happened between Jesus and his God and Father on the cross, it is necessary to talk in trinitarian terms. The Son suffers dying, the Father suffers the death of the Son. The grief of the Father here is just as important as the death of the Son."[21]

As this quotation from *The Crucified God* indicates, Moltmann's early reflections on the cross, while deliberately pursuing a trinitarian interpretation, elaborate that trinitarianism in terms of the Father and Son only, a problem pointed out by some critics of Moltmann's early work.[22] The Holy Spirit is mentioned in the discussion in *The Crucified God*, but only briefly and almost in passing. Moltmann has been describing the "deep conformity between the will of the Father and the will of the Son in the event of the cross" that results from Jesus' obedience to the Father (Mk 14:36) and leads to his experience of godforsakenness on the cross. Father and Son are thus engaged in a mutual surrender that indicates a deeper underlying unity between them even and especially at the moment of most extreme "separation" as the Son dies in godforsakenness. Moltmann continues, "What proceeds from this event between Father and Son is the Spirit which justifies the godless, fills the forsaken with love and even brings the dead alive, since even the fact that they are dead cannot exclude them from this event of the cross; the death in God also includes them." The presence of the Spirit in the event of the cross is thus understood in terms of what results from this event, the grace and mercy that flow forth upon lost human beings from the surrender of Father and Son.[23] While this is by no means negligible, it is not yet a full explication of the role of the Spirit in the cross as a trinitarian event.

But Moltmann's work in the following years reflects ongoing development in his thinking on pneumatology. In both *The Church in the Power of the Spirit* (1975) and *The Trinity and the Kingdom* (1980) he makes use of Hebrews 9:14, which says that Christ, "through the eternal Spirit, offered himself without blemish to God," to support his point that it is *through the Spirit* that the surrender of both Father and Son takes place. "The Holy Spirit is therefore the link in the separation. He is the link joining the bond between the Father and the Son, with their separation."[24] In and through the Spirit, their separation is in identity with their union: the separation of the cross is the actualization of their union of will in their mutual surrender. The moment of their deepest separation can be the moment of their deepest union because this is encompassed and empowered by the Holy Spirit: "The power which leads him into abandonment by the Father is the power which at the same time unites him with the Father."[25] That the Father and Son are engaged in a "single surrendering movement"[26] is possible because the surrender of each, which issues in this single movement, is motivated and activated out of the same source and the same energy, the Spirit of God.

The Kenotic Role of the Spirit

With *The Way of Jesus Christ* (1989), a significant advance has
been achieved by Moltmann: this, his major work on christology, is
set entirely in a pneumatological key. The entire event of the coming
of Christ, especially as depicted in the synoptic gospels, takes place in
and through the Holy Spirit and cannot be understood apart from the
activity of that Spirit.[27] Jesus' very identity and existence are defined
by his unique experience of the God he knows as Abba, and the presence to him of Abba is uniquely mediated through the presence and
power of the Spirit.[28] Since the Spirit is God's own creative and salvific
power, the abiding presence of the Spirit in Jesus means "the true
beginning of the kingdom of God, and of the new creation in history."[29] The Spirit is the divine agency that gives shape and force to
Jesus' ministry, the power in which he proclaims the kingdom of the
Father and brings healing and wholeness to human beings. The synoptic gospels make a point of showing that Jesus and his mission are
rooted in and guided throughout by God's Spirit—for example, in his
anointing by the Spirit for ministry at his baptism, an anointing that
Luke makes explicit in the scene at the synagogue at Nazareth (4:18-
21). For Moltmann, what makes Jesus' course specifically "messianic" is that the One who leads him along this way is the Spirit of
God.[30] God's messiah is essentially defined by his *openness* and *surrender* to the leading of the Spirit.

This activity of the Spirit provides the context in which to view
Jesus' surrender to the Father's will on the cross:

> [T]he Spirit who was Jesus' active power now becomes his
> suffering power. . . . The sufferings of Christ are also the suffer-
> ings of the Spirit, for the surrender of Christ also manifest[s] the
> self-emptying of the Spirit. The Spirit is the divine subject of
> Jesus' life-history; and the Spirit is the divine subject of Jesus'
> passion history.[31]

This means that it is the Spirit of God that leads, guides, inspires, and
empowers Jesus' course in dying as in living. Just as it is in the presence of the Spirit that Jesus knows God as Abba, it is in that same
presence that Jesus surrenders to the supreme contradiction of that
knowledge, his godforsakenness, in giving himself over to the will of

the Father. The Spirit who has been the dynamic energy of God in his ministry is now the mysterious presence that empowers him to confront the absence of the Father. However, as the quote above indicates, in empowering the surrender of the Son, the Spirit empties itself also. The mutual surrender of Father and Son entails a *kenosis* of the Spirit. Not only is the Spirit the divine energy behind the surrender of Father and Son and the gracious outpouring of eternal life that issues from that event; what these affirmations, profound enough in themselves, entail is that the Spirit, too, is surrendered and surrenders itself.

In *The Spirit of Life* (1991) Moltmann's primary focus is pneumatology. Its treatment of the Spirit's involvement in the event of the cross builds on the foundations laid in the earlier works. Because it is in and through the Spirit that Jesus knows himself to be the "beloved Son" of Abba—for "the Spirit is the real determining subject of this special relationship of Jesus' to God, and of God's to Jesus"[32]—the mutual surrender of Father and Son takes place within the context of Jesus' possession by the Spirit. The imagery suggests that the Spirit encompasses or mediates the relation of the Father to Jesus and Jesus to the Father and thus plays a determining role in what happens within their relationship in the event of surrender. This means that the "rupture" in their relationship must also have an impact on the One who is its "determining subject."[33] But also emphasized is that the entire course of the Spirit's history with Jesus, and not just the event of the cross, involves a *kenosis* of the Spirit. Moltmann draws on Jewish rabbinic theology of the *Shekinah* to develop the idea that the pouring out of the Spirit on Jesus and its abiding presence with him entails a self-emptying and self-limitation for the Spirit:

> The phraseology about the "descent" of the Spirit on Jesus, and its "resting" on him, suggests that the Spirit should be interpreted as *God's Shekinah*. What is meant is the *self-restriction* and *self-humiliation* of the eternal Spirit, and his feeling identification with Jesus' person and the history of his life and suffering—just as, according to the rabbinic idea [of the *Shekinah*], God's Spirit has committed itself to the history of Israel's life and sufferings.[34]

By dwelling in Jesus, the Spirit partakes of all the limitations and humiliations of Jesus in his human condition and in his experience of suffering as messianic Son. As the temptation narratives indicate, the meaning of Jesus' sonship is not defined by worldly force and power, but by openness to the Spirit and, eventually, by suffering. If the Spirit abides in Jesus and, as the *Shekinah* idea suggests, accompanies and guides him on his course, then it also enters with him into his suffering and death.[35]

> And if the Spirit accompanies him, then it is drawn into his sufferings, and becomes his *companion* in suffering. The path the Son takes in his passion is then at the same time the path taken by the Spirit. . . . [The Spirit] participates in his human suffering to the point of his death on the cross. . . . Through the Shekinah, the Spirit binds itself to Jesus' fate, though without becoming identical with him.[36]

Moltmann notes that the "Gospel of Mark tells the history of Jesus as the history of the Spirit with Jesus."[37] This history begins with the descent of the Spirit at Jesus' baptism in which Jesus comes to know that he is the "beloved Son" (1:10-11) and God is "Abba." When Jesus calls on Abba in Gethsemane (14:36), what is implied is this overarching context of the Spirit's presence (in other words, that Jesus says "Abba" because of the Spirit). In its own way Gethsemane is another trial (temptation) about the meaning of Jesus' sonship and, once again, this sonship comes to be defined by surrender to Abba and to the leading of the Spirit. The cry to Abba in Gethsemane leads Moltmann to claim:

> This means that Mark is giving a pneumatological interpretation to Jesus' passion. . . . What begins with his baptism through the operation of the Spirit ends in his passion through the operation of the Spirit. The Spirit which "leads" Jesus into the wilderness is beside him, sustaining him in his suffering from God. . . . Whereas in Jesus' baptism God calls Jesus "my beloved Son," in Gethsemane Jesus responds by addressing him as "Abba, dear Father." Both the call to life and the response in dying are given "in the Spirit." Jesus goes in the Spirit and through the Spirit to his death. And that means, in the awareness that he is the messianic son of God whom baptism with the Spirit has designated him to be.[38]

What Moltmann only hints at here, but can be inferred, is that it is the Spirit who drives Jesus' dying cry of protest on the cross.[39] The Spirit sustains Jesus' faith in Abba to the end, which is what makes the experience of abandonment so terrible. Jesus suffers this in the Spirit, and the Spirit suffers it with him. The Spirit is the source of Jesus' protest against God's self-contradiction and the power that makes it possible for him to die upholding that protest in the throes of godforsakenness. The Spirit goes with him into godforsakenness, which means that on the most fundamental level his relation with the Father is sustained by the Spirit even when it is experienced as broken in every other sense. Only God's Spirit of "indestructible life" (Heb 7:16) can sustain their connection in brokenness and cause it to transcend the ultimate death of abandonment by God.

Moltmann notes an interesting inversion in Mark. Beginning in Gethsemane, and from there until his death in abandonment, Jesus experiences God as "the hidden, absent, even rejecting Father." But it appears that at the same time Jesus has a "growing certainty of his messiahship, to the point when he publicly acknowledges it before Pilate (15:2), an acknowledgment which then leads to his execution, and to the title 'king of the Jews' over the cross."[40] I would add that this building movement toward the confirmation of Jesus' identity climaxes in the centurion's confession, "Truly this man was the son of God!" (15:39), which is given precisely in reaction to Jesus' dying cry of abandonment and the breathing out of his spirit.[41]

As Moltmann interprets it, "This growing certainty of his messiahship is a clear sign of the presence of God's Spirit in the absence of God the Father which Jesus experienced."[42] Jesus' understanding of his messiahship has always been conditioned by the Spirit, as has his relation with the Father. When the Father is now silent, the only thing that can possibly sustain his continuing openness to the Father and account for his paradoxically increasing assurance of his mission (and for his protest against God's self-contradiction) is the presence of the Spirit. In the face of Jesus' evident final abandonment by God, it might also be suggested that the presence of the Spirit is the only way to account for the centurion's profession that Jesus is God's son. It is surely no accident that the centurion's profession echoes the Father's declaration at Jesus' baptism. Is this meant to signify the presence, in the mode of mystery and suffering and surrender, of the Father and Spirit, precisely at the moment of the Son's abandonment (namely, that the centurion, through the Spirit, says what the Father may not)? Or is it a deliberate reminder of Jesus' foundational experience of sonship (his baptism) and, hence, of the terrible awesomeness of the Father's surrender of the Son?

Moltmann notes once again that the Epistle to the Hebrews also affirms the pneumatological dimension of the cross in stressing that Christ offers himself "through the Spirit" (9:14).

> The value of the sacrifice does not depend solely on the one surrendered. It has to do with the mode of surrender too. And in this happening Christ is determined through the eternal Spirit. The Spirit is not something he possesses. It is the power that makes him ready to surrender his life, and which itself sustains this surrender.[43]

In Hebrews Christ is both the one who offers (high priest) and that which is offered: through the power of the Spirit, he is not merely passive victim, but active subject in offering the perfect covenantal sacrifice. So,

> It is not the Romans who are the real controlling agents in Christ's passion and death, and not even death itself. It is Christ himself who is the truly active one, through the operation of the divine Spirit who acts in him. In "the theology of surrender," Christ is made the determining subject of suffering and death through the Spirit of God.[44]

The Spirit empowers and accompanies Jesus in his suffering—and therefore suffers with him, not in the same way, but in a way distinctive to the Spirit. The Spirit is Jesus' "strength in suffering" and "the 'indestructible life' in whose power Jesus can give himself vicariously 'for many.' "[45] The Spirit is there as Jesus dies, "his companion in suffering"[46] who "suffers the suffering and death of the Son, without dying with him. So what the Spirit 'experiences'—though we must not overstress the metaphor—is surely that the dying Jesus 'breathes him out' and 'yields him up' (Mk 15:37; stronger, Jn 19:30)."[47] Moltmann cites a suggestion by E. Vogelsang: "Of such a kind was Christ's death cry: as his senses left him and he went down to death, the Holy Spirit interceded for him, with inexpressible groanings, helping his weakness also."[48] This reference to Romans 8:26 suggests that Jesus' death cry encompasses (or is encompassed by?) the groaning of the Spirit, groaning with him as it is breathed out (surrendered) by him.

As he dies, Jesus surrenders the Spirit who has been with him from the beginning, who has shaped his very identity and life, and whose presence has been the "place" where he has found Abba. Matthew (27:50) and Luke (23:46) speak of his yielding up and breathing out his spirit, the latter transforming the cry of abandonment in Mark and Matthew into the supreme expression of surrender to the Father: "Father, into thy hands I commit my spirit!" It is interesting, although Moltmann does not stress this, that John 19:30 uses "delivering up" language (*paredōken*) to speak of Jesus' surrender of his spirit, language that is used elsewhere to speak of the handing over or surrendering of the *Son* (for example, Jn 19:16; Rom 8:32). Whether or not the gospel texts about Jesus giving up his spirit are to be interpreted as referring to the Holy Spirit, it is surely not inappropriate to speak of his surrender of the Holy Spirit at the moment when he must let go of everything that the presence of that Spirit has meant to him.

This overview of the development of Moltmann's pneumatological interpretation of the cross yields the following synthesis: what is actualized and manifested on the cross is a comprehensive pattern of *kenosis*, of surrendering and being surrendered. The Father gives his own beloved Son to the world and for the world through the Holy Spirit—even to the point of letting go of the Son in the event of godforsakenness. The life-giving Spirit, obedient to the loving will of the Father, empties itself into the world in its descent and indwelling in Jesus—even to the point of partaking in Jesus' life and sufferings and being yielded up in death. Jesus empties himself into the world and submits to the leading of the Holy Spirit and the will of the Father—even to the point of letting go of the beloved Father in death and giving up the Spirit in whose power his life has been lived. The phrases "to the world," "for the world," and "into the world" are significant. As has been stressed, the cross is the consequence, not so much of divine prearrangement, as of the history of God's kenotic engagement with the world and specifically with human beings. Because God has given the Son and Spirit to and for the world, there is a sense in which we may speak of God's *surrendering* them to the world. In the very act of seeking out wholehearted and authentic engagement with human beings, God opens up the radical possibility that what is offered in love will be accepted or rejected by creaturely freedom. In giving over the Son and Spirit, God has truly laid Godself open to the world; God has made Godself vulnerable—surrendered—to the world's response.

The Grieving of the Spirit

What this review of Moltmann's thought has provided is a perspective from which to understand the vulnerability and, hence, the grieving of the Spirit. The Spirit is vulnerable, first of all, by virtue of its self-investment in the world. The cross, and the history of the Spirit with the Son of which it is the culmination, reveal the Spirit as the One who both empowers and surrenders or, better, empowers precisely by surrendering. The Spirit is the supremely kenotic One, empowering Christ's self-giving in life and in death precisely by that Spirit's own giving of self. Surely the language about the Spirit's being Jesus' "strength in suffering" and maintaining the Father's and Son's profound communion of will at the very moment when they are most "separated" from each other suggests that the Spirit "spends" itself, pours out itself, empties itself in order that the Father's gift of the Son for the world might be accomplished.

Second, the Spirit is vulnerable because this self-spending is invested in that which is Other than God. Our reflections on the event of the cross have shown how "expensive" the divine openness to the world can be for God. If the sending of the Son and the Spirit, the meaning of which receives its sharpest focus in the cross, is the culmination of God's self-giving openness to the world, it means that this event is a key to understanding the entire history of God with the world. Although it is not possible to trace it in detail here, this history, from the very beginning of creation until its eschatological fulfillment, is one of self-emptying on God's part, a self-emptying empowered and mediated by the Spirit. From the very beginning, God's generous love has graciously turned toward that which is Other, granting it being, autonomy, and freedom. This means "making room" for the Other to *be Other*: God commits Godself to standing by that which has been granted existence and freedom and to being faithful to these gifts. In this, God's love has made itself vulnerable to being thwarted, so that bringing creation to the fulfillment God desires for it may cause this love to suffer. God's creative love is what makes possible and sustains the freedom by which it can be acted upon by the Other. This is what Moltmann means when he says, "Creative love is ultimately suffering love because it is only through suffering that it acts creatively and redemptively for the freedom of the beloved. Freedom can only be made possible by suffering love."[49] So bringing creation to salvific fulfillment "in the midst of humanity's history of disaster . . . is anything but effortless. . . . [It] comes into being out of God's 'labour and travail.' "[50]

What does this specifically mean for the Spirit? God is present in the travail of creation not only because the Son has become incarnate in its very reality, but also because God has poured out the Spirit to give it life. God, the source of all life, brings forth creation by giving it room to be and breathing forth the Spirit. The Spirit, God's own power of life, brings all other life into being, flowing in all things, giving them their life. Through this Spirit of life, God "goes out" of God and enters into communion with God's Other. In Moltmann's words, "The reciprocal inhabitation of humans in God and of God in humans . . . is effected in the 'community of the Holy Spirit.' "[51]

If God's Spirit is given as gift to be the source of the life of creation, it means that the Spirit is involved, personally and immediately, in creation's history of freedom. The Spirit is poured out in empowering creation's being, autonomy, and freedom, and so is caught up in the playing out of its destiny. As the life-giving energy that connects God and creation in dynamic relationship, the inexhaustible Spirit "spends" itself in bearing their mutual give and take. The Spirit is the indwelling presence of God in a broken and incomplete creation striving toward fulfillment, giving itself to keep creation alive all through its history of death. The God who is unfathomable love is present even in the world's darkest times and places, as well as in its goodness and growth, and the Spirit is the form that this presence takes within creation's tortured, fragile, endangered, unfinished history. This means that the Spirit's very being is opened and poured out into the world, and is expended in maintaining its life. The Spirit's very being is intimately involved in every aspect of creation and its history and in the minute-by-minute living, suffering, and dying of every creature.

By reason of its indwelling all of creation, the Spirit subjects itself to all that creation undergoes and to all the conditions of creaturely existence. The Spirit enters into the incompleteness, the ongoing development, and the brokenness of creation in order to bring it to the fullness of life, sustaining through the pain and nurturing the growth of all things as they strive for fulfillment. Within the being of every creature, the Spirit yearns for its freedom from sin and death and for its life in abundance (Rom 8:19-23). In the *kenosis* of the Spirit, God is poured out into creation, to partake as intimately as possible in its life. In the Spirit, God is closer to us than our own self because the Spirit is the life of our life.

Yet this presence of God takes the form of hiddenness, suffering, and subjection to the conditions of creaturely existence, so that God may be with us where we are now without violating our human reality. Through the *kenosis* of the Spirit, God dwells in creation in a way that does not overwhelm its creaturely autonomy and freedom, its otherness and particularity, but rather fosters them. Moltmann stresses the relational import of this self-emptying: "By virtue of God's unselfish love, God permeates all creatures and makes them alive. In this way God lives in the creation community and allows the community of all God's creatures to live in God."[52] This "permeation" is actualized in and through the Holy Spirit. The Spirit's very being is kenotic, because it gives itself to bring God's presence into the world and to bring the world—as world—into God.

The Spirit, thus, has an intimate, personal self-investment in the world for the sake of the very great love of God for God's creation. Paul's statement that "the Spirit itself intercedes [for us] with inexpressible groanings" (Rom 8:26 NAB) follows closely upon the affirmation that "all creation is groaning in labor pains even until now; and not only that, but we ourselves, *who have the firstfruits of the Spirit*, we also groan within ourselves as we wait for adoption, the redemption of our bodies" (Rom 8:22-23 NAB, emphasis mine). The connection cannot be accidental: the groaning and travail of creation are infused with the groaning and travail of the Spirit laboring to bring the new creation to birth out of subjection to "futility" and "slavery to corruption" (Rom 8:20-21 NAB). It is the very gift of the first fruits of the Spirit that sharpens our yearning for the fulfillment it promises. From within creation and within our own beings the Spirit labors and groans against all the conditions that impede creation's fullness of life, especially death.

Thus, the Spirit is brought to grief because this self-investment in the world is an investment of love, and love, by its very nature, is vulnerable. If we would try to begin to understand the grieving of the Holy Spirit, we need to consider the labor of a mother giving birth, her unspeakable delight in every minute detail of the precious little life entrusted to her care, the utterly selfless, self-expending devotion she pours out so that her child will be healthy and safe, her kenotic self-sacrifice in one day letting go so that the child may achieve self-actualization, autonomy, and freedom—and then the unbearable agony of seeing that beloved child violated, humiliated, tortured, maimed, lost, or killed. If the Spirit is indeed as intimately involved in creation's life as we have claimed, it means that creation's pain is the Spirit's pain. When God's beloved creatures are abused, treated with contempt and violence—with "bitterness and wrath and anger and clamor and slander [and] malice" (Eph 4:31)–the Holy Spirit of God grieves. And perhaps the grief is all the more profound because the violence is inflicted by creatures upon each other, *all* of whom—victims and perpetrators alike—are loved, held in being, and empowered in freedom by the Spirit. Life is costly, love is costly, and the Spirit is the One who pays the ultimate price, spending self in order to make possible the life of the Other, and risking what openness to that Other might bring.

While it might be objected that, in all of this, biblical metaphors are being applied too literally, I would counter that perhaps we are inclined not to take them seriously enough. Biblical metaphors convey depths of meaning that sometimes cannot be expressed in any other way. If it is true that on one level the metaphors should be taken less than literally—does God *literally* empty Godself?—on another level, they should be taken much more than literally. These images are pointing to something that is true about God, and it is this deeper truth, the truth behind the metaphor, that is in fact the point. By touching a chord that reverberates deeply in us, the image of the grieving of the Holy Spirit of God communicates a dimension of God's love that opens out into a fuller and richer reality of love. Divine love is not limited to the human dimensions of love, but is infinitely greater. Put simply, we grieve because we love: whatever element of love's intensity is expressed in grief, that element of God's love must be infinitely richer. The grieving of the Spirit is God's passionate, tenderhearted (Eph 4:32), vulnerable love, bearing the world in its suffering. The exhortation not to grieve the Holy Spirit of God is one of profound seriousness: any assault upon any part of creation impinges upon the One who holds it in life and loves it dearly.

Notes

[1]Unless otherwise noted, all biblical quotations are taken from the Revised Standard Version.

[2]Catherine Mowry LaCugna, *God for Us: The Trinity and Christian Life* (New York: HarperCollins, HarperSanFrancisco, 1991).

[3]It is beyond the scope of this paper to rehearse the history of the discussion of divine impassibility. One of the best treatments of this topic is that by J. K. Mozley, *The Impassibility of God: A Survey of Christian Thought* (Cambridge: Cambridge University Press, 1926). More recently, in *The Descent of God: Divine Suffering in History and Theology* (Minneapolis: Fortress Press, 1991) Joseph M. Hallman has also examined nuances in the classic insistence on impassibility. Another survey and analysis is given by Hans Küng in *The Incarnation of God: An Introduction to Hegel's Theological Thought as Prolegomena to a Future Christology*, trans. J. R. Stephenson (New York: Crossroad, 1987), especially in the excurses at the end of the book. For a discussion of the influence of Greek philosophical ideas on the formation of the Christian concept of God and the problems this raises, see Wolfhart Pannenberg, "The Appropriation of the Philosophical Concept of God as a Dogmatic Problem of Early Christian Theology," in *Basic Questions in Theology: Collected Essays*, vol. 2, trans. George H. Kehm (Philadelphia: Fortress Press, 1971), 119-83.

[4]Terence E. Fretheim, *The Suffering of God: An Old Testament Perspective*, vol. 14 of *Overtures to Biblical Theology* (Philadelphia: Fortress Press, 1984), 36-37.

[5]Ibid., 47-49.

[6]Augustine, *De Trinitate* 15.27-32; 5.12.

[7]Jürgen Moltmann, *The Way of Jesus Christ: Christology in Messianic Dimensions*, trans. Margaret Kohl (San Francisco: HarperCollins, 1990), 91-92.

[8]*Roman Missal* (New York: Catholic Book Publishing Co., 1964), 375.

[9]*The Compact Edition of the Oxford English Dictionary* (1971), s.v. "grieve," "grief."

[10]Fretheim, *The Suffering of God*, 112. For his discussion of divine grief, see especially 109-13.

[11]Jürgen Moltmann, *The Source of Life: The Holy Spirit and the Theology of Life*, trans. Margaret Kohl (Minneapolis: Fortress Press, 1997), 19-22.

[12]Ibid., 22-25; idem, *God in Creation: A New Theology of Creation and the Spirit of God*, The Gifford Lectures 1984-85, trans. Margaret Kohl (San Francisco: Harper & Row, 1985), 9-12.

[13]Moltmann, *The Source of Life*, 13-14.

[14]For the theology of the surrender of the Son, see especially Jürgen Moltmann, *The Trinity and the Kingdom: The Doctrine of God*, trans. Margaret Kohl (San Francisco: Harper & Row, 1981), 80-83.

[15]Ibid., 78.

[16]Jürgen Moltmann, *The Crucified God: The Cross of Christ as the Foundation*

and Criticism of Christian Theology, trans. R. A. Wilson and John Bowden (New York: Harper & Row, 1974), 4, 153. Moltmann takes the cry of abandonment in Mark's passion narrative seriously. His position is that Mark's bleak account is probably closest to what actually happened and that the cry of "Why?" from Psalm 22 captures what Jesus would have experienced in terms of dying apparently cursed and abandoned by God (146-53).

[17]Moltmann, *The Trinity and the Kingdom*, 79.

[18]Moltmann, *The Crucified God*, 150-51.

[19]Moltmann, *The Trinity and the Kingdom*, 81.

[20]Moltmann, *The Way of Jesus Christ*, 173.

[21]Moltmann, *The Crucified God*, 243.

[22]Carl E. Braaten, "A Trinitarian Theology of the Cross," *The Journal of Religion* 56 (1976): 118; D. Lyle Dabney, "The Kenosis of the Spirit: Continuity Between Creation and Redemption," a paper delivered at the meeting of the Karl Barth Society of North America at the American Academy of Religion annual meeting (San Francisco, Nov. 21, 1992), 16-19; idem, "The Advent of the Spirit: The Turn to Pneumatology in the Theology of Jürgen Moltmann," *Asbury Theological Journal* 48 (Spring 1993): 81-107. In the latter article, Dabney analyzes the background for this "neglect" of the Spirit in the wider context of the Western theological tradition, and credits Moltmann's later efforts to forge new trails of exploration into the "presence" of the Spirit.

[23]Moltmann, *The Crucified God*, 243-44.

[24]Moltmann, *The Trinity and the Kingdom*, 82.

[25]Jürgen Moltmann, *The Church in the Power of the Spirit: A Contribution to Messianic Ecclesiology*, trans. Margaret Kohl (New York: Harper & Row, 1977; reprint, San Francisco: HarperCollins, 1991), 95.

[26]Moltmann, *The Trinity and the Kingdom*, 82.

[27]Moltmann, *The Way of Jesus Christ*, 73-78.

[28]Ibid., 73.

[29]Ibid., 92.

[30]Ibid., 138-39.

[31]Ibid., 174.

[32]Jürgen Moltmann, *The Spirit of Life: A Universal Affirmation*, trans. Margaret Kohl (London: SCM Press, 1992), 61.

[33]Dabney, "The Kenosis of the Spirit," 40, 46, reflects along a similar line on the impact of the cross on the Spirit, suggesting that the separation between Father and Son entails "the coming to grief, . . . the profoundest frustration and nullification of the work of the Spirit," but tempering this with the affirmation that this "discontinuity" is encompassed by an even greater "continuity" made possible by the power and self-emptying of the Spirit.

[34]Moltmann, *The Spirit of Life*, 61, emphasis in original.

[35]Ibid., 61-62.

[36]Ibid., 62, emphasis in original.

[37]Ibid., 63.

[38]Ibid., 63-64.

[39]Moltmann stresses the despair in Jesus' death cry in order to argue that Jesus truly enters with lost human beings into the depths of godforsakenness. While I agree with the theological importance of this solidarity with humanity, I believe that the "Why hast thou forsaken me?" is a cry, not so much of despair as of protest: one who insists on asking "Why?" has not given up hope, but is "hoping against hope." The cry of Psalm 22 calls on God to be faithful to Godself. If Jesus had truly given up on God, he would have died quietly, in apathy. His loud cry of "Why?" is not a surrender to hopelessness but a protest, an insistence that God *be* *God*. Samuel E. Balentine, *The Hidden God: The Hiding of the Face of God in the Old Testament, Oxford Theological Monographs* (Oxford: Oxford University Press, 1983), notes that lament psalms, such as Psalm 22, are characterized by complaint and protest, often expressed in the form of accusatory questions, against God's self-contradictory behavior (especially absence) that has resulted in peril for the sufferer. This would support the argument that Jesus' cry is a protest provoked precisely by who God is supposed to be and by Jesus' past relationship with God.

[40]Moltmann, *The Spirit of Life*, 65.

[41]Moltmann discusses implications of the paradox that the Gentile centurion's confession is made in response to Jesus' cry and death in godforsakenness, in *The Crucified God*, 147, 193-95, but does not elaborate on the Spirit's role in this.

[42]Moltmann, *The Spirit of Life*, 65.

[43]Ibid., 63.

[44]Ibid.

[45]Ibid., 64.

[46]Ibid., 62.

[47]Ibid., 64.

[48]E. Vogelsang, *Der angefochtene Christus bei Luther* (Berlin, 1932), 66, following Luther, *WA* 5:58, 18, quoted in Moltmann, *The Spirit of Life*, 64.

[49]Moltmann, *The Trinity and the Kingdom*, 60.

[50]Moltmann, *God in Creation*, 89.

[51]Jürgen Moltmann, "God Is Unselfish Love," in *The Emptying God: A Buddhist-Jewish-Christian Conversation*, ed. John B. Cobb, Jr., and Christopher Ives, *Faith Meets Faith Series* (Maryknoll, N.Y.: Orbis Books, 1990), 120.

[52]Ibid., 121.

Part II

NARRATING THE ACTION
OF THE SPIRIT IN A DIVIDED
WORLD AND WOUNDED CHURCH

Mediating Repentance, Forgiveness, and Reconciliation: What Is the Church's Role?

Robert J. Schreiter

How is one to understand the Church's role in mediating repentance, forgiveness, and reconciliation from a communicative point of view? One must begin, I believe, with events that have brought these themes around reconciliation to the foreground. In the last fifteen years four sets of events have shaped this area of concern. The first set was the end of authoritarian regimes in many parts of the world, beginning with the end of the national security states in Latin America, going on to the collapse of the Soviet bloc in Central and Eastern Europe, and culminating in the end of apartheid in South Africa. All of these events seriously damaged lives and the social fabric in these societies. In all of these, the Church has played a role: most prominently in places like Chile and South Africa, most sadly in the case of Argentina where the bishops did next to nothing during the violence.

Closely following this first set of events is a second group: These are the civil wars that broke out in Africa, the Balkans, Sri Lanka, Indonesia, and elsewhere. Where wars used to be waged between the combatants of two countries locked in battle, most wars today are fought within a single country's borders, and the civilian population suffers the greatest casualties. Moreover these wars are fought in countries that often are already poor, and become even poorer as a result. There are about ten million refugees in the world today who have fled across borders in hopes of safety. There are tens of millions more who are displaced in their own country. One wonders if some of these countries will find any stability in the near future. Here again, one can identify the action of the Church in a number of ways. In the cases of the Balkans, Sri Lanka, and Indonesia, the Church has found itself in situations of interreligious contact and, sometimes, conflict. In African conflicts, the role of the Church has been less prominent although visible, notably in Rwanda.

A third set of events has to do with coming to terms with the past. It was sparked especially by the United Nations' proclamation of 1992 as the Year of Indigenous Peoples. Native peoples in the Americas, in Australia, and in South Asia spoke out about the abuses in the past perpetrated by colonial powers. Reparations have been called for. Certainly this has raised awareness; whether anything is changing all that much remains to be seen, now more than ten years later. Again, with these events, the Church has found itself on different sides. However, it has been more frequently on the side of wrongdoing, as stories of abuse in mission schools, especially in North America and Australia, have come to light.

The fourth and final set of events has been the sexual abuse scandals in the Roman Catholic Church. The latest wave began with the revelation of the sexual abuse of religious women in Africa, and perhaps reached its peak in 2002 with the disclosure of hundreds of cases of sexual abuse of minors by United States clergy. Cases of sexual abuse by clergy have surfaced also in several countries in Europe as well as in Australia. These events have been prominent in the consciousness of many as of late.

Faced with this litany of woes, it is not surprising that themes of healing and reconciliation have taken on special significance and urgency in our world today. There was very little literature—theological or otherwise—on these matters fifteen years ago. Today these are words one hears everywhere.[1] Theologians are compelled to try to address these events by exploring the theological (and other) resources upon which we might draw. Most importantly, we are called upon to help the Church clarify and focus its own role, bringing the resources of the tradition to bear upon the reconstruction of societies and the healing of individuals after these traumatic events, and helping the Church to see the consequences of its own involvement in wrongdoing.

This presentation addresses the Church's role in healing and reconciliation in these areas today by focusing on how the Church might become a more communicative body, using its resources for healing and reconciliation. Obviously, within the short compass of this presentation, all that can be done is sketch out the general shape of such a role. It is impossible to take up all these different matters, or address in any detail the different situations in all the inhabited continents of the world. Moreover, in addressing conflict, trauma, and wrongdoing, each situation has its unique history. Even efforts at reconstruction cannot be drawn from a single template. Nonetheless, the continuing urgency of examining how the Church might carry out this important "ministry of reconciliation" (2 Cor 5:19) is a task, it seems to me, that we as theologians need to pursue in our research and in our teaching.

I begin with some general thoughts about how the healing and reconciliation needed in the areas noted above fit in with the long-term ministry of reconciliation of the Church. Then I will look at three aspects of this process: apology, repentance or reparation, and forgiveness. The final section will return to the broader theme of reconciliation and the Church's role in it. This is all examined in light of the overall theme of the communicative action of the Holy Spirit in the Church and in the world.

The Church's Ministry of Reconciliation

"All this is from God, who reconciled us to himself through Christ, and has given us the ministry of reconciliation" (2 Cor 5:18 NRSV). This sentence from Paul's Second Letter to the Corinthians provides one of the clearest warrants for the Church's claim to a ministry of reconciliation. God is reconciling a broken and alienated world to God's self. This came through the action of Christ. And from that flows— from God through Christ—a ministry of reconciliation. This ministry finds its special place in the forgiveness of sins, given by God first to Christ, and given by the risen Christ to the Church. For Roman Catholics, this has found a special focus and discipline in the sacrament of reconciliation, although surely baptism and Eucharist must be counted as sources of reconciliation as well. Pope John Paul II convened a Synod of Bishops to explore this topic, which led to the post-synodal apostolic exhortation *Reconciliatio et Paenitentia* in 1984.

In view of this theological point, the Church's ministry has focused on the wrongdoer, bringing the wrongdoer to repentance and back into communion with God. That is and will always remain at the center of the ministry of reconciliation. But in the four sets of events mentioned above—the end of totalitarian political rule, the consequences of civil war, coming to terms with the colonial past, and the clergy sexual abuse scandal—more is needed. Victims of these traumatic events have to be cared for as well. The Church has most frequently addressed this need through its social ministries of alleviating hardship and suffering. But what has become evident today, even for those who carry out this social ministry through relief and development work, is that there must be attention to more than the material conditions of catastrophe, oppression, and abuse. Work to rebuild shattered lives and societies figures into this as well. To that end, in 1995 the member organizations (now more than one hundred and fifty of them) of Caritas Internationalis mandated the General Secretariat to develop training in reconciliation that could be used by their workers in the field. What was needed was not only skills and strategies, but theology and spirituality as well.

The point where skills and strategies, on the one hand, and theology and spirituality, on the other, come together is in bonds of trust and communication. All of the traumatic events mentioned above have to do with the sundering of trust—between a people and its society, between peoples, between individuals and institutions. Reconciliation, when all is said and done, is about the restoration of trust; not the return to the *status quo ante*, since that can never happen. New bonds of trust must be put in place.

Those bonds must be built in a safe and trustworthy way. Communication is central here—communication that does not damage victims again, communication that can be trusted. This, it seems to me, is central for how the Church must carry out and communicate its ministry of reconciliation in these settings. It also stands as the fundament of communicative action, defined by philosophers like Habermas, and theologians like Edmund Arens, Helmut Peukert, and Bernd Jochen Hilberath.[2] Or put in another way, by the Dutch Amnesty International lawyer Daan Bronkhorst, the truth must be spoken in a way that corresponds to the facts, in a way that I can understand it, by a source whom I can trust.[3] Trustworthy communicative action by the Church is essential for the Church's maintaining its catholicity today, living and acting as it does in a world with dense networks of communication. I will return to this at the end of this essay.

Elements of Reconciliation after Conflict

In this second part, I wish to look at three elements in the reconciliation process, namely, apology, repentance or reparation, and forgiveness. While these may be considered in this sequence as the ideal form of reconciliation—apology of wrongdoers, followed by their repentance and reparation, culminating in forgiveness by victims—it frequently does not happen that way. Wrongdoers may deny that they have done anything wrong (General Agusto Pinochet in Chile, for example). The wrongdoers may no longer be present or may even be dead and so cannot apologize (as has been the case in some of the clergy sex abuse cases). In poor countries ravaged by war, few or no resources may be available to restore what victims have lost. Forgiveness can happen at times even when there is no apology or repentance; a number of such cases can be found in the documents of the Truth and Reconciliation Commission's proceedings in South Africa. This must be kept in mind. Each potential case of reconciliation is different, and the elements can appear in different sequences.

Apology

A number of things can be said about apology in the reconciliation process and the Church's use of it. Regarding the latter, Pope John Paul II's dramatic apology on the first Sunday of Lent in the Jubilee Year 2000 caught worldwide attention.[4] It was reported at the time that this series of apologies for past misdeeds by members of the Church was very controversial within the Roman Curia. The International Theological Commission, at the direction of Cardinal Ratzinger, issued a document entitled "Memory and Reconciliation: The Church and the Faults of the Past" at a news conference a few days before the Pope's prayer service of apology.[5] It is a very nuanced document in many ways, trying to specify the presuppositions and conditions for the Church engaging in apology. It draws not only on sources in the tradition, but engages contemporary hermeneutical philosophy, with the overall goal of achieving communion between the alienated parties through a fusion of their respective horizons (*Horizontverschmelzung*). It takes up the question of the difficulty of establishing the truth, the intent to create a more common belonging, and the building up of communion. It is especially sensitive to the question of history and change of mentalities.

Papal apology is a modern phenomenon. Before Paul VI, the last time it has been used was by Hadrian VI, who apologized in 1522 to those involved in the Reformation for actions of the Roman Curia.

Along with the apologies of John Paul II, I want to note two others: that of the United Church of Canada in 1988 to the First Nation peoples of Canada for having exploited them, and a similar one a few years later by the Oblates of Mary Immaculate, also in Canada. Both of these were directed especially to the physical and sometimes sexual abuse of Native children in mission schools.

The pope's apology certainly caught attention, and stands as a model for other church leaders. But there was a procedural difference from the two Canadian examples. In both of them, the apology was constructed *with* the victims. The wrongdoers (or their institutional successors) were led through a process wherein instances of abuse were recounted along with the consequences this had for the lives of those abused children. In following this pattern, two important communicative actions emerge in the apology process. First, the wrongdoers get deeper insight into the brokenness of victims by hearing their stories. Very often the victims themselves experience catharsis and even healing in the process of their story telling. Second, it means that apology becomes more than a performative speech act (as good as that is). It portends in addition a changed relationship, part of going together to a new place or, to use Paul's words in Second Corinthians, becoming a "new creation." In the case of the UCC process, it took three years of dialogue to produce the apology.

This is not to downplay the importance of the speech act of apologizing. What I am trying to underscore here is the importance of a more profound and thoroughgoing communicative action, namely, creating a new, long-term relationship. There was a brief instant of that in the meeting of U.S. Catholic bishops with victims of sexual abuse at the bishops' assembly in June 2002. Individual bishops have devoted more time to this. But my point is that for an apology to be healing and a portent of reconciliation, it cannot be done hastily, no matter how sincere and committed the wrongdoer might be.

A second point about apology as communicative act involves the kind of ecclesiology presupposed when apology is done on behalf of the Church. This came to attention outside the Roman Catholic Church with the 1998 document "We Remember: A Reflection on the 'Shoah' " issued by the Commission for Religious Relations with the Jews of the Pontifical Council for Christian Unity.[6] While making great strides in acknowledging the failure to do good, one sentence rankled many readers, Jewish and Christian alike: "We deeply regret the failures of the sons and daughters of the Church." This document, the product of long preparation, was issued at a time when there was controversy around what role Pius XII did or did not play with regard to European Jews at the time of the *Shoah*. In this and in other places, the document appears to oscillate between wanting to speak on behalf of the entire (Catholic) Church, but to impute guilt only to individuals (the Church's "sons and daughters") rather than to the institution itself. A good deal of attention has been given both to the theology that seems to underlie this view of the Church, as well as to its reception both within and outside the Church.[7] Theological reasons can be adduced for making a distinction between the Church as the spotless bride of Christ or the body of Christ (and therefore, sinless) and its members (who are capable of sin). Historical reasons can be given as well (namely, polemics between Catholics and Reformers about the nature and condition of the true church). And even cultural reasons can be offered (more collectivist societies, such as those found in the Mediterranean region, who have a strong sense of honor and shame). However, there are at least two good reasons to reconsider such a division between the Church as institution and the members of the Church.

First, there is the problem of social sin or "sinful structures." There have been repeated attempts since the middle of the twentieth century to elaborate carefully a theology of social sin, sin of the world, and structural injustice. These attempts both distinguish and relate the sins of individual moral subjects to the consequences of those sins as they come to be embedded in groups and institutions.[8] While it is individuals who sin, an individual's identification with social relations and institutions through complex patterns of attribution may set up patterns by which not sinning, in the midst of those institutions, becomes all but impossible. For example, there is a legal question today about how much moral responsibility a soldier or groups of soldiers have in situations of human rights abuses.[9] Another case would be one in which leaders identify themselves not only with an institution but also somehow become emblematic of it (as in the case of absolute monarchies). Can one sanction such an identification with an institution in this regard? In the debates swirling around Pope Pius XII during the Second World War, can one, in light of this possibility, absolve the Catholic Church from responsibility for his actions?

The issues of consequences of sin becoming thus embedded and the modes of complete identification of person and institution there-

fore raise the question: Can or must one speak in an admittedly analogous manner of "sinful structures in the Church"? And if so, should
not the Church as institution apologize? I am not a specialist in ethics
and will go no further here. But from the point of view of communication, if the receiver consistently cannot get the message intended by
the speaker, the problem may be larger than the skill of the speaker in
communicating. The problem may be the incomprehensibility of the
message itself.

A second point that needs to be examined in light of communicative action is the difficulty that many people have in grasping the theological distinction between the Church and its sons and daughters.
This is easier to comprehend in a collectivist society, where honor,
shame, and "face" are attributed to the social entity, be it family, nation, or Church. The preservation of the larger entity is always para-
mount. It is more difficult to comprehend in an individualistic society,
where social patterns of honor and shame are less salient. On the one
hand, some people see it as a distinction without a difference. This is
particularly the case in democratic societies where the nation is not a
monarch, but rather the people themselves are. It has been noted by
Rosemary Radford Ruether and others that when Americans hear the
theological term "the people of God," what they are also hearing is
"We the people," the opening words of the U.S. Constitution. This
may be theologically imprecise, but it is, I believe, in this country, a
common perception.

On the other hand, those same people can and do make this distinction in other instances. In the recent sexual abuse scandal, most American Catholics appeared to be able to distinguish between the Church
they love and are committed to, and sinful priests and bishops who
had either perpetrated these crimes or worked to cover them up. Church
attendance appears not to have fallen (although financial contributions have) as a result of the scandals. People identify with a "church"
that is not described adequately and solely by its hierarchy. This was
evident when the bishops made an appeal to the whole church in the
United States to engage in a day of penitence. The reaction was tepid.
Most likely this was so because many people did not feel that the
whole church was the problem, but very specific persons and practices within it.

I am not arguing here that intelligibility should be reduced to the
lowest common denominator or to what the "market" will bear; but

rather that, over time, frames of reference change, and what is accepted at one time may be less so at a later point. The International Theological Commission itself speaks of "paradigm changes" (par. 5.1) and quotes the Holy Father on matters of cultural conditioning. To be sure, there is no truck here with cultural relativism, but rather a realization of how profound these social effects can be. We need continually to examine our modes and manners of communication within the Church, and also its reception.

Repentance and Reparation

Repentance and reparation are dimensions of the second aspect of the reconciliation and healing process. They are public, symbolically laden acts that intend to communicate remorse about what has been done in the past. They look backward to the event, trying to engage in some restorative rebuilding, but also forward in proclaiming that such events must never be allowed to happen again. This is the *nunca mas* (never again) that arose out of Latin America after the end of civil wars and the ideology of the national security state, and the "never again" crying out from the ashes of the Holocaust.

I am speaking of the two concepts of repentance and reparation together. They constitute two ideas, which in a more detailed presentation would need to be distinguished. Repentance requires some form of speech and may be accompanied by other public actions. Reparation may entail financial or other payments to victims, but may also be largely symbolic in its relation to past events. Here, in the interest of communicative action, I wish to concentrate on the symbolic dimension. To do that I will describe two responses to the calamities of the Second World War. Both have to do with how to respond to the horror of the concentration camps of that period.

The first has to do with Dachau, one of the first concentration camps opened by the Nazi government, right outside the city of Munich. Here all kinds of "undesirable" elements from the German population were incarcerated: intellectuals, clergy, politicians, and Jews. Many of them met their deaths there. After the liberation of the camp in 1945, it was decided to leave part of it standing as a lasting remembrance to the horrors that happened there. The intent was not only to preserve the memory, but also to educate subsequent generations so that such atrocities would never happen again.

In 1961, a group of Carmelite nuns requested and received permission to establish a Carmel there, where the sisters would pray in perpetuity in reparation for the crimes committed. It was established on the north end of the camp and dedicated to the redeeming blood of Christ. To my knowledge, it stands there to this day.

In 1998, a group of Polish Christians attempted to establish a similar convent near the Auschwitz concentration camp in Poland. They also wished to erect a cross—again in reparation for the even greater atrocities committed there. This time, although given tentative permission by the cardinal primate of Poland, a huge controversy broke out. Central to the issue was that, at Auschwitz, it had been predominantly (although not exclusively) Jews who had been murdered. Establishing a Catholic presence there exacerbated the still very vulnerable relations between Catholics and Jews. Eventually, with Vatican intervention, the project was dismantled.

Why the different reactions? Although both were concentration camps instituted by the Nazi government of Germany, the populations who were interned and murdered were largely different. Dachau held mainly German citizens, some of whom were Jews. At Auschwitz, it was principally Jews who were killed. The presence of German nuns at Dachau allowed some measure of what "Memory and Reconciliation" calls "common belonging"—Germans praying for German victims persecuted by other Germans. Poles were complicit in many instances with the Germans in the persecution of Jews. Allowing Catholic Polish nuns the same venue at Auschwitz was a "disconnect," so to speak. Jewish survivors and the descendants of the dead there would be losing some symbolic control over the site of their suffering. Differing theologies of repentance and forgiveness between Judaism and Christianity likely would also play a role. But even without trying to discern more clearly the differences here, one can see why this was not a communicative action; it distorted rather than repaired relationships. Wisely, the Vatican intervened.

Repentance is a symbolic communicative action, as is also, to a great extent, reparation. Repentance has to occur in symbolically appropriate and culturally intelligible forms if it is to communicate what it intends. Reparation as a communicative action can never bring back the *status quo ante*, for history has been irrevocably changed. Nor can repentance and reparation bring back the dead. In engaging in repentance and reparation, the Church needs to attend to *who* is repenting, what the *relationship* is between the two parties, and the *message* that is circulating.

Forgiveness

Forgiveness is a very complex phenomenon, the object of much study and scrutiny today. Pope John Paul II highlighted its importance in making it the theme of his Message for the World Day of Peace in 1997.[10] "Forgiveness studies" has blossomed in the past ten years as a branch of psychology in the United States.[11]

I would like to focus on two aspects of forgiveness: the role of memory and the role of reconstruction. Forgiveness is not a form of amnesia; it is not about forgetting what has happened. The adage "forgive and forget," while well intended, is singularly bad advice. To ask someone to forget a traumatic event of the past is, in effect, to victimize them once again. We cannot forget; but we can remember in a different way. The quality of memory, and how it relates the conflicted parties to the past event, is the real focus of forgiveness. One of the most common definitions of forgiveness now circulating is that forgiveness is about overcoming resentment about the past. One continues, in memory, to have a relationship with past events and even with the people who have perpetrated those events. But in forgiving, one is no longer held hostage to the past. Overcoming resentment does not mean condoning past acts. Nor does forgiving necessarily entail renouncing the possibility of punishment; punishment may be a communicative action that says to the larger public that such acts will not be tolerated in the future. Forgiveness, then, involves a shift in perspective toward the past, not an erasure of it.

The quality of memory, then, is what is at stake in the act of forgiveness. Memory expresses itself in how the story of the past is narrated. It is concerned, first of all, with telling the truth about the past. Often, in situations of conflict, the narrative of the past is distorted to justify the actions of the wrongdoer. What has to be sorted out after the conflict is over is what really did happen. This accounts for the genesis of the Truth and Reconciliation Commissions that are now operating around the world. Originally, these were called Justice and Reconciliation Commissions. But the realization quickly dawned that there could be no justice until the truth had been established; hence, the change of the name and the focus.[12]

With the establishing of the truth, the second step is revising the narrative. Narrative here is not only a matter of truth-telling. What is embodied in the narrative also is the quality of the relationship between the parties. A not uncommon action to be undertaken after the end of conflict is that histories have to be rewritten. This has been one goal in postwar Bosnia and Herzegovina: to rewrite the history of that country in the school curriculum. The narration of the relation of Croats, Serbs, and Muslims has to be recast if memory is not to become the source of violence once again. A comparable example is how the image of the Native American in film has changed in the course of the last thirty years in the United States.

Forgiveness is an essential element in the reconstruction of society, in creating a different kind of future. Archbishop Desmond Tutu enshrined this idea in the very title of his memoir of serving as chair of the South African Truth and Reconciliation Commission: *No Future Without Forgiveness*.[13] Without giving up resentment, the relationship with the past cannot change. Without a change in that relationship, there can be no future different from the past.

Going back to the Holy Father's apologies during the Jubilee Year, one can understand why seeking forgiveness is so important. Without forgiveness, there can be no change in relationships and therefore no future together. Because forgiveness was so central to the ministry of Jesus, and has been entrusted to the Church by him, it plays a pivotal role in the Church's ministry of reconciliation. But because it is central does not make forgiveness something easily achieved. It is hard work.

In reflecting on this, one must keep in focus both forgiving and being forgiven. By going back to our own experience of being forgiven, we learn something about the dynamics of the act of forgiveness. The two are clearly linked to each other in the Lord's Prayer. Seeking forgiveness provides a certain discipline about truth-telling (in this instance, about ourselves), which creates the space for something different to happen.

The Church's Role in Reconciliation

In his afterword to a collection of essays on the Church's role in reconciliation, Gregory Baum notes a number of salient features, which recur in accounts of the Church's involvement in reconciliation.[14] Most

generally, everyone assumes that the Church has a role in reconciliation processes by nature of its heritage and ministry, but rarely has it
been exercised effectively. Part of that is due to the fact that issues of
post-conflict reconciliation have rarely received the attention among
church leaders that they deserve. Church leadership generally has had
little preparation for assuming roles in these processes. Given the complexity and even ambiguity of what people mean by reconciliation,
this is hardly surprising. Yet we cannot be content with remaining at
this level of ignorance and lack of expertise.

Reconciliation, which involves the healing of victims and the reconstruction of societies, is more than a set of strategies and skills.
Because it is a participation in the work of God, reconciling the world
in Christ, it must also be a spirituality, a way of living deeply within
the divine Mystery. To elaborate that spirituality goes beyond the scope
of this presentation.[15] What I would like to focus upon in this concluding section is the communicative quality of three aspects of the reconciliation process and the Church's role within them.

The Creation of Safe Spaces

The reconstructive work of reconciliation begins with the creation
of safe and hospitable spaces within which the work of reconciliation
can take place. In post-conflict situations or after the experience of
trauma, social (and physical) spaces are needed where victims can
begin to reflect upon their shattered lives. These spaces must be such
that the victims are not victimized again. The experience of violence
and trauma underscores for us how unsafe the world is. A space must
be created wherein victims do not have to fear for their safety. This
space is both social and physical. It is social in that there must be
persons with whom victims can feel safe to begin to explore their
wounds. To that end, a communicative action for the Church can be
the creation of "healing circles"[16] or "listening circles"[17] where the
traumatic past can be unfolded. These spaces must not only be safe;
they must also be hospitable and welcoming. And this hospitality must
be in words and practices intelligible to the victims, not just to those
extending hospitality. The combination of safety and hospitality in-
stills some measure of trust for the victim. As was noted at the beginning of this presentation, it is trust that is taken away in the acts of
violence.

For the Church to play a significant role in reconciliation its own space must be safe and hospitable again, both socially and physically. The ancient idea of taking sanctuary in the Church reflects this idea. Hospitality in the Church prepares victims for the experience of grace. The use of church space for meetings of truth and reconciliation commissions and the calling upon of church leaders to lead processes of reconciliation both point to that ministry which has been entrusted to the Church.

The first question to be raised about the Church's role is, therefore, whether or not the Church is a place of safety and hospitality. In the case of the sexual abuse of minors by clergy, the Church has clearly become a very dangerous place. In some instances in Rwanda, people took refuge in church buildings, only to be turned over to massacre by the pastor. A purification of church space and of its leadership may be necessary. An example of this happened in Argentina when the bishops made a formal apology to the Argentine people. Standing with portraits of two heroic bishops who had been assassinated, Angelelli and Romero, they confessed: "We ask you for pardon, for we have not been like them."[18]

A Site of Ritual and Symbol

Ritual and symbol play a crucial role in the practice of reconciliation. This is so because the realities that are being addressed in reconciliation are often of such enormity that words, by themselves, are simply inadequate. How does one express what it means to have lost loved ones in conflict? What can compensate for the loss of language and culture among colonized indigenous peoples? How are the lives of sexually abused children re-established? We need to resort to a discourse of ritual action and symbolic representation to give voice not only to our emotions about what has happened, but also as a vehicle for our hopes for the future. By many accounts, the inauguration of Nelson Mandela as President of South Africa was such a moment. When the swearing of the oath of office was completed, there was a fly-over by the South African Defense Forces. Many people who were present at the ceremony as well as those who watched it on television had the same experience: those jet fighters are ours now and no longer oppress us. Pope John Paul's action at Yad Vashem and at the Western Wall during his visit to Jerusalem spoke more eloquently than sheaves of documents.

The Church is a treasure trove of rituals and symbols. These need to be enlisted in the communicative dimension of reconciliation.[19] I have already noted something of the symbolic dimensions of processes of repentance and reparation. These communicative acts do not reinstate the past, but are important means of mediating between past and present, and then in turn creating something of a new future. How the Church can enlist its penitential practices and its celebration of the Sacrament of Reconciliation figure into this. At the same time, it has been noted that the Church has been more adept at dealing with wrongdoers than with victims. It was suggested to me recently that perhaps we might take a cue from the Orthodox churches and from Hispanic piety. In the Western church, Holy Saturday is a kind of ellipsis between Good Friday and the Easter Vigil in the Triduum. Perhaps it might become, along the lines of mourning of the dead Christ as commemorated in Orthodoxy and among Latino/a populations, a time to gather victims into the Paschal mystery of Christ's own descent among the dead.

Reconnecting

Certainly central to Roman Catholic ecclesiology are notions such as communion and catholicity. One can imagine the process of reconciliation as drawing upon the deeply communicative dimension of the Trinitarian life that stands at the center of communion ecclesiology, and the clearly communicative character of what makes catholicity a global presence and reality. Reconnection is what reconciliation is about, exemplified for us dramatically in John 21:1-19, where Jesus forgives the denials of Peter and entrusts to Peter the care of the most vulnerable of Jesus' followers, his lambs. Finding ways to create life-giving bonds in a globalized world, which is at once more dense in its patterns of communication and more alienating and excluding in its economic practices, is certainly one of the challenges to the Church's understanding of its ministry of reconciliation.

Conclusion

Thinking of how the Church can mediate acts of apology, of repentance and reparation, and of forgiveness in reconciliation today can be daunting, given the scope and extent of the brokenness of our world.

But in those reflections, we need to remember that it is God who is reconciling the world, not ourselves. We participate in this ministry as fragile instruments. What is nonetheless clear is that if the Church is to have credibility in these times, it must take up this ministry for the sake of fidelity to its calling and embrace of the world God loves so much. In many ways, our communicative actions toward that world will speak louder than our words—or at least give greater voice to that Word that God has spoken among us in Christ.

Notes

[1]Two especially helpful works here are Gregory Baum and Harold Wells, eds., *The Reconciliation of Peoples: Challenge to the Churches* (Maryknoll, N.Y.: Orbis Books, 1997) and R. Scott Appleby, *The Ambivalence of the Sacred: Religion, Violence, and Reconciliation* (Lanham, Md.: Rowman & Littlefield, 2000).

[2]Among the literature I have in mind here is Jürgen Habermas, *Theorie des kommunikativen Handelns* (Frankfurt: Suhrkamp, 1981); Edmund Arens, *Christopraxis. Grundzüge theologischer Handlungstheorie* (Freiburg: Herder, 1992); Helmut Peukert, *Wissenschaftstheorie–Handlungstheorie–Fundamentaltheologie* (Düsseldorf: Patmos, 1976); Bernd Jochen Hilberath and Matthias Scharer, *Kommunikative Theologie: Eine Grundlegung* (Mainz: Grünewald, 2002).

[3]Daan Bronkhorst, *Truth and Reconciliation: Obstacles and Opportunities for Human Rights* (Amsterdam: Amnesty International, 1995), 145f.

[4]The text of his apology can be found in *Origins* 29 (March 23, 2000): 645, 647-648.

[5]The text may be found in *Origins* 29 (March 16, 2000): 625-644.

[6]This text may be found in *Origins* 27 (March 26, 1998): 669, 671-675.

[7]See Bradford Hinze, "Ecclesiastical Repentance and the Demands of Dialogue," *Theological Studies* 61 (2000): 207-238; Robert J. Schreiter, "The Church as Sacrament and as Institution: Responsibility and Apology in Ecclesial Documents," in Judith Banki and John Pawlikowski, eds., *Ethics in the Shadow of the Holocaust: Christian and Jewish Perspectives* (Chicago: Sheed & Ward, 2001), 51-60.

[8]See, for example, Piet Schoonenberg, *Man and Sin* (Notre Dame, Ind.: University of Notre Dame Press, 1965), and more recently, Jon Sobrino, "The Winds in Santo Domingo," in Alfred Hennelly, ed., *Santo Domingo and Beyond* (Maryknoll, N.Y.: Orbis Books, 1993), 174f.; idem, "El perdón, Tres perspectives desde El Salvador," *Spiritus* 42 (March 2001): 7-20.

[9]The case of the Dutch Blue Helmets (U.N. peacekeepers) at Srebenica in 1995 is an example.

[10]The text can be found in the December 18, 1996 edition of the English language *L'Osservatore Romano*, 3, 8.

[11]A good introduction to this is Robert Enright and Joanna Northcott, eds., *Exploring Forgiveness* (Madison: University of Wisconsin Press, 1998).

[12]See Robert J. Schreiter, "Wahrheitscommissionen im Spannungfeld von Wahrheit, Gerechtigkeit, und Versöhnung," in Gerhard Beestermöller and Hans-Richard Reuter, eds., *Politik der Versöhnung* (Stuttgart: Kohlhammer, 2002), 197-230.

[13]Desmond Tutu, *No Future Without Forgiveness* (New York: Doubleday, 1999).

[14]Gregory Baum, "A Theological Afterword," in Baum and Wells, *The Reconciliation of Peoples*, 184-192.

[15]I have tried to do that in *The Ministry of Reconciliation: Spirituality and Strategies* (Maryknoll, N.Y.: Orbis Books, 1998).

[16]See Robert J. Schreiter, "Entering the Healing Circle: The Practice of Reconciliation," in Stephen Bevans, Eleanor Doidge, and Robert J. Schreiter, eds., *The Healing Circle: Essays in Cross-Cultural Mission* (Chicago: Chicago Center for Global Ministries, 2000), 176-188.

[17]Robert J. Schreiter, "Creating Circles of Listening in a Parish," *Initiative Report* 3 (March 2001): 3-6.

[18]Cited in Sobrino, "El perdón," 9.

[19]For helpful insights into this see Herbert Anderson and Edward Foley, *Dangerous Stories, Mighty Rituals* (San Francisco: Jossey Bass, 1998).

The Mission Has a Church:
Spirit, World, and Church in Luke-Acts

Dennis Hamm

If we search the New Testament for narrative paradigms of the relationships among Spirit, world, and church, Luke emerges as our best provider. To be sure, each of the evangelists tells the story of Jesus in a way that reflects an incipient ecclesiology. Mark has his pericope about the true family of Jesus, his portrait of flawed disciples, and his parable about the household waiting for the return of its master (13:33-36). Matthew has his speeches—the Sermon on the Mount showing what healing and praying should look like, the mission speech sending the twelve apostles into a hostile world trusting in "the spirit of [their] Father" (10:20), and the speech on church order, with its disciplinary protocol wrapped in the "care package" of the parables of the compassionate shepherd and the cautionary tale of the unforgiving servant. And John has his advanced pneumatology and his profound symbolism of the church as the temple of Jesus' body.

Luke, however, goes a giant step further when it comes to ecclesiology. The hints he gives about church in his gospel he spells out in paradigmatic narratives in his second volume, the Acts of the Apostles. This essay explores Luke's portrayal of the mission of the Spirit-driven church in three ways. First, spelling out the implications of two phrases in Gabriel's announcement, I review in broad strokes Luke's narrative theology about the en-Spirited church in the world. Second, I focus on two passages that, though they are largely neglected in discussions about the role of the church in the world, can contribute powerfully to that conversation. They are Jesus' farewell discourse in the Lukan account of the Last Supper (22:24-30) and his portrayal of the community at prayer in Acts 4:23-35. Finally, I suggest how these examples of narrative ecclesiology can contribute to our contemporary efforts to understand the Spirit-led mission of the church in our world.

Luke's Pneumatology of the Church on Mission

Before I explicate the two chosen passages, let me review Luke's pneumatology of the church on mission in broad summary statements.

The first words about Jesus in Luke's gospel refer to the power of the Holy Spirit and reach their full meaning only in Luke's second volume, his story of the church. Gabriel's announcement of Jesus' conception by the Holy Spirit (Lk 1:35) promises that "he will inherit the throne of David his father" (v. 32), an echo of Nathan's prophecy in 2 Samuel 7:13 and of Psalm 132:11. Of course Jesus inherits nothing of the kind in the remainder of the third gospel. Only in his second volume does Luke show how this promise materializes when he has Peter say on Pentecost, "But since he [David] was a prophet and knew that God had sworn an oath to him that he would set one of his descendants upon his throne, he foresaw and spoke of the resurrection of the Messiah. . . . Exalted at the right hand of God, he received the promise of the Holy Spirit from the Father and poured it forth, as you see and hear" (Acts 2:30-33). And so, on the occasion of this pilgrim feast of Pentecost when Jews gather "from every nation under heaven" (2:5) to celebrate the giving of the Law at Sinai, Peter interprets the miracle of communication (everyone hearing the disciples "proclaiming in their own tongues the mighty acts of God," v. 11) as a sign of the resurrection of Jesus and the end-time outpouring of the Holy Spirit. Luke's worldwide horizon comes through the narrative not only in his enumeration of sixteen geographical areas in verses 9 through 11 but also in his implication that this Pentecost experience is a reversal of the scattering and confusion of Babel (Gn 11:7-9). As Babel was a scattering by way of a *confusion* of tongues (and in the Septuagint version of Genesis 11:9 the very name Babel is rendered *Synchysis* (Confusion), the multilingual crowd gathered from the diaspora is "confused" (Acts 2:6, *synechythē*) by their miraculous ability to *understand*.

This blessing of Jews from "every nation under heaven" (Acts 2:5) is also a fulfillment of the covenant with Abraham. Early in Genesis, that promise was already presented as a reversal of Babel. The collective arrogance of "all the earth" (LXX Gn 11:1) was expressed not only in their plan to construct a tower with its "top up to heaven," but also in their ambition to "make a name for ourselves" (v. 4). God's fresh start with Abram and Sarai reverses the initiative of name making: "I will make you a great nation and *I* will bless you and *magnify your name*" (12:2). And the divine purpose for this one nation is the blessing of *all* nations: "And in you shall *all* the tribes [*phylai*] of the earth be blessed" (12:3). Thus the Pentecost blessing is the reversal of Babel because that is the ultimate vocation of Israel as expressed in the covenant with Abraham. That Luke has all these connections in view becomes clear at the end of Peter's second speech, the one after the healing of the man born lame in Acts 3. Toward the end Peter says, "You are the children of the prophets and of the covenant that God made with your ancestors when he said to Abraham, 'In your offspring all the families of the earth shall be blessed' " (Acts 3:25, echoing Gn 12:3; 18:18; 22:18).

Thus, by spelling out the implications of a single clause in the Annunciation ("he will inherit the throne of his father David") as it is explicated by the two-volume Lukan narrative, we see that it is linked to Luke's understanding of Spirit and world. As a consequence of the death and resurrection of Jesus, the end-time gift of the Spirit of God becomes available for the healing of the world's confusion. And how does "church" figure in this process? The next clause in Gabriel's message addresses precisely that question.

"And he will rule over the house of Jacob forever, and of his kingdom there will be no end" (Luke 1:33). "House of Jacob" is a biblical epithet for the twelve tribes of Israel, especially as gathered by the Servant of YHWH (see Is 49:6). As in the case of inheriting the throne of David his father, Jesus does no such reigning in the course of the gospel narrative. His choice of a core group with the symbolic tribal number twelve *points* in that direction, but it takes the events immediately before and after Pentecost, understood in the light of an enigmatic prophecy during the Last Supper, to indicate just how Jesus gets to reign over the house of Jacob.

The Commissioning of the Servant Leaders at the Last Supper (Luke 22:24-30)

Most scholarship on the Lukan account of the Last Supper has focused on 22:19c-20, with its interpretation of the body as "given for you," the mandate to "do this as *my* memorial," and the mention of the second, post-prandial cup, explained as "the *new* covenant in *my* blood." As a question of text criticism, this so-called "longer version" has been established as an authentic part of Luke's gospel.[1] More pertinent to our discussion is what comes next, the altercation and the farewell discourse, which is clearly a product of Luke's redaction and composition.

Mark frames *his* account of the "institution narrative" (Mk 14:22-25) with the prophecy about the betrayal of one of the twelve (vv. 17-21) on one side, and the prophecy about the disciples' scattering and Peter's denial (vv. 27-31) on the other. In contrast, Luke chooses to postpone the word about betrayal until after the meal proper, so that the prophecies about betrayal (Lk 22:21-22) and denial (vv. 31-33, omitting Mark's reference to the scattering of all) now frame the material about discipleship (vv. 23-30).

After the prophecy of betrayal (vv. 21-22), Luke introduces a startling note: "Then an argument broke out among them about which of them should be regarded as the greatest"—which the attentive reader recognizes as a repetition of the altercation mentioned at Luke 9:46, in the context of the second passion prediction ("The son of man is to be handed over to men"). In the second chapter Luke has provided dramatic plausibility for this surprising interruption by introducing verse 23 as a response to the prediction about his betrayal by someone at table with them: "And they began to debate among themselves who among them would do such a deed."

Next comes the mention of the who-is-the-greatest quarrel. What follows immediately is Jesus' instruction about true greatness, which Luke has *postponed* from its place in the Markan sequence, the aftermath of the third passion prediction, where Luke *omits* the episode of the ambition of James and John (Mk 10:35-40; see Lk 18:31-43) and the teaching on true greatness (Mk 10:41-45), which he saves for this moment at the supper. Luke paraphrases Mark 10:43 in a way that accents the new way leadership is to be exercised among his disciples: "Rather, let the greatest among you be as the youngest, and the leader [*ho hegoumenos*] as the servant [*ho diakonōn*]. . . . I am among you as one who serves [*ho diakonōn*]" (Lk 22:26b, 27c).

The next three verses, rarely included in discussions of Luke's ecclesiology, are in fact crucial to his narrative theology of Spirit, church, and mission to the world. "It is you who have stood by me in my trials; and I confer a kingdom on you, just as my Father has conferred one on me, that you may eat and drink at my table in my kingdom; and you will sit on thrones judging the twelve tribes of Israel" (Lk 22:28-30).

First, note that this passage climaxes with the promise of "judging the twelve tribes of Israel." This, obviously, is a version of a Q saying found in a quite different context in Matthew, that of Jesus' response to Peter about the rewards of discipleship ("Jesus said to them, 'Amen, I say to you that you who have followed me, in the new age, when the Son of Man is seated in his throne of glory will yourselves sit on twelve thrones, judging the twelve tribes of Israel' " [Mt 19:28]). In Matthew's context the saying clearly refers to the disciples' sharing in Jesus' glory at the Parousia.

Here in Luke's context of the Last Supper, however, coming as it does after Jesus' exhortation to his disciples against desiring to dominate ("The kings of the Gentiles lord it over them [*kyrieuousin autōn*] . . . but among you it shall not be so" [Lk 22:25a, 26a]), the saying points to quite another meaning. Given Luke's sensitivity to the Septuagintal resonances of Greek words, it is likely that Luke intends *krinontes* ("judging") to be heard in the sense of the sort of "judging" exhibited in the book of Judges ("*Kritai*"), where the verb refers to the leadership, or ruling, of the twelve charismatic leaders raised up to lead the twelve tribes of Israel between the conquest period and the emergence of kings (see, for example, LXX Judges 4:4 [Deborah]; 12:7 [Jephthah]; 15:20 and 16:31 [Samson]). That meaning of "judging" is indeed compatible with Jesus' teaching on servant-leadership.[2]

That they are to lead "twelve tribes of Israel" has a specific resonance within the narrative of Luke-Acts. Indeed, the phrase links directly with Gabriel's "house of Jacob" (Lk 1:33)—i.e., the end-time restoration of the twelve "tribes of Jacob" to which the oracle of God refers in Isaiah 49:6. As we have seen, Acts 1-2 interprets the messianic community of Jews gathered "from every nation under heaven" as precisely that end-time restored remnant of the twelve tribes.

If this reading of verse Luke 22:30 is correct, the preceding verses support that understanding. "And I confer [*diatithemai*] a kingdom on you, just as my Father has conferred [*dietheto*] one on me, that you may eat and drink at my table in my kingdom . . ." (vv. 29-30a). The Greek verb used here for conferring, or appointing, a kingdom (*diatithemai*) is cognate with the word for "covenant," *diathēkē*. Indeed, the one other place the verb is used in Luke-Acts refers to the covenant of promise that God made with Abraham. After the healing of the man born lame at the Beautiful Gate, Peter speaks to the *andres Israelitai* (Acts 3:12). He calls them "sons of the prophets and of the *covenant which God made [hyioi . . . tēs diathēkēs hēs dietheto ho theos]* with your fathers when he said to Abraham, 'In your offspring all the families of the earth shall be blessed' " (v. 25). This statement quotes the divine promise to Abraham after the binding of Isaac (Gn 22:18 [echoing 12:3]) and to Isaac at Genesis 26:4.

This promise of a kingdom that is the Father's and Jesus' is surely the same reality expressed in the final words of the risen Jesus at Luke 24:49—"And behold I am sending the promise of my Father upon you; but stay in the city until you are clothed with power from on high." And this promise takes its contextual meaning from Luke 11:13 and 12:32. At 12:31-32, Luke elaborates the Q saying about seeking the kingdom of the Father with this sentence: "Do not be afraid any longer, little flock, for your Father is pleased to *give you the kingdom*." Coming as it does not long after 11:13 ("If you, then, who are wicked, know how to give good gifts to your children, how much more will the Father in heaven *give the holy Spirit* to those who ask him?"), kingdom and Spirit are linked, if not equated.[3] The idea that Jesus' pledge to send the "promise of my Father" refers to the gifts of the divine Spirit and kingdom is confirmed at the outset of Acts 1:3-4. There Luke tells of the risen Jesus appearing to the apostles for forty days, "speaking *about the kingdom of God.*" "While meeting with them, he enjoined them not to depart from Jerusalem, but to wait for '*the promise of the Father* about which you have heard me speak; for John baptized with water, but in a few days you will be baptized with *the Spirit*' " (Acts 1:4-5). Thus the "promise of the Father" is equated with the gift of the Holy Spirit. In the immediate context that endowment of the Spirit is an illustration of what it means that Jesus was "speaking about the *kingdom of God.*" So the promise of the Father is kingdom and Spirit.

Does Luke really want his audience/readers to equate the coming of the kingdom of God with the gift of the Holy Spirit at Pentecost? The reference at the Last Supper to eating and drinking at Jesus' table in his kingdom is a further clue. Does this sharing of table fellowship refer to the heavenly banquet? Or does Luke understand the table fellowship to be unfolding among the Jerusalem Christian community after Easter? Luke's narrative points to the latter. Peter, in his speech to Cornelius's household, says of the apostles' experience of the risen Jesus that they "ate and drank with him after he rose from the dead" (Acts 10:41). This could be read as a reference to the table fellowship implied in the resurrection appearances at Luke 24:30 (on the road to Emmaus) and vv. 41-43 (with the Emmaus two, the eleven, and those with them). But Acts 1:4 suggests more. The participle that the NAB translates "while he was with them"—*synalizomenos*—and occurring only here in the New Testament, means "to eat at the same table, with focus on fellowship," with the root sense of "eat salt with."[4] This suggests that Jesus' reference to eating and drinking at his table in his kingdom refers to the post-Easter experience of the apostles. By extension, it would seem also to point to the table fellowship of the church in general, when they knew him in "the breaking of the bread" (Acts 2:42, 46; 20:7, 11—all in the light of Luke 24:35). To be sure, Luke subscribes to an eschatological scenario that includes the fullness of the coming of the kingdom of God with the final appearance of the Son of Man (Lk 21:36); yet that reign has been inaugurated with his own preaching and healing ministry (11:20 [kingdom of God at hand]; 17:21 [kingdom of God among you]). The continuation of that ministry by the Jerusalem church is the continuation of the Spirit-driven mission promised in the Lukan account of the Last Supper in the word about the disciples' "ruling" of the twelve tribes restored at Pentecost. It is a sign of Luke's remarkable realism that he couches this robust prophecy in an editorial unit that is framed by the prophecies about betrayal and denial and a reference to petty squabbling. Yet Luke eases the burden of the news of Peter's coming denial with the further promise of prayer for Peter's post-Easter rehabilitation: "But I have prayed that your own faith may not fail; and once you have turned back, you must strengthen your brothers" (22:32).

There is more, of course, to the Lukan account of the Last Supper. But the foregoing analysis should be enough to indicate that Luke's version of this event plays an integral part in his narrative ecclesiology. Clearly, Luke wants his readers to celebrate "the breaking of the bread" (his phrase for the Lord's Supper or the Eucharist; see Lk 24:35; Acts 2:42; 20:7, 11) with heightened awareness about their identity as members of the church. As the restored Israel of the end time, they are heirs of the promises to Israel. In the full context of Luke-Acts, that means they share Israel's mission to be a "light to the nations." The hope is that, though they are as weak as the denier Peter and as fractious as the original Twelve, God will accomplish this daunting task through the power of the Holy Spirit accessed through prayer.

The Prayer of a Challenged Community (Acts 4:23-31)

The Acts of the Apostles abounds in examples of the post-Pentecost church, with its rehabilitated servant-leaders, implementing its Spirit-driven mission to the world. Consider the cameo descriptions of community life (2:42-47; 4:32-35; 5:12-15), the good example of Barnabas (led by the Spirit to share property, 4:36-37) and bad examples of Ananias and Sapphira (whose dishonesty is called "lying to the Holy Spirit" and "testing the Spirit of the Lord," 5:1-11), the ministry of Philip (8:4-40), the call and healing of Saul (9:1-19), Peter's divinely managed outreach to the household of Cornelius (Acts 10), and the Council of Jerusalem (Acts 15). But one of the richest examples of this narrative ecclesiology is the (largely neglected) account of the prayer of the community and its "Pentecostal" aftermath in Acts 4:23-32.[5]

This passage is especially pertinent to our theme of Spirit, church, and world in that it portrays the original messianic community of Jerusalem confronted by rejection and then, after gathering in prayer, empowered by the Holy Spirit to live a robust community life and to reach out in a mission of healing and bold preaching. The episode is unique in Luke's work in that it is the only portrayal of the Christian community at prayer that provides the *content* of that prayer (indeed, in that regard it is unique in the whole of the New Testament). At the same time, the prayer portion (vv. 24b-30) is very much of a piece with the rest of Acts in that, although it is a prayer and thus not usually compared to the speeches of Acts, it contains the kind of biblical interpretation characteristics of those speeches—the *pesher*. A *pesher* is a kind of interpretation that abounds in the Dead Sea Scrolls; it is an interpretation of an ancient text as fulfilled in recent or current events in the interpreting community. The prayer of Acts 4 does precisely that. After invoking God as Creator (v. 24), it quotes the first two verses of Psalm 2 (the Septuagint version, with its past tense) in verses 25-26. Then, in reverse order, or chiastic fashion, it applies the language of the Psalm to the agents and events entailed in the arrest, trials, and crucifixion of Jesus. The carefully crafted form of this *pesher* can be seen in the following schema (the words of the psalm that receive interpretation in the *pesher* appear in italics):

A "Why did *the Gentiles* rage? And *the peoples* plot vain things?
   B The *kings* of the earth stood up, and the *rulers*
     C *gathered* together
      against the lord and against his *anointed*

     C' For in truth they *gathered* in this city
      against your servant Jesus, whom you *anointed*,
   B' Herod [a king] and Pontius Pilate [a ruler]
A' with *the Gentiles* [the Romans] and *the peoples* Israel, to do
   what your hand and your will long ago had planned to take place"
   (vv. 25b-28).

It helps that verse 7b of the psalm ("You are my son; today I have begotten you") had already become part of Christian appropriation of this messianic psalm. The experience of the resurrection had enabled them to recognize Jesus as the psalm's royal "son of God" who reports that word spoken to him upon his accession to the throne (see Acts 2:36 and 13:33).

At this point, where historical application becomes petition, the community prayer departs from the wording of the psalm. Yet the prayer does not simply leave the rest of Psalm 2 behind; it *subverts* the arrogant and belligerent tone of the psalm. Given the strong language in the remainder of Psalm 2 about divine jeering, mockery, wrath, and the shattering in store for those who would resist the Lord and his anointed, one has every reason to expect that a community prayer that begins by quoting the first two verses of Psalm 2 would continue by calling down divine wrath upon their adversaries. Instead, they pray to be empowered "to speak your word with all boldness" (Acts 4:29). And, given the biblical connotations of the divine "hand" extended to punish those who resist the exodus (as in Ex 3:20; 7:5; or Dt 26:8), when the prayer continues, "as you extend your hand . . . ," we might expect something like, "as you extend your hand with new plagues to smite our adversaries." But no, the prayer continues, "as you extend your hand in *healing*, and signs and wonders are performed through the name of your holy servant Jesus" (Acts 4:30).

The phrase "signs and wonders" resonates intertextually in two powerful ways. First, and most immediately, it echoes the "wonders" and "signs" of the Joel quotation of Acts 2:19 applied, *pesher*-fashion, to Jesus' ministry at 2:22 and then to that of the apostles at 2:43, interpreting their healing work as signs that "the last days" (2:17) had been inaugurated. And so, here they are praying for a continuation of that end-time ministry. Second, linked with the language of God extending his "hand," the phrase "signs and wonders" recalls the exodus signs and wonders (as in Ex 7:3; 11:9; 11:10; Dt 6:22; 7:19; 11:3; 29:2), interpreting their healing ministry as an extension of Jesus' ministry and therefore as a continuation of the new exodus he began. They pray for this healing ministry to be done "in the name of your holy servant [*pais*]" Jesus, calling Jesus by the same title used earlier in the prayer regarding David, "servant" (v. 25), thereby implying that their work will be similarly empowered by the Holy Spirit (v. 25; see Acts 2:33; 10:38 [Jesus]; 4:8 [Peter]). Indeed, Luke describes the immediate response to the prayer as an infilling of the Holy Spirit and an empowerment "to speak the word of God with boldness." When Luke writes that the place where they were gathered was "shaken" [*esaleuthē*], he uses a term with apocalyptic connotations (see Lk 21:26) to indicate that this empowerment manifests the end-time outpouring of the Spirit of God. That they should pray for these signs and wonders to be done "through the name" of Jesus refers, in the context of Acts, to these things as signs precisely of the resurrection of Jesus (see Acts 3:15-16 and 4:8-10).

Reference to Psalm 2 is still operative. Not only has Jesus' death fulfilled Psalm 1:1-2; his resurrection and the signs and wonders done in his name have demonstrated in a transcendent way the universal reign adumbrated in the rest of the psalm. The link between resurrection and kingly reign also sits at the heart of Peter's Pentecost proclamation (Acts 2:30-32).

The description of Christian *koinonia* that follows (Acts 4:32-35) is, along with 2:42-47, often isolated from its context, the better to contemplate it as a cameo picture of early Christian community life. But this practice, reinforced by modern editors' insertion of a bolded subheading like the NAB's "Life in the Christian Community," should not distract from Luke's implied intention: the unity of minds and hearts and the spontaneous sharing of possessions to meet the needs of all, like the power to heal and to preach boldly, are *consequences* of the Spirit's empowerment accessed through the community prayer.[6]

These gifts are the fulfillment of what Jesus had referred to as "the promise of my Father"—the Holy Spirit and kingdom—i.e., participation in the reign of Jesus the Messiah by empowerment to continue his healing and preaching ministry.

Some Implications for an En-Spirited Church in the World Today

We have made just three soundings regarding Spirit, world, and church in Luke-Acts—two verses from Gabriel's announcement, the Lukan account of the Last Supper, and the prayer of the community in Acts 4. Are these segments of Lukan narrative ecclesiology still paradigmatic for thinking about Spirit, world, and church today? I suggest the following five implications.

1. Followers of Jesus can expect to be challenged by betrayal, denial, and duplicity in their midst. Like Mark and Matthew, Luke includes Jesus' prophecies about an insider's betrayal and Peter's denial. But whereas Mark and Matthew use those references to frame their accounts of the supper itself, Luke uses them to frame Jesus' teaching on servant leadership. In this way Luke associates the issues of betrayal and denial more directly with the subject of the exercise of authority in the leadership of the community. Similarly, in the description of community prayer and *koinonia* in Acts 4, Luke follows immediately with the contrast between the good example of Barnabas's generosity with the bad example of Ananias and Sapphira's duplicity, thereby showing that the ideal portrait of 4:32-34 has been (and will be) vitiated by human frailty. The Spirit of God can be resisted and even "lied to," yet such duplicity will not carry the day.

2. Ecclesial leadership that places honor and power above service violates the spirit of the Lord's Supper, and is therefore totally out of place in a community formed by the Eucharist. Luke drives this home in his account of the Last Supper by repeating at 22:24 the apostles' argument about which of them should be regarded as the greatest (first mentioned at 9:46) and by postponing to the Last Supper the teaching on authority as service that Mark placed after the third prediction of the passion and resurrection. This surely stands as a caveat to anyone in a pastoral office today who would sacrifice service of the faithful in the defense of the honor and authority of office. It would also challenge anyone who would foster vocations to the priesthood by empha-

sizing status and privilege over service and solidarity.

3. These narrative paradigms illustrate the perennial reality that the healing and preaching mission of the church to the world is a process initiated by the Creator through the power of the Holy Spirit working with agents who open themselves to that power through prayer. Although Luke does not mention the Holy Spirit explicitly in his Last Supper account, he does speak of conferring a "kingdom" on the disciples as his Father has conferred one on him (Lk 22:29-30). The remainder of Luke-Acts makes it evident that the promise of kingdom begins to be fulfilled with endowment of the Holy Spirit's power at Pentecost, and thereafter as needed. Before Jesus foretells Peter's threefold denial (Lk 22:34), he speaks of his prayer for Peter's (post-Easter) rehabilitation (22:32). Here, Luke's reader learns to associate the gift of the Spirit with prayer, following Luke's version of Jesus' reception of the Holy Spirit by the Jordan while he was praying (Lk 3:21), along with the Pentecostal Spirit upon the one hundred and twenty at prayer in Acts 1-2. The further gift of the Spirit in response to the prayer of Acts 4, with its empowerment for mission and community life, comes not as a unique moment but as a picture of "business as usual." To take Acts 4:23-34 not as a mere report but as a paradigm would help us integrate worship and mission in the church today.[7]

4. The community prayer of Acts 4:24-30 addresses God as both creator and redeemer. At a time when some (for example, Matthew Fox) would force a dichotomy between "creation theology" and "redemption theology," Luke, like most biblical authors, is clear that it is the creator who rescues. The "maker of heaven and earth and all that is in them" is also the one who heals creation through the death and resurrection of Jesus and through the church that continues his mission to the world.

5. Luke's narrative theology is clear that the mission of the church is not merely self-maintenance but bold outreach. When Jesus commissions the Twelve to implement the kingdom, Luke's two-volume story illustrates the reality that this mission entails the Spirit of God reaching out through the church to a dark and ailing world. Jesus of Nazareth implements Israel's vocation of being a "light for revelation to the Gentiles" (Is 49:6; Lk 2:31; Acts 13:47; 26:13, 18, 23) and a blessing to "all the families of the earth" (Gn 12:3; 22:18; Acts 3:25) only when he becomes the risen Lord working through the renewed

Israel that is the church. The paradigmatic narratives of Acts make it clear that this is the work of the Spirit. This is a reminder to Christians today that our interdenominational and intra-denominational frictions and factions will be resolved only to the extent that we open ourselves to the Spirit of God and commit ourselves more fully to the pursuit and sharing of God's truth and to the service and healing of the world around us.

Do we wonder about the mission of the church today? Attention to Luke's narrative theology can help us yield to a kind of Copernican revolution that understands that the divine mission has a church, through which the Spirit of God would renew the world despite our sinfulness and frailty.

Notes

[1] For a review of the text-critical question, see Bruce M. Metzger, *A Textual Commentary on the Greek New Testament* (2nd ed.; New York: American Bible Society, 1994), 148-50.

[2] The earliest example of this reading of Luke 22:29-30 that I am aware of is that of J. Jervell, "The Twelve on Israel's Thrones," in his book *The Divided People of God: A New Look at Luke-Acts* (Minneapolis: Augsburg, 1972), 75-112. See also J. Fitzmyer, *The Gospel According to Luke (X-XXIV), Anchor Bible* 28A (Garden City, N.Y.: Doubleday & Co., 1985), 1415; and also L. T. Johnson, *The Gospel of Luke, Sacra Pagina Series*, vol. 3 (Collegeville, Minn.: Liturgical Press, 1991), 345-46, 349.

[3] That this equation of divine reign and Holy Spirit was evident early in the tradition receives support from that fascinating variant reading for Luke 11:2 (the kingdom petition) appearing in two twelfth-century manuscripts and the citations in fourth- and fifth-century patristic writers: "Thy holy Spirit come upon us and cleanse us." For details, see Metzger, *A Textual Commentary on the Greek New Testament*, 130-31.

[4] F. W. Danker, *A Greek-English Lexicon of the New Testament and Other Early Christian Literature,* 3rd ed. (Chicago: University of Chicago, 2000), *s.v. synalizomenos.*

[5] For a more detailed exegesis of this passage, see my article, "Acts 4:23-31— A Neglected Biblical Paradigm of Christian Worship (Especially in Troubled Times)," *Worship* 77 (May 2003): 225-37. Much of what follows here regarding this passage derives from that study.

[6] Similarly, the first "cameo" of Christian life, Acts 2:42-47, is also narrated as a consequence of the repentance, baptism, and reception of the Holy Spirit that followed upon Peter's Pentecost preaching (2:37-41).

[7] This point is elaborated in Hamm, "Acts 4:23-31," 234-37.

The Spirit and the Church in a World at War:
The Promise and Challenge of Nonviolent Action

Elizabeth Groppe

There was, one imagines, a somber air in the Senate Chamber as
my senator stood to address his colleagues: "After careful consideration, meditation and prayer to the Holy Spirit for enlightenment and
wisdom," he stated, "I rise today in support of the resolution before
us."[1] The date was October 4, 2002, and the resolution in question
authorized the war against Iraq. My senator sent me a transcript of this
speech in response to a letter I had written about the impending war,
and I wish I could have a conversation with him someday to hear
more about his theological reasoning and his criteria for discernment
of spiritual wisdom. For the time being, his statement has led me to
reflect on the issue of war through the prism of pneumatology.

Much of the debate about Christianity and war revolves around the
interpretation of the teaching and example of Jesus Christ. Does fidelity to Jesus' injunction to love our enemies (Mt 5:44) require that we
put away the sword, as Jesus instructed the disciple who struck the ear
of the slave of the high priest (Lk 22:50-51; Mt 26:51-52)? Does our
profession that Jesus Christ is the Messiah who inaugurates the era
when "nation shall not lift up sword against nation, neither shall they
learn war any more" (Is 2:4) commit us to the complete renunciation
of warfare, as the bishops and theologians of the early church maintained? Or are there occasions when participation in warfare is ethically justified by Christian responsibility for the common good, as
Augustine and the subsequent just war theory affirm?[2]

In this short essay I cannot begin to do justice to these complex and
important questions, but what I hope to do in at least a preliminary
fashion is to bring a pneumatological perspective to bear on discern-

ment about warfare. An analysis of warfare from the perspective of
the theology of the Holy Spirit does not remove the difficult ethical
challenges posed by Jesus Christ's teachings and witness in the gospels, yet it does enable us to be more explicit about a number of theological issues that pneumatology brings into focus. In this essay, I will
examine the phenomenon of warfare through the prism of some of
the prominent pneumatological themes in the New Testament and in
the work of pneumatologists Yves Congar and Jürgen Moltmann:
conversion, freedom, truth, sacrifice, discipline and order, communion, and vitality and life. My reflections presume that the problems
of injustice and racism that defensive wars and liberation struggles
have sought to redress are very real and serious. I also presume that
the practice of nonviolent action advanced by Mahatma Gandhi,
Martin Luther King, Jr., and others has a vital contribution to make
to theological and ethical inquiry about responses to tyranny, and I
incorporate their work and witness into my analysis. I will conclude
with some reflections on the mission of the church in the world today.

Conversion

Our human sinfulness is at the root of war and constitutes the major obstacle to peace. Greed, lust for power, blinding political ideology, hatred of the "other," vengefulness—these are the demons of
warfare and tyranny. According to scripture and tradition, it is the
mission of the Holy Spirit to bring this sin to our consciousness and
call us to conversion. The promised Paraclete "will convince the world
concerning sin" (Jn 16:8). As Yves Congar explains in his trilogy, *I
Believe in the Holy Spirit*:

> [The Holy Spirit] makes us, at a level that is deeper than that of
> mere regret for some fault, conscious of the sovereign attraction
> of the Absolute, the Pure and the True, and of a new life offered
> to us by the Lord, and he also gives us a clear consciousness of
> our own wretchedness and of the untruth and selfishness that fills
> our lives. We are conscious of being judged, but at the same time
> we are forestalled by forgiveness and grace, with the result that
> our false excuses, our self-justifying mechanisms and the selfish
> structure of our lives break down.[3]

The context of God's call to conversion from sin is not the threat of retribution or vengeance but the *attraction* of the Pure and the True. Judgment is inseparable from the outstretched arm of mercy, and the Paraclete is not only our prosecutor but also our pardoner (Jn 20:21-23; Acts 2:38).[4] As Rowan Williams writes, "It is not so much that we repent and are then forgiven, as that, forgiven, we learn to repent."[5]

What, then, of the aggressors of war? What of dictators and tyrants? Defensive warfare may be undertaken with the presumption that aggressors and dictators can be converted from their oppressive behavior by the threat of bodily or lethal harm to their person or their loyalists. Historically, however, there is little evidence that threats of harm or even death are effective means of converting hearts. On the contrary, violent action against aggressive or dictatorial powers typically intensifies their belligerence and repression. This was the case in Tsarist Russia in 1905 when the gains made by a nonviolent strike for better working conditions and more democratic government were lost in the repressive response to a violent uprising; it was true in Basque Country in the 1980s, in Sri Lanka in the 1970s and 1980s, and in the civil wars in Central America in the 1980s.[6] *Amandla!*, a documentary film about resistance to apartheid in South Africa, includes interviews with men who served in the government forces during the apartheid years. When they saw throngs of indigenous Africans marching toward them, chanting and singing, bearing (some of them) weapons, they felt afraid, they said, and they fired into the crowds. These were not hardened militants, but young men barely twenty, overcome with fear.[7] During the bombing raids of World War II, Briton Cyril Connolly wrote, in parody of 1 John 4:18, "Perfect fear casteth out love."[8] Yet without the experience of love, Congar's pneumatology suggests, conversion is impossible.

But is conversion really possible under any circumstances? Many an aggressor or dictator has seemed impervious to conversion and remained unabashedly unrepentant when confronted with the atrocities he or she has committed.[9] And yet it is precisely a religious faith in the *possibility* of conversion that undergirds the theory and practice of nonviolent action developed by Mahatma Gandhi and Martin Luther King, Jr. Gandhi abjured any form of action that might arouse fear in an opponent. Rather, he insisted, "Our motto must ever be gentle persuasion and a constant appeal to the head and heart."[10] His method of *satyagraha* called upon the people of India to disobey unjust laws and to willingly accept imprisonment as a consequence; he enjoined them to accept bludgeons at British hands and to refuse to retaliate. Gandhi believed that when the British witnessed the voluntary suffering of the Indian people—a suffering that they themselves, the British, had inflicted on unarmed men and women—their hearts would be troubled and their consciences moved. "Real suffering bravely borne melts even a heart of stone."[11] Inspired by Gandhi, Martin Luther King, Jr. promised his white southern persecutors that he and his nonviolent army would meet their physical force with soul force. He proclaimed:

> Do to us what you will, and we will continue to love you. We cannot in all good conscience obey your unjust laws, because noncooperation with evil is as much a moral obligation as is cooperation with good. Throw us in jail, and we shall still love you. . . . One day we shall win freedom, but not only for ourselves. We shall so appeal to your heart and your conscience that we shall win *you* in the process, and our victory will be a double victory.[12]

There is some evidence that the practice of nonviolent action as developed by Gandhi and King does indeed have the power to change hearts. In 1960, for example, the white mayor of segregationist Nashville, Tennessee, stood on the front steps of City Hall and, in response to a pointed question from university student Diane Nash, acknowledged before a nonviolent assembly of four thousand civil rights marchers that discrimination based on skin color is morally wrong.[13] In Le Chambon-sur-Lignon, France, during the genocidal reign of Nazism in Europe, the nonviolent witness of pastor André Trocmé, his wife Magda, and their rural village converted some members of the Vichy police and leaders of the German troops stationed at Le Puy, who turned a blind eye to the evidence that the villagers of Le Chambon were sheltering Jews.[14] Conversions of this character, of course, may not always be forthcoming. Yet, as Peter Ackerman and Jack Duvall demonstrate in *A Force More Powerful*, a remarkable study of the use of nonviolence in the twentieth century, nonviolent action can remove dictators from power even against their own will when nonviolence is organized in a manner that permeates an entire society, as popular struggles against Marcos, Pinochet, and Milosevic attest.[15] The exercise of any political authority requires the cooperation of the populace governed, and widespread nonviolent noncooperation with a repressive regime can bring political change even if there is no immediate conversion of a tyrant's heart. Nonviolent deposition of a tyrannical or unjust government leaves open the possibility for legal action against the offenders, encounters between oppressors and their victims in this new context, and gradual movement toward conversion.

Freedom

The Holy Spirit, Congar observes in his survey of the Christian pneumatological tradition, works through all things and in all things without doing violence to anyone and without abrogating human freedom. Commenting on the book of Wisdom, which describes the Spirit as intelligent, holy, subtle, and penetrating of all things (7:22-23), Congar writes:

> The Spirit, who is both one and transcendent, is able to penetrate all things *without violating or doing violence to them.* . . . The Spirit, then, is unique and present everywhere, transcendent and inside all things, subtle and sovereign, able to respect freedom and to inspire it. The Spirit can further God's plan, which can be expressed in the words "communion," "many in one" and "uniplurality." At the end, there will be a state in which God will be "everything to everyone" (1 Cor 15:28), in other words, there will be one life animating many *without doing violence* to the inner experience of anyone, just as, on Mount Sinai, Yahweh set fire to the bush and it was not consumed.[16]

The Holy Spirit is more intimate to us than our own hearts, nearer to us than our own thoughts—and yet never violates us or overpowers us, never destroys our freedom, never coerces a response. "We are led by another," Congar states in an interpretation of Aquinas, "who does not act without us and does not use violence."[17] As the Eastern tradition maintains, the Spirit works in synergy with our own human will.[18] "Now the Lord is the Spirit, and where the Spirit of the Lord is, there is freedom" (2 Cor 3:17).

Hannah Arendt distinguishes violence from power, strength, force, and authority by its instrumental character.[19] A violent act abrogates the free will of another and makes of a human person a mere instrument or object. Warfare, by definition, is coercive, and coercion is an intentional part of military strategy. General Rios Montt, president of Guatemala during a period in which the government's war against its indigenous population reached the level of genocide, proclaimed that Guatemala was in need of a change and "the change consists precisely in this: to impose *your* will on another."[20] A manual of military policy published by the U.S. National Defense University is entitled *Shock and Awe: Achieving Rapid Dominance*, and it defines the desired military dominance as:

> the ability to affect and dominate an adversary's will both physically and psychologically. Physical dominance includes the ability to destroy, disarm, disrupt, neutralize, and to render impotent. Psychological dominance means the ability to destroy, defeat, and neuter the will of an adversary to resist; or convince the adversary to accept our terms and aims short of using force. The target is the adversary's will, perception, and understanding.[21]

The manual makes no distinction between use of this strategy for aggressive or defensive warfare. Ethically one must distinguish between these two forms of combat, but phenomenologically the process of military engagement is the same: physical force or psychological means are used to destroy, neutralize, or render impotent the will of another human being.

Is nonviolent action really that different? "If Mandela believed that nonviolent action is the opposite of force," write Ackerman and Duvall in *A Force More Powerful*, "he was not right—it is, in fact another form of force."[22] The nonviolent struggles that Ackerman and Duvall chronicle aimed to change the will and behavior of adversaries, or, if change was not forthcoming, to force them by nonviolent resistance to act against their will. Churchill insisted he would never give up India, the jewel of the British imperial crown; Marcos never wanted to accept the true outcome of the election he sabotaged in the Philippines; Pinochet was unwilling to abdicate his brutal rule of Chile; and the Soviet Union did not want to grant rights or liberties to the labor movement in Communist Poland. The nonviolence of Gandhi, the Filipino people, the populace of Chile, and the Solidarity movement aimed just as surely as *Shock and Awe* to disrupt and disarm the adversary. And yet, Gandhi would insist, there is a fundamental difference between nonviolent and violent forms of disruption. Brute force and Gandhian *satyagraha* are both fundamental laws of the universe, but they are laws of a very different character, and only the latter is worthy of the human being and capable of sustaining human civilization.[23] *Satyagraha* means the firmness or force (*agraha*) of love and truth (*satya*), but "[i]n Satyagraha there is not the remotest idea of injuring the opponent."[24] The power of nonviolence is a force that does not aim to destroy or to violate, even as it seeks to disarm. "My method," Gandhi explained, "is conversion, not coercion, it is self-suffering, not the suffering of a tyrant. I know that method to be infallible."[25] Thousands of Solidarity members refusing to labor in the shipyards and industries of Communist Poland until they are granted better working conditions and the right to organize is a form of force or social pressure, but it is a kind of force that leaves open the possibility for the active cooperation and conversion of others.

Truth

In the dramatic forensic setting of John's gospel, the Holy Spirit is the Paraclete, the Advocate, the champion of truth: "I will ask the Father, and he will give you another Advocate, to be with you forever. This is the Spirit of truth, whom the world cannot receive, because it neither sees him nor knows him. You know him, because he abides with you, and he will be in you" (Jn 14:15-17; cf. Jn 15:26; 16:13). The first letter of John reiterates: "the Spirit is the one that testifies, for the Spirit is the truth" (1 Jn 5:6). According to St. Paul, the Spirit knows what is of God (1 Cor 2:11) and imparts spiritual truth and wisdom (1 Cor 2:12-14). Patristic and medieval theologians were unanimous in their position that the Holy Spirit is the principle of all true knowledge.[26] "*Omne verum,*" wrote Ambrosiaster, "*a quocumque dicitur, a Spiritu Sancto est.*"[27] In the words of Thomas Aquinas, "to make the truth manifest belongs uniquely to the Holy Spirit (*convenit proprietati Spiritus sancti*)."[28]

Motivations to engage in warfare are many and varied, but historically one of these motives has been to fight for something that one holds to be true. In this sense, one could argue that warfare is compatible with the workings of the Spirit. And yet, in 1917, Senator Hiram Johnson declared, in words that are oft-repeated, that the first casualty of war is truth itself.[29] There is something about the very character of warfare that seems inimical to truth. Before combat even begins, truth may be surrendered in order to mobilize the necessary political support for war. At the time of this writing, there is compelling evidence that truth was indeed a casualty in the campaign of the Bush and Blair administrations for a war against Iraq.[30]

War planners and strategists, moreover, emphasize the importance of deception in the conduct of war. The military planning manual *Shock and Awe* states that in order to achieve strategic aims and military objectives, "deception, confusion, misinformation, and disinformation, perhaps in massive amounts, must be employed."[31] The manual reminds us that Sun Tzu, the famed Chinese military writer of 500 B.C.E., maintained that all warfare is based on deception.[32] From the Trojan horse to the German U-boats that carried a cargo of human limbs that could be released to the surface of the water to lure the Allies into thinking that their submarines had already been hit, deception has been a common part of military strategy.

In reporting the events precipitating war, the story of a war's progress, and the narration of a war's history, truth may suffer as well. War news is often censored or even twisted both to serve strategies of combat and the political need to maintain support for a war from those who are paying for the combat with their taxes and their children's lives.[33] Perhaps, suggests veteran war correspondent Chris Hedges, the populace may even welcome and invite a distorted narration of war if it is one that can wrap their lives in purpose, meaning, and a banner of nobility. Hedges cites Lawrence LeShan's *The Psychology of War*, which differentiates between the "mythic reality" and "sensory reality" of wartime. Sensory reality sees warfare for what it truly is, while mythic reality imbues the intentional killing and mayhem of warfare with a transcendent or heroic meaning.[34] The sensory reality of war is ineluctable to the soldier in the trenches, the child burned with napalm, or the Baghdad mother whose son has no limbs. But this is not the reality most of us see. "[T]he lie in war," writes Hedges, "is almost always the lie of omission. The blunders and senseless slaughter by our generals, the execution of prisoners and innocents, and the horror of wounds are rarely disclosed, at least during a mythic war, to the public."[35] War, moreover, can warp language itself, and it invites a mythologization that censors historical memory and silences the critique and self-scrutiny necessary to a healthy society and the pursuit of truth.[36]

One of the most dramatic differences between war and nonviolent action is that nonviolent theory and practice insist upon truthfulness. *Satyagraha*, the very name of Gandhi's nonviolent method, can be translated as "truth force," and Gandhi describes his discovery of nonviolence as the fruit of "my experiments with truth."[37] Gandhi was uncompromising in his conviction that truth and honesty should structure all political life, and he did not hesitate to discuss even the boldest of his plans for Indian independence in broad daylight.[38] In warfare, Gandhi observed, both sides typically claim the truth of their own cause, and brute force is not a discriminating arbitrator.[39] The method of *satyagraha* may not completely safeguard us from self-delusion and falsehood, but it is, Gandhi believed, the surest path toward truth, for if we take action in the name of a cause that was not the noble truth we had once believed it to be, it is we and we alone who suffer for our delusion, as our method of action prohibits the doing of harm to others. Sir Chimanlal Setalvad, an official of the Hunter Committee, questioned Gandhi about his campaign for truth:

Q. Who . . . is to determine the truth?

A. [Gandhi] The individual himself would determine that.

Q. Different individuals would have different views as to Truth. Would that not lead to confusion?

A. I do not think so.

Q. Honest striving after Truth is different in every case.

A. That is why the non-violence . . . was . . . necessary. . . .
Without that there would be confusion and worse. [All] terrorism is bad whether put up in a good cause or bad. [Every] cause is good in the estimation of its champion. General Dyer (and he had thousands of Englishmen and women who honestly thought with him) enacted Jallianwala Bagh [a massacre in which British forces opened fire on nonviolent Indian protestors] for a cause that he undoubtedly believed to be good. He thought that by that one act he had saved English lives and the Empire. That it was all a figment of his imagination cannot affect the valuation of the intensity of his conviction. . . . In other words, pure motives can never justify impure or violent action.[40]

Pure motives are superior to impure motives, but they do not preserve us from egregious error or deathly falsehood in time of war. Nonviolence, Gandhi maintained, is a safer course to navigate if one hopes to abide in the Spirit of truth.

Sacrifice

According to the letter to the Hebrews, it was through the Holy Spirit that Jesus Christ gave his life on the cross for our redemption. In the theology of priesthood and sacrifice of this anonymous letter, Christ offered himself without blemish to God "through the eternal Spirit" (Heb 9:14). Warfare is inextricable from sacrifice; men, women, and even children are called off to battle and honored for the sacrifice they make to their nation.[41] This sacrifice is voluntary when men and women purposively enlist in the military to serve a cause they believe to be true, but, increasingly, the sacrifices of warfare are involuntary—youth are conscripted into armies, or civilians, who constitute up to 95 percent of the casualties in contemporary civil conflicts, are killed or maimed by bombs, napalm, landmines, or other instruments of war.[42] One might postulate, at least, that those who voluntarily sacrifice their lives as combatants are acting in the sacrificial power of the Holy Spirit through whom Jesus Christ gave his life on the cross.

René Girard, however, argues that such an interpretation of warfare obscures a fundamental dimension of the revelation of the gospel and indeed of the letter to the Hebrews itself, which proclaimed that the sacrifice of Jesus Christ puts a definitive *end* to *all* sacrifice. The passion of Christ, according to Girard, employs the cultural mechanisms of religious and social violence in order to subvert them and reveal their illegitimacy. The scapegoat, the victim immolated on the altar of social and political necessity, is revealed in Christ as the innocent lamb before whom all the mythologies of sacred violence unravel. Christians, Girard acknowledges, have been slow to recognize the meaning of our own revelation, and we ourselves have even become perpetrators of persecution and religiously motivated violence. The true meaning of the passion nonetheless remains embedded in the very structure of the gospel and the history of the world, and it is the Holy Spirit—the Paraclete, the advocate of the victim—who is gradually revealing to us the meaning of our own religious identity:

> The Spirit is working in history to reveal what Jesus has already revealed, the mechanism of the scapegoat, the genesis of all

mythology, the nonexistence of all gods of violence. In the language of the Gospel the Spirit achieves the defeat and condemnation of Satan. . . . [T]he Spirit is necessary in history to work to disintegrate the world and gradually discredit all the gods of violence.[43]

If it is the work of the Holy Spirit to discredit the gods of violence, nonviolent action is indeed one venue of the Spirit's action, for nonviolent resistance to evil has historically served to discredit the violence of the persecutors. The British colonial rule of India lost legitimacy in the eyes of the world when British soldiers struck down row after row of unarmed Indians marching peacefully to protest Britain's exclusive control over salt production, and the segregationist policies of the Southern United States lost validity in the eyes of the public when scores of black men and women were beaten, rounded up, and imprisoned because they had seated themselves, nonviolently, at a lunch counter in a downtown department store.

Discipline, Order, and Harmony

Paul enjoined the early Christian communities to "live by the Spirit" (Gal 5:16), and he promoted a discipline—an ordering and harmony of life—rooted in the mystery of Christ crucified and risen. In Paul's vision, the Spirit of Christ enables us to rightly order our passions and desires such that we live not by the works of the flesh—fornication, impurity, licentiousness, idolatry, enmity, strife, jealousy, anger, quarrels, dissension, factions, envy, drunkenness, carousing (Gal 5:19-20)—but rather by the fruits of the Spirit. These, Paul explains, are love, joy, peace, patience, kindness, generosity, faithfulness, gentleness, and self-control (Gal 5:22). All Christians should live together bearing one another's burdens, and if someone falls into transgression they should be restored to a path of holiness in a spirit of gentleness (Gal 6:1).

Military life is very disciplined and orderly—Gandhi himself recognized the value of this dimension of military practice.[44] But war has its own ethos, and many forms of self-discipline unravel in the fog and fear of war. Drunkenness or drug-induced states are common means by which combat soldiers try to cover their fear or overcome their inhibitions.[45] John Garcia, an American soldier in Okinawa, consumed a quart and a half of whisky daily: "It was the only way I could kill," he explains. "I'd get up each day and start drinking. How else could I fight the war?"[46] Women are often exploited when lonely soldiers have recourse to prostitution. Moreover, writes the late war correspondent Elizabeth Neuffer, "war and rape often go hand in hand," as Homer's *Iliad* and the subsequent history of warfare attest.[47] The mayhem and disorder spawned by war permeate an entire society. War is a suspension of the customary norms of civilized behavior, and this can corrode the normal disciplined patterns of community life. The looting and chaos in the streets of Iraq is only the most recent example of this phenomenon.

Nonviolent action, like military training, requires intensive discipline and preparation. When Christian ethicist Bernard Häring proposed during the height of the Cold War that nations transition from a policy of nuclear deterrence to a strategy of nonviolent civilian-based defense, he noted that men and women with military training could make an important contribution to the success of the new nonviolent "army" with their habits of discipline and order.[48] The forms of discipline and training required for nonviolent action, moreover, go beyond the forms of discipline necessary for military service, since one must learn not only to strategize and organize and work collaboratively with others, but also to withstand fear, derision, and even lethal danger without anger or hatred or violence.

Indeed, the practice of direct nonviolent action requires an intensification of self-discipline and civil behavior, in contrast to the suspension of social norms so common in warfare. The aftermath of a nonviolent campaign should find a society more harmonious, more orderly, and more disciplined rather than more chaotic and riotous. Gandhi was very intentional about this. His ambition, he explained, was much greater than simple independence from the colonial rule of the British Empire—he envisioned the true self-rule of the Indian people.[49] This could be achieved not by a violent overthrow of the British by a military force, but by the slow, patient work of the entire nation whom Gandhi encouraged in disciplines such as prayer, fasting, manual labor, democratic decision making, outreach to the "untouchables" to dissolve the caste divisions of his society, and bridge-building between Hindus and Muslims. According to Ackerman and Duvall, Gandhi's movement of nonviolent civil disobedience did indeed transform its participants and forged a new civil spirit in the nation.[50] This, they conclude in their survey of the history of nonviolent movements in the twentieth century, is not the exception but the rule. In Poland, in South Africa, in the American South—indeed, wherever nonviolence is employed with deliberate, sustained organization and effort—the populace emerges strengthened in the disciplines of democracy and civil society. In contrast, they maintain, no military insurrection or violent coup post-World War II has extended freedom to the people in whose name power was claimed.[51] "Looking back," they observe:

> political scientists and historians have seen a relationship between the way a nation overcomes authoritarian or outside rule and its ability to sustain civil society and democracy. When nonviolent action is used to achieve power, the people have to develop abilities and exemplify the spirit that are later critical in governing: empowering individuals to take public action, building consensus on behalf of common objectives, and insisting that laws and leaders derive from people's consent. Nonviolent power becomes not only the means of achieving change; it becomes the first line of defense for a society's most sacred values.[52]

Nonviolent power is also a line of defense for the sacred values St. Paul identified as the fruits of the Holy Spirit: love, joy, peace, patience, kindness, generosity, faithfulness, gentleness, and self-control (Gal 5:22).

Communion

"Put things in order, listen to my appeal, agree with one another, live in peace: and the God of love and peace will be with you," St. Paul concludes his letter to the Corinthians. His final blessing invokes "the grace of the Lord Jesus Christ, the love of God, and the communion (*koinōnia*) of the Holy Spirit" (2 Cor 13:11-13). Communion emerges as the quintessential mark of the Spirit in Congar's survey of the history of pneumatology. The Holy Spirit, Congar explains, unites us to one another not simply by virtue of our common humanity but through a common participation in the very life and love of God. In the Spirit of God, persons of every time, place, race, and culture are incorporated into the body of Christ through the One who is "unique and present everywhere, transcendent and inside all things, subtle and sovereign, able to respect freedom and to inspire it."[53] The Spirit of love takes living roots in every person in a strictly original and personal way, bringing persons to communion by respecting and even stimulating their diversity.[54] "Communion is precisely unity without uniformity, the harmony or symphony of diverse voices. There is nothing more sublime, nothing more concrete."[55]

There is surely a certain kind of unity in warfare. War unites a society in a common effort under the shadow of a common threat, and it forges enduring bonds between the members of military units and civilian supporters, many of whom look back with reverie at the camaraderie they once enjoyed.[56] Chris Hedges served as a war correspondent for the *New York Times* during the war in Bosnia in 1995, and he recalls an encounter with a beautiful young woman named Ljiljana who had suffered terribly during the war. She had lost her father, her cheeks were hollow, and her teeth were decayed and broken. And yet, as she and her friends looked back on the war some weeks after it had ended, they admitted that those days:

> may have been the fullest of their lives. . . . Once again they were, as perhaps we all are, alone, no longer bound by that common sense of struggle, no longer given the opportunity to be noble, heroic, no longer sure what life was about or what it meant. That old comradeship, however false, that allowed them to love men and women they hardly knew, indeed, whom they may not have liked before the war, had vanished.[57]

That old comradeship—"however false." Why this qualification? What is "false" about the camaraderie of wartime? According to Hedges, who speaks from his frontline experience of multiple wars in many countries, war generates a false unity because it merely camouflages undercurrents of social alienation and dislocation—it does not heal them.[58] From a pneumatological perspective, moreover, the social unity of wartime is a false comradeship because it is a unity based on a polarizing opposition between human groups rather than a truly inclusive communion: it is a unity of us vs. them, nation vs. nation, race vs. race, creed vs. creed. Persons on our side are celebrated as heroes, while those on the opposing side are dehumanized. The dead on our side are mourned and martyred, while grief for the dead among the enemy becomes unthinkable. This is not the unity of the Holy Spirit, whose Pentecostal gift of the understanding of languages across the boundaries of nation and race reversed the divisions of the human family wrought by pride and arrogance at Babel.[59]

Nonviolent action, like warfare, generates a spirit of fellowship and common purpose among its participants, a sense of nobility and the meaningfulness of life. Sometimes it can also draw lines of opposition between groups of people: the Indians vs. the British, integrationists vs. segregationists, and so on. Yet both Gandhi and King distinguished carefully between the systems of imperialism and segregation they opposed and the human persons who implemented these systems, persons whom they refused to dehumanize or demonize, persons from whom they desired not separation but conversion. "We must resolutely refuse," wrote Gandhi, "to consider our opponents as enemies of the country. Whilst we may attack measures and systems we may not, must not, attack men."[60] King, in turn, insisted that "While abhoring segregation we shall love the segregationist. This is the only way to create the beloved community."[61]

Life and Vitality

On the day of resurrection, Jesus Christ, crucified by the Roman empire, was "made alive in the Spirit" (1 Pet 3:18). In the Holy Spirit, Paul proclaims, we too may share in this new life: "If the Spirit of life who raised Jesus from the dead dwells in you, he who raised Christ from the dead will give life to your mortal bodies through his Spirit that dwells in you" (Rom 8:11). As Jürgen Moltmann reflects, "God's mission is nothing less than the sending of the Holy Spirit from the Father through the Son into this world, so that this world should not perish but live."[62] During World War II, Moltmann was captured while serving in the German army. He struggled with desolation and shame in POW camps until a chaplain gave him a Bible, where he discovered the psalms of lament. The story of this POW camp experience prefaces Moltmann's *The Source of Life: The Holy Spirit and the Theology of Life*, in which he articulates a pneumatology of life, vitality, and joy:

> The Gospel of John tell us quite simply what it is that is brought into the world from God through Christ: *life*. "I live, and you shall

live also" (John 14:19).For the Holy Spirit is "the source of life" and brings life into the world—whole life, full life, unhindered, indestructible, *everlasting* life. . . . The sending of the Holy Spirit is the revelation of God's indestructible *affirmation* of life and his marvelous *joy* in life.[63]

The Spirit of Christ who is the "resurrection and the life" (Jn 11:25) conquers death, gives the grace of life eternal, and enlivens and animates our temporal, earthly existence. For Moltmann, the flourishing of all creatures, the vitality of human community, the sensuousness of beauty, the holism of body and soul, and the healing of illness are all signs of the new creation being wrought by the Spirit of the resurrection, the Spirit who raised Jesus Christ from the dead.

Wars of self-defense and wars of liberation are waged for the protection of life, and in this sense one could argue that defensive warfare is consistent with the movement of the Spirit. Yet the very ethos of war is not life and vitality but destruction and death. Hedges notes that Freud identified two instincts that lure human beings: *eros*, an instinct for love and intimacy, and *thanatos*, an impulse for annihilation. War may seductively wrap itself in the mantle of *eros* as soldiers march off to battle in the name of those they love, but it is *thanatos* that triumphs in the heat of war when destruction itself becomes alluring and enticing. Hedges witnessed this phenomenon in El Salvador, Nicaragua, Guatemala, the Sudan, the Punjab, Iraq, Bosnia, and Kosovo. "The eyes of the soldiers who carry this orgy of death are crazed. They speak only in guttural shouts. They are high on the power to spare lives or take them, the divine power to destroy."[64] During World War II, American poet John Peale Bishop wrote that the greatest tragedy of the war "was not that it made so many dead men, but that it destroyed the tragedy of death."[65] Reverence for life, respect for the absolute preciousness and godliness of human persons, was drowned in the rivers of blood that flowed through Europe.

The power of *thanatos* cannot be countered effectively with words and rhetoric but only with direct action that witnesses to the holiness of life by rescuing persons from death and by refusing to do harm. Philip Hallie, haunted by memories of the exploding white phosphorus warheads he had fired during World War II and troubled by research on human cruelty he had conducted in the postwar years, was near suicide when he happened upon an account of Le Chambon, the

French Huguenot village of André and Magda Trocmé. Le Chambon, as a village, exercised nonviolent resistance against the Nazis and rescued five thousand Jewish men, women, and children from death. "I was seeing spontaneous love that had nothing to do with sheer, brute power," he recalls. "I was seeing a new reality, undergoing a revelation. Here was a place where help came from love, not from force."[66] Reaching up to scratch his cheek, he discovered that he was in tears.[67] The people of Le Chambon "would not give up a life for any price. . . . For them, human life had no price; it had only dignity."[68]

Conclusion

"War is hell," said General Sherman. There is, then, nothing original or novel about an argument that war is, in so many ways, antithetical to the work of the Holy Spirit. And yet, even though Sherman's maxim has become part of our cultural discourse about warfare, we cloak war in the language of justice and righteousness and celebrate war as something noble and patriotic. At this time in history, it is particularly important that Christians in the United States scrutinize warfare very carefully and honestly evaluate our national policies from an ethical and theological perspective. Examination of warfare through the prism of pneumatology, which I have done here only in a limited and preliminary manner, suggests that war obscures and obstructs the presence of the Spirit of Christ in our world. War inhibits conversion. It operates through deception, disorder, and the offering of innocent victims to the sacrificial gods of violence. Warfare fractures communion, destroys life, and courts *thanatos*.

Where does this leave us in a world of tyrants and dictators, a world of increasing injustice and polarization, a world of terrorism and hatred? These threats and dangers are all too real, and as Christians we have a responsibility to respond actively. The legacy of Gandhi and King reveals that there are ways other than war to confront tyranny, racism, and injustice—paths more in keeping with the Spirit of freedom, truth, communion, and life. But the nonviolent action that Gandhi and King preached and practiced is not an easy, instant cure for our fractured world. It must be complemented by other means in order to nurture peace, such as the strengthening of global justice, international law, and international institutions of arbitration.[69] Nonviolent action, moreover, requires prayer, discipline, training, organization, coordination, and broad participation. It cannot be accomplished by isolated persons acting alone. James Lawson traveled the South in the late 1950s with the Fellowship of Reconciliation, training and advising people in nonviolent methods to resist racial segregation and advance civil rights. He emphasized "the necessity of fierce discipline and training and strategizing and planning and recruiting and doing the kinds of things you do to have a movement. That can't happen spontaneously. It has to be done systematically."[70] This presents a tremendous challenge—and a tremendous opportunity—for the Christian churches.

"Peacemaking," the U.S. Catholic Bishops state in *The Challenge of Peace,* "is not an optional commitment. It is a requirement of faith. We are called to be peacemakers, not by some movement of the moment, but by our Lord Jesus" (#333). One concrete way in which we can exercise this requirement of faith is through the training and mobilization of the church, the body of Christ and temple of the Holy Spirit, in the practice of nonviolent action.[71] There is great precedent for this undertaking. Christian churches were indispensable to the Civil Rights movement in America in the 1960s; people met in churches to pray, study, organize and attend training sessions in nonviolence. The support of the Catholic Church and Pope John Paul II was critical to the success of the nonviolent Solidarity movement in Poland, and the People Power movement in the Philippines could not have removed Marcos from office without the widespread involvement of the Catholic faithful, the leadership of Cardinal Sin, and the voice of Catholic Radio Veritas. The nonviolent movement against apartheid in South Africa is unimaginable without the radiant face of Archbishop Desmond Tutu.

In a world where tyranny and injustice have not yet been vanquished across the globe, the Christian churches, in company with people of other religious faiths, must learn from this legacy and carry it forward through the implementation of programs to educate, train, and mobilize people of faith in the exercise of nonviolent action.[72] The Catholic Church, as the largest worldwide body of Christians—a body that crosses all national boundaries—has an especially important role to play in this regard.

Last October, when the Congress of the United States voted to initiate a war against Iraq, abruptly halting the U.N. weapons inspections that were underway, my senator ended his address on the Senate floor with this invocation: "May the Holy Spirit enlighten the leaders of the

world to understand the true meaning of the Second Great Command-
ment to love thy neighbor as thyself and may God continue to bless
America as we go forward."[73] The neighbors whom we are to love as
ourselves include the people of Iraq and the men and women in the
United States military. At the time of this writing, it is estimated that
between 5,000 and 10,000 Iraqi civilians have been killed by our war.[74]
Dead are 423 American servicemen and women and at least 1,178 are
wounded.[75] The number of Iraqi military casualties is unknown. Hospitals are ill-equipped to treat the wounded.[76] High rates of cancer and
birth deformities, suspected to be a legacy of the depleted uranium
first used in the Persian Gulf War, continue.[77] American soldiers show
signs of psychological trauma and long to go home.[78] Ancient, irreplaceable artifacts of the history of Iraq, and, indeed, of human civilization itself, have been looted. Saddam Hussein is no longer in power,
but democracy is nowhere in sight. One journalist describes Iraq as a
"land ruled by chaos."[79] No evidence that Hussein actually possessed
weapons of mass destruction—the primary reason given for the war—
has been found.[80] Anger seethes throughout the region and threatens
to generate more terrorism against the United States.[81] The cost of the
war and the subsequent occupation will be at least $157 billion, money
that will not be available to fight AIDS in Africa, or bring full em-
ployment in America, or convert our economy from fossil fuel to re-
newable energy. Meanwhile, the various proposals that were put forth
for the nonviolent containment and deposition of Saddam Hussein are
now only a muted part of history.[82] Kenneth Overberg, a Jesuit moral
theologian and one of my colleagues, has fittingly taken words from
the psalmist, printed them in bold, and pinned them to the bulletin
board outside his office door: "Be gracious to us, O Lord. Enter our
lament in your book; store every tear in your flask" (Ps 56:8).

Notes

[1] Senator George V. Voinovich, "Statement on Iraq Resolution," *Congressional Record* 148 (4 October 2002): S9944.

[2] On the history of Christian ethics with respect to issues of nonviolence and war, see Lisa Sowle Cahill, *Love Your Enemies: Discipleship, Pacifism, and Just War Theory* (Minneapolis: Fortress, 1994).

[3] Yves Congar, *I Believe in the Holy Spirit*, trans. David Smith (New York: Seabury, 1983), 2:123.

[4] Congar, *I Believe in the Holy Spirit*, 2:122-24.

[5]Rowan Williams, *Christian Hope and Christian Life: Raids on the Inarticulate* (New York: Crossroad, 2001), 24.

[6]Peter Ackerman and Jack Duvall, *A Force More Powerful: A Century of Nonviolent Conflict* (New York: Palgrave, 2000), 13-59, 457-68.

[7]*Amandla! A Revolution in Four Part Harmony*, Artisan Entertainment, Santa Monica, California, 2002. Despite this incident, the film defends the use of violence by the liberation movement in South Africa. Ackerman and Duvall, in contrast, do not believe the armed struggle was essential to the overturning of apartheid—it was very easily neutralized by the far superior force of the apartheid regime. What was essential was the nonviolent mass organization and mobilization of the people that made arbitrary and oppressive rule impossible. Ackermann and Duvall, *A Force More Powerful*, 349 and 368.

[8]Paul Fussell, *Wartime: Understanding and Behavior in the Second World War* (New York: Oxford, 1989), 276.

[9]See, for example, Hannah Arendt, *Eichmann in Jerusalem* (New York: Viking Press, 1964). On denial on the part of the murderers in the Rwandan genocide, see Philip Gourevitch, *We Wish to Inform You That Tomorrow We Will Be Killed with Our Families* (New York: Picador, 1998), 305.

[10]Mahatma Gandhi, *The Essential Gandhi: An Anthology of His Writings on His Life, Work, and Ideas*, ed. Louis Fischer (New York: Random House, 1962), 147.

[11]Ibid., 79.

[12]Martin Luther King, Jr., *Strength to Love* (Philadelphia: Fortress, 1981), 56.

[13]Ackerman and Duvall, *A Force More Powerful*, 327.

[14]Philip Hallie, *Lest Innocent Blood Be Shed: The Story of the Village of Le Chambon and How Goodness Happened There* (New York: Harper and Row, 1979), 114. *Weapons of the Spirit*, a documentary film about Le Chambon, is available for classroom use from http://www.chambon.org/weapons.htm.

[15]Ackerman and Duvall, *A Force More Powerful*, 369-396, 279-302; Roger Cohen, "Who Really Brought Down Milosevic?" *New York Times Magazine*, 26 November 2000, 43-47, 118, 148. *A Force More Powerful* was the basis for a three-hour PBS documentary of the same title in the year 2000. In 2002, a documentary about Milosevic entitled *Bringing Down a Dictator* was also produced. These films are available for classroom use from Films for the Humanities and Sciences at 1-800-257-5126.

[16]Congar, *I Believe in the Holy Spirit*, 2:17. My emphasis.

[17]Ibid., 2:136. Reference is to Aquinas's discussion of human freedom vis-à-vis God's inspiration in ST Ia IIae q. 9, a. 4 and 6; q. 68, a. 3, ad 2; IIa IIae, q. 23, a. 2; q. 52, a. 1, ad. 3.

[18]On this point, see Congar, *I Believe in the Holy Spirit*, 2:121.

[19]Hannah Arendt, *On Violence* (New York: Harcourt, Brace & World, 1969), 46.

[20]*When the Mountains Tremble*, 90 min., New York, New Yorker Films, 1983, updated 1993.

[21]Harlan K. Ullman and James P. Wade, *Shock and Awe: Achieving Rapid*

Dominance (National Defense University Press, 1996), Introduction, 4. Available at www.dodccrp.org.shockIndex.html, accessed 2 February 2003.

[22]Ackerman and Duvall, *A Force More Powerful*, 368.

[23]Gandhi, *The Essential Gandhi*, 79-80.

[24]Ibid., 77-78.

[25]Ibid., 164.

[26]Congar, *I Believe in the Holy Spirit*, 2:219, 2:226 n. 25.

[27]"All truth, no matter where it comes from, is from the Holy Spirit." Cited in Congar, *I Believe in the Holy Spirit*, 2:219. Reference is to *PL* 17, 245.

[28]Aquinas, *In Ioannem* 14, 4 (no. 1916). Translation by Bruce Marshall, *Trinity and Truth* (New York: Cambridge, 2000), 181.

[29]Cited in Chris Hedges, *War Is a Force That Gives Us Meaning* (New York: Public Affairs, 2002), 62.

[30]Spencer Ackerman and John B. Judis, "Deception and Democracy: The Selling of the Iraq War," *The New Republic* 228, 30 June 2003, 14-18, 23-25; Andrew Buncombe and Raymond Whitaker, "Ministers Knew War Papers Were Forged, Says Diplomat," *The Independent* on-line edition, accessed 29 June 2003.http://news.independent.co.uk/low_res/story.jsp?story=419982&host=3&dir=62, accessed 6/29/03; Richard Norton-Taylor and Nicholas Watt, "No 10 Knew: Iraq No Threat," *The Guardian* on-line edition (19 August 2003): http://politics.guardian.co.uk/kelly/story/0,,1021534,00.html, accessed 8/20/03. A survey conducted by the Program on International Policy Attitudes, based at the University of Maryland, concluded that a majority of Americans had accepted at least one of three common pieces of misinformation about Iraq, which greatly contributed to popular support for the war policy. See http://www.pipa.org, accessed 10 October 2003.

On distortion of evidence prior to the Persian Gulf War in 1991, see Scott Peterson, "In War, Some Facts Less Factual: Some US Assertions from the Last War on Iraq Still Appear Dubious," *Christian Science Monitor* 94, 6 September 2002, 1, 14. Moreover, in studying the history of Hussein's tyranny in Iraq, it is disturbing to learn that the United States supported Hussein in the 1980s when there was ample evidence that he not only possessed but actually employed chemical weapons; he was at that time our ally in the region, and fidelity to the truth of human rights was subordinated to political expediency. See Samantha Powers, "Iraq: 'Human Rights and Chemical Weapons Use Aside,' " *America in the Age of Genocide* (New York: Basic Books, 2002), 170-245.

[31]Ullman and Wade, *Shock and Awe*, Introduction, 4.

[32]See Sun Tzu, *The Art of War*, trans. Samuel B. Griffith (New York: Oxford, 1963), 53, 66, 106.

[33]With respect to the war against Iraq, see for example Robert Fisk, "How the News Will Be Censored in This War," *The Independent* online edition (25 February 2003): http://argument.independent.co.uk/low_res/story.jsp?story=381438&host=6&dir=140, accessed 26 February 2003.

[34]Lawrence LeShan, *The Psychology of War* (New York: Helios, 2002, 1992), 31.

[35]Hedges, *War Is a Force*, 22. See also Fussell, " 'The Real War Will Never Get in the Books,' " in *Wartime*, 267-97.

[36]Hedges, *War Is a Force*, 62-82, 122-41. On the relationship between deception and violence see also Miroslav Volf, *Exclusion and Embrace: A Theological Exploration of Identity, Otherness, and Reconciliation* (Nashville: Abingdon, 1996), 233-274.

[37]Gandhi, *The Essential Gandhi*, 278; Gandhi, *An Autobiography: The Story of My Experiments with Truth* (Boston: Beacon Press, 1993).

[38]Gandhi, *The Essential Gandhi*, 136.

[39]Ibid., 138.

[40]Ibid., 132.

[41]According to Kumar Rupesinghe and Sanam Naraghi Anderlini, it is estimated that between 200,000 to 250,000 children, both girls and boys, are fighting wars today. See *Civil Wars, Civil Peace: An Introduction to Conflict Resolution* (Sterling, Va.: Pluto Press, 1998), 2.

[42]The statistic on civilian casualties is from Rupesinghe and Anderlini, *Civil Wars, Civil Peace*, 2.

[43]René Girard, *The Scapegoat*, trans. Yvonne Preccero (Baltimore: John Hopkins University Press, 1986), 207. See also Gil Baillie, *Violence Unveiled: Humanity at the Crossroads* (New York: Crossroad, 1995).

[44]Gandhi, *The Essential Gandhi*, 315.

[45]Fussell, *Wartime*, 97.

[46]Ibid., 101.

[47]Elizabeth Neuffer, *Key to My Neighbor's House: Seeking Justice in Bosnia and Rwanda* (New York: Picador, 2001), 272. For detailed documentation of one recent instance of the use of rape as an instrument of war, see Joanne Csete, *The War Within the War: Sexual Violence Against Women and Girls in Eastern Congo* (New York: Human Rights Watch, 2002).

[48]Bernard Häring, *The Healing Power of Peace and Nonviolence* (New York: Paulist Press, 1986), 114.

[49]Gandhi, *The Essential Gandhi*, 164, 166.

[50]Ackerman and Duvall, *A Force More Powerful*, 107.

[51]Ibid., 459.

[52]Ibid., 491. For an excellent theoretical analysis of war and the undermining of democracy, see Kenneth Melchin, "Stretching Towards Democracy: Theology and Theory When Talk Becomes War," forthcoming in the 2003 *Proceedings of the Catholic Theological Society of America*.

[53]Congar, *I Believe in the Holy Spirit*, 2:17.

[54]Ibid.

[55]Congar, *Esprit de l'homme, Esprit de Dieu*, Foi Vivante, no. 206 (Paris: Cerf, 1983), 54.

[56]See LeShan, "The Human Attraction to War," in *The Psychology of War*, 21-31.

[57]Hedges, *War Is a Force*, 7.

[58]Ibid., 9. On this point Hedges references George Orwell, *1984* (San Diego: Harcourt, Brace Jovanovich, 1949), 35.

[59]Congar, "Pneumatologie dogmatique," in *Initiation à la pratique de la théologie*, ed. Bernard Lauret and François Refoulé (Paris: Cerf, 1982), 2:499 and 2:499 n. 36.

[60]Gandhi, *The Essential Gandhi*, 148.

[61]King, *Strength to Love*, 56.

[62]Jürgen Moltmann, *The Source of Life: The Holy Spirit and the Theology of Life*, trans. Margaret Kohl (New York: Fortress Press, 1997), 19.

[63]Ibid. Emphasis in original.

[64]Hedges, *War Is a Force*, 171.

[65]Cited in Hallie, *Lest Innocent Blood Be Shed*, 274.

[66]Hallie, cited in Patrick Henry, "Remembering the Rescuers," *First Things* 102 (April 2000): 13-16.

[67]Hallie, *Lest Innocent Blood Be Shed*, 2-4.

[68]Ibid., 274.

[69]See, for example, Glen Stassen, ed., *Just Peacemaking: Ten Practices for Abolishing War* (Cleveland: Pilgrim Press, 1998). For a discussion of this book by a variety of theologians and additional bibliography see *Journal of the Society of Christian Ethics* 23 (Spring/Summer 2003): 169-284. For reflection on the structural causes of war, see Howard Richards, "A Logical Plan for Peace," available at www.howardri.org.

[70]Ackerman and Duvall, *A Force More Powerful*, 315.

[71]For a vision of the integration of Catholic social teaching and the lived practice of the Christian faithful, see Margaret R. Pfeil, "Called and Gifted: Charism and Catholic Social Teaching" (paper presented at the conference "New Things": Catholic Social Teaching and the Twenty-First Century, University of Notre Dame, Notre Dame, 4-7 April 2002). For one example of a Christian organization currently engaged in nonviolent action at various places around the globe, contact Christian Peacemaker Teams, PO Box 6508, Chicago, IL 60680.

[72]On nonviolence in the world religions, see Daniel L. Smith-Christopher, *Subverting Hatred: The Challenge of Nonviolence in Religious Traditions* (New York: Orbis, 2000); Marc Gopin, *Between Eden and Armageddon: The Future of Religion, Violence, and Peacemaking* (New York: Oxford University Press, 2000); Thich Nhat Hanh, *Being Peace* (Berkeley, Calif.: Parallax Press, 1987); Eknath Easwaren, *A Man to Match His Mountains: Badshah Khan Nonviolent Soldier of Islam* (Petaluma, Calif.: Nilgiri Press, 1984); Murray Polner and Naomi Goodman, eds., *The Challenge of Shalom: The Jewish Tradition of Peace and Justice* (Philadelphia, Pa.: New Society, 1994).

[73]Voinovich, "Statement on Iraq Resolution," S9946.

[74]Peter Ford, "Survey Pointing to High Civilian Death Toll in Iraq: Preliminary Reports Suggest Casualties Well Above the Gulf War," *Christian Science Monitor* online edition, 22 May 2003, http://www.csmonitor.com/2003/0522/p01s02-woiq.htm, accessed 10 October 2003.

[75]"Killed in the Line of Duty," http://more.abcnews.go.com/sections/us/Primetime/IRAQ_Casualties.html, accessed10 October 2003; Jason Burke and Paul Harris, "America's Hidden Battlefield Toll," *The Observer* online edition, 14 September 2003, http://observer.guardian.co.uk/print/0,3858,4753236-102275,00.html, accessed 14 September 2003.

[76]Doctors Without Borders, "U.S. Fails to Fulfill Obligation to Support Health System in Iraq Posing Threat to Health of Iraqi People" (Press release, 2 May 2003): http://www.doctorswithoutborders.org/pr/2003/05-02-2003.shtml, accessed 6 May 2003.

[77]Elizabeth Neuffer, "Iraqis Trace Surge in Cancer to US Bombings," *Boston Globe* (26 January 2003): A11.

[78]Bob Graham, "I Just Pulled the Trigger," *London Evening Standard* online edition (19 June 2003): http://www.thisislondon.co.uk/news/articles/5402104?source=Evening%20Standard, accessed 6/30/03; Leonard Greene, "AWOL State of Mind: Calls from Soldiers Desperate to Leave Iraq Flood Hotline," *New York Post* online edition (5 October 2003): http://www.nypost.com/news/nationalnews/7316.htm, accessed 10 October 2003.

[79]Suzanne Goldenberg, "A Land Ruled by Chaos," *The Guardian* online edition (4 October 2003): http://www.guardian.co.uk/print/0,3858,4767215-103681,00.html, accessed 10/6/03.

[80]See David Cortright, Alistair Miller, George Lopez, and Linda Gerber, "Unproven: The Controversy Over Justifying War in Iraq," (Fourth Freedom Forum, June 2003), available at http://www.fourthfreedom.org/php/t-d-index.php?hinc=Unproven.hinc, accessed 10 October 2003.

[81]Niko Price, "Many Iraqis Turn Anger Toward the U.S.," *The Guardian* online edition, 17 April 2003, http://www.guardian.co.uk/worldlatest/story/0,1280,-2573029,00.html, accessed 4/17/ 03; Caroline Overington and Maggie Farley, "US Aggression Breeds Terror: UN Chief," *Sydney Morning Herald* online edition, 24 September 2003, http://smh.com.au/articles/2003/09/23/1064083001492.html, accessed 26 September 2003.

[82]For one proposal for nonviolent deposition of Saddam Hussein, see Priscilla Elworthy, "Bomb-Catching," *New Internationalist* 360 (September 2003): 24-25. Elworthy is chair of the Oxford Research Group, which develops nonviolent methods for global and local security. See also David Cortwright, George Lopez, and Alistair Miller, "Winning Without War: Sensible Security Options for Dealing with Iraq" (Fourth Freedom Forum, 2002), available at http://www.fourthfreedom.org/php/t-si-index.php?hinc=www_report.hinc, accessed 10 October 2003.

"Tongues as of Fire":
The Spirit as Paradigm for Ministry
in a Multicultural Setting

Maria Teresa Morgan

The church speaks all languages in the catholicity of witness.[1] In the mystery of God's self-communication, the Word becomes flesh and abides with us, becoming incarnated, encrypted, and uttered in the manifold expressions and possibilities of "every tongue, people, and nation" (Rv 7:9).

The word of salvation is carried out to all nations by the church, for the church is by its very nature missionary and universal (*Ad Gentes*, 2). It is missionary because it is "the Church of the Trinity" (*Lumen Gentium*, 2-4; *Ad Gentes*, 2-4; *Gaudium et Spes*, 40; *Unitatis Redintegratio*, 2, 6), taking its origin in the sending forth of the Son and the Holy Spirit. It is universal because as it is born in the communion and mission of trinitarian love, it is also sent forth beyond the boundaries of time and place to preach the gospel to all nations. The universality of this mission is brought into sharp relief in the pluriform cultures of our contemporary American reality, not only in society at large, but also as these cultures evidence themselves in the local church.[2] Today, "every city and nation is becoming a nation of nations."[3] Globalization, along with political and economic instability, is forcing the migration of large numbers of people to the United States, as well as to Canada, the United Kingdom, and most Western European countries, bringing a proliferation of cultures and languages. The ensuing multiculturalism offers different perspectives, even as it produces conflicts and tensions; it also represents an important challenge to the living out of faith in our world.

A ministerial experience within an increasingly diverse ecclesiological reality involves an uneasy tension between ethnocentrism and ethnodiversity. Language, and more specifically speech, which is the event of language,[4] is a key element in the challenge and gift that multiculturalism presents. Ministering in an environment where Creole, French, Portuguese, and Spanish are spoken alongside English has made me acutely aware of the importance of language as symbol, not only in its semantic dimension, but also as emblematic of identity, of divisions, and of the often untapped potential for mutual enrichment among diverse monolingual groups. If culture is mediated by the language in which it is spoken, it is also true that language is more than words; it encompasses stories, images, songs and dance, food, dress, and ways of worshiping.

For this reason I have chosen the theme of the Spirit's gift of tongues as a paradigm for ministry in a multicultural setting. I will consider the gift of tongues from the perspective of the New Testament prophetic proclamation tradition, rather than from that of the ecstatic, or glossolalia tradition.[5] This paper examines the biblical images of the Pentecost account, presenting these images as the foundational model for ministry in a multicultural church. Based upon the patristic affirmation that Pentecost reverses the division of Babel and drawing from the pneumatology of Yves Congar and George Montague, this paper will consider the possibilities and the challenges of diversity.[6] It will address how the Spirit may be speaking to the church through the diverse cultures and languages of contemporary America. It will also analyze the images present in the Pentecost account, seeking to discover therein a ministerial model for unity in multiplicity. The revelatory and perhaps even religious nature of language will be presented through three biblical passages: the Tower of Babel (Gn 11:1-9), the Exodus/Sinai event (Ex 19-20; Dt 4:10-15; 5:24), and Pentecost (Acts 2:1-12) giving particular attention to how the images in the narratives of Genesis, Exodus, and Deuteronomy culminate in the Lucan account of the Pentecost. The paper will identify how these passages underline the role of language in salvation history. The pneumatological model proposed for consideration will move from the exclusivity evidenced at Babel to the inclusivity manifested at Pentecost.

Pneumatology is dependent on praxis, for, as Yves Congar asserts, the theology of the Spirit, like all theology, develops out of the lived experience of the church.[7] In order to contextualize the pneumatology developed in this paper, I will consider first two issues that emerge directly from the life of the local church in which I minister. These two issues are cultural pluralism and the relationship between the church and cultures. Though the issues presented here are particular to the church of south Florida, they have a wider reach due to the varied cultural configurations of major cities in the United States.

A Nation of Nations: From the Melting Pot to Cultural Pluralism

The term "cultural pluralism" originated with Horace M. Kallen, a professor at the New School for Social Research. In 1954, he proposed the concept of cultural pluralism to identify a process by which diverse cultures retained their specific characteristics while establishing a relationship with other cultures and ethnic groups.[8] Kallen's ideas have not been incorporated as a way of life in the United States. Indeed, sociological research shows that for all immigrant groups, full assimilation occurs in three generations.[9] The term cultural pluralism, however, has been redefined and has become part of our language to indicate loosely the diversity of cultures that co-exist, sometimes uneasily, in major cities in the United States.[10]

The experience of life in south Florida embodies the postmodern understanding that language is constitutive of reality and not just a reflection of it.[11] The encounter of diverse peoples, languages, and cultures are an experience of daily life in Miami Dade and the surrounding counties. According to the census bureau, 51 percent of Miami Dade County's 2.3 million residents were born outside of the United States and two of every three residents speak a language other than English at home.[12] These figures designate the greatest percentage of foreign-born residents living in any metropolitan area in the United States. The same trend is evidenced in neighboring counties. In Broward County, a quarter of its 1.6 million residents were born in a country other than the United States and one in four does not speak English at home. In Palm Beach County, 17 percent of its 1.1 million residents are foreign-born; one in five homes speak a language other than English. The multiculturalism of south Florida is considered an economic strength in a global economy as well as a source of tensions among the various ethnic and language groups.

A recent NBC poll of six hundred residents from Miami Dade, Broward, and South Palm Beach counties demonstrated that most residents believe the multicultural proliferation of the past decade has been detrimental to the quality of life in south Florida. Almost one-third of the participants pointed to language as the cause. Almost half of the native English speakers favor an "English only" requirement at the workplace, although this rule would be illegal.[13] Native English speakers resent bilingual requisites at the workplace while non-native English speakers complain about being belittled for their accents and grammatical mistakes. More than half of the non-native English speakers said they experience discrimination at work because of their accent or their imperfect English. The evidence indicates that language creates barriers and is symptomatic of those barriers. Thus, the "Babelian paradigm" is often predominant in the manner in which people relate, or fail to relate, in south Florida.[14] For the majority of residents, the multiplicity of languages has a negative and punishing effect because it prevents and perverts understanding among the different groups, fostering dispute, animosity, and violence.

The regional, cultural, and linguistic diversity I have just presented is not unique to south Florida, for multiculturalism and multilingualism are found in every major city of the nation. The process of enculturation makes English the predominant language for the third generation. But demographers advise us to make peace with cultural diversity, for as the children and grandchildren of immigrants become enculturated, new waves of immigrants will continue to come to our nation due to globalization and economic and political instability.[15]

If the United States has become a gathering of many ethnic and linguistic groups, it follows that the local church reflects this reality. The question must then be asked as to what is the relationship between the church and the cultural milieu in which it is localized. Before proceeding further, it is essential to clarify the choice of two terms: cultures and the church.

The Relationship between the Local Church and Cultures

I have chosen the term "cultures" rather than "culture" because the former represents a more diversified and dynamic understanding of interaction and engagement than the latter; it is also more reflective of the diversity in American society and the reality of the local church.[16] Cultures is also the term used in most ecclesial documents.[17] According to Bernard Lonergan, culture represents a classicist and static notion.[18] The term cultures, on the other hand, is more reflective of an empirical notion and the fluidity of socialization.[19] I have chosen the term "church" over "faith" or "gospel" because "church" is the locus where faith and the gospel are made concrete in the lived experience of the Christian community (*Lumen Gentium*, 23, 26).[20] My use of the word "church" refers primarily but not exclusively to the Roman Catholic Church. The term church as I use it in this paper reflects the ecclesiology of *koinonia*, or communion, proposed by Vatican II, an ecclesiology that is inclusive and respectful of differences (*Lumen Gentium*, 2, 4, 8, 9; *Ad Gentes*, 19).[21] The term church is also representative of conciliar ecclesiology wherein the local church is seen as the realization of the one, holy, Catholic Church (*Lumen Gentium*, 13). This pre-eminence of the local church was seen by Karl Rahner to be the most novel ecclesiological contribution of the council.[22]

A third term, inculturation, is key to illumining our understanding of the relationship between the church and cultures. Inculturation denotes the bringing of the church to life in the culture(s) of the local community. It is a process that applies not only to missiology, but to the particular church of every community. The ecclesiology of *koinonia* promoted by Vatican II contributed greatly to the development of inculturation.[23] The integration of faith and culture began cautiously with Pius XII, was fostered by John XXIII, and culminated in the second chapter of *Gaudium et Spes*, where the interdependence between faith and culture was elucidated and embraced.[24] Paul VI's *Evangelii Nuntiandi* is widely considered the Magna Carta of the relationship between faith and culture. John Paul II has continued to foster the quest for the integration of the gospel message in the manifold expressions of cultures.

The historical consciousness of Vatican II reflected in the conciliar and papal documents indicates that one cannot conceive of a ministry that disassociates the church from cultures. Paul VI called this disassociation "the drama of our time" (*Evangelii Nuntiandi*, 20).[25] The second chapter of *Gaudium et Spes* makes clear that the church assumes the diversity of the cultures of the people in a specific place. Using the beautiful analogy of the seed "which is the word of God" growing out of a particular geographical soil, *Ad Gentes* proposes that the cultural specificity of a region forms part of the theology of the local church (*Ad Gentes*, 22). The local church thus constitutes the privileged space for inculturation, for it is there that the gospel encounters the people. The question then is, how does inculturation take place at the local level of the faith community?

The process of inculturation involves the integration of the Christian experience with the cultures present in the local church. The lived Christian experience that emerges from this process is both an expression of the cultures of the people and the manifestation of *koinonia* that becomes a gift of the local church to the universal church.[26] In the concrete experience of cultural diversity within the local church in which I minister, there is a struggle as inculturation seeks to foster a new lived experience. When I have given presentations on the topic of ministry in a multicultural society, I have encountered much resistance and pain among the participants. I suspect that other communities experience these same tensions. The issue of language often distills the cultural animosity present in the local church. Different ethnolingual groups cling to their language in worship and in ministries, judging other groups as threats. Being able to speak the language of minority people liberates them[27] from the experiences of anonymity and dislocation.[28] Indeed, history has proven that language is part of the "dangerous memory" of a people.[29] For the dominant culture, other languages are seen as transgressing the boundaries of national identity. Thus, often in the local church, each cultural group remains exclusive of the others. This division and animosity was evidenced recently in a walk-out by some members of a local parish during a bilingual homily. In this instance, the language issue was the trigger. The paradigm of Babel was the model.

We see then that the tensions and linguistic polemics that exist in our multicultural society carry over into the local church. From our fractured ecclesial communities emerges the need to develop a praxis of engagement that draws its source from the Spirit, the source of unity.[30] I propose that the Pentecost account can provide us with metaphors for the scriptural and theological underpinnings of a praxis of engagement and inclusivity.[31] This paradigm will move us from the cacophony of Babel to the cohesiveness of Pentecost. With this in mind, I will now proceed to consider the images present in the accounts of the Tower of Babel, the Exodus/Sinai event, and Pentecost. I have chosen these passages because an early tradition included them in the triennial cycle of readings for Pentecost. I have also chosen them because different strands of the narratives are carried over and woven into each successive account. This continuity is expressed through the references to fire, to the word of God and the words of humanity, to multiple languages and to the gift of the covenant, which for Christians reaches its full manifestation with the outpouring of the Spirit at Pentecost.

The Divisive Nature of Languages: Genesis 11:1-9

The biblical account of the Tower of Babel is the first to be considered. This passage introduces the etiology of nations. Migration, the attempt to build a select society, and the resulting scattering of peoples and languages provide a drama where fear, ambition, and their punishing consequences play dominant roles. The story begins with a worldview in which linguistic conformity is a condition for unity. "The whole world spoke the same language, using the same words . . . one people, all speaking the same language" (Gn 11:1, 6). It continues with a story of migration and two projects undertaken for the purpose of dominance and exclusivity.[32] "While people moved eastward they came upon a valley in the land of Shinar and settled there. They said to one another, 'Come, let us mold bricks and bake them in the fire.' . . . Then they said, 'Come, let us build ourselves a city and a tower with its top in the sky and so make a name for ourselves; otherwise we shall be scattered all over the earth' " (Gn 11:2-4). Confusion and dispersion come about as punishment in the form of diversity: "The Lord came down to see the city and the tower. . . . Then the Lord said . . . 'Let us then go down and there confuse their language, so that one will not understand what the other says,'. . . The Lord scattered them thence all over the earth" (Gn 11:5, 7, 8).

The divisive nature of language is evident here: sin has shattered it into multiplicity, resulting in disintegration and the formation of nations. The Septuagint and the New Testament employ three Greek terms to designate a people. The first is *ethnō*, indicating nations in the political sense and referring to humanity separated from God. In general, it refers to "the others." The second term is *laos*, which describes the people of God. Finally, one finds the term *ochlos*, meaning the multitude, the marginalized and despised to whom Jesus showed a preferential option.[33] In Genesis 11:9 nations are considered as *ethnō*—"terrestial realities of the flesh"—manifested in different languages and awaiting the redemption of Pentecost when they will become *laos*.[34] Just as sin and division are revealed in the proliferation of languages, we will later see that the Spirit's theophany at Pentecost brings about union through the very diversity of languages (Acts 2:8).[35] For this reason, the Fathers of the church saw in Pentecost a reversal of Babel.

The revelatory and perhaps even religious nature of language is evidenced in the account of Babel, in the Exodus/Sinai narrative, and at Pentecost. In the first, it is presented as the alienating result of sin. The division of tongues is a curse brought upon humans because of their presumption, preventing communication and fostering disarray, dispute, and separation from God and from one other. In the second, the interchange of words between God and the people of Israel seals the covenant (Dt 5:4-28). Post-biblical rabbinical theology affirms that God's covenant word at Sinai is communicated in all the languages of the world.[36] At Pentecost, language will serve as an epiphany of redemption. In eschatology, it will be manifested in the gathering of all the nations "out of every tongue"(Rv 7:9).[37]

I will now proceed to examine the Exodus/Sinai account giving particular attention as to how the images present in the narrative reveal the cultic nature of language, in this instance, as revelatory of the covenant. At Babel, the fire at the brickyard of human presumption ultimately forges the punitive words that divide the nations. At the Holy Mountain, the fire at the core of God's utterance gathers the people of Israel into a covenantal relationship that will be offered to all nations through the communication of the flaming word into many languages.

The Word at the Heart of the Fire: Deuteronomy 5:24[38]

The Lucan account reflects a Christian tradition that establishes a close connection between the giving of the Law at Sinai and the gift of the Spirit at Pentecost.[39] In later Judaism the Jewish feast of Pentecost commemorated the covenant at Sinai.[40] It is possible that Luke, being familiar with this tradition, intended to present the Spirit as the new and universal covenant (Jer 31:31; Ez 36:26, 27) given to all people.[41]

The cluster of symbols found in Exodus 19, 20:18-22, 24:17; Deuteronomy 4:10-15, 32-36; 5:4, 24; and Acts 2:1-13 elucidates Montague's intuition that "biblical revelation is not primarily propositional but symbolic."[42] The scrutiny of images in the theophanies at Sinai and on Pentecost reveals striking confluences between the phenomena of sound, word(s), and hearing with the manifestation of fire.[43] Vesting fire upon the word of God carries powerful allusions that bear witness to the consuming, transforming, and unifying quality of God's revelation. The analogy of the word of God as the word of fire illumines and ignites the biblical imagination from the Pentateuch to the New Testament. In Exodus 19:18 and Deuteronomy 4:33, 36; 5:4, 24 this image conveys the power, passion, and permanence of the covenant between God and Israel. Luke will harness the force of this symbol to describe how the tongues of humanity are enkindled by the Spirit so that all may hear of the wonders of God (Acts 2:3, 4, 11). I will proceed by considering the development of the rich symbols of the Sinai account in rabbinical theology and conclude by introducing Luke's masterful gathering of these symbols and traditions in the Pentecost account.

The rich lode of images embedded in the Exodus/Sinai account weaves oracular and auditory phenomena with the image of fire. The Exodus narrative relates visual experiences (Ex 24:17), but the predominant references are to sound, speaking, hearing and fire (Ex 19:5-9, 13, 16, 18; 20:18, 19). The Deuteronomist Sinai synthesis (Dt 4:2-40) makes no mention of a visible manifestation but rather of "hearing" God's word from the heart of the fire.[44] Word, covenant, and fire shape variegated metaphors that persisted in post-biblical Judaism and are garnered in the Lucan account. The talmudic and Judaic post-biblical tradition not only continue the association of the Law with speech and with flame,[45] but also allude to the universality of the covenant by commenting on the multiple languages of its manifestation.[46] Philo associates God's gift of the Law and the communication of speech by fire, describing how the divine voice at Sinai elicited a special sound in each person and turned into flame.[47] According to rabbinic theology, first developed with the Targum on Deuteronomy 33:2, God's voice at Sinai divided into "seven voices and then went into seventy tongues."[48] The universality of the covenant is affirmed by underscoring the transmission of God's Law into all the languages of the world "so that all people would receive the Law in their own language,"[49] for the seventy languages corresponded to the seventy Gentile nations listed in Genesis 10:2-31.[50]

The rich symbols of the Sinai covenant and tradition, sound, wind, fire, and languages, are incorporated into the Pentecost account, manifesting thus the inclusiveness of all nations and languages in God's gift of the new covenant. At Pentecost, the voice of the Spirit becomes the intelligible word of the covenant.

The Gift of Tongues at Pentecost: Acts 2:1-12

Just as in Genesis, when God transforms the raging force of chaos and gives it to humanity as a blessing, at Pentecost the Spirit tames the chaos of language and through tongues of fire puts its power at the service of humanity so that the gospel may be heard by "people from every nation and language" (Rv 7:9) and be proclaimed by people in their own languages.[51]

The gift of tongues at Pentecost is interpreted by commentators both as ecstatic prayer, indicating the pre-conceptual speech of glossolalia, and as a form of prophecy, enabling the speaker to announce the "signs and wonders" of God (Acts 2:11).[52] As mentioned in the introduction, the gift of tongues is considered here from the latter perspective.

The connection between the tongues of fire, the gift of tongues, and the proclamation of the gospel is demonstrated in Acts 2:1-13. The manifestation of the Spirit in "tongues as of fire" (Acts 2:3) evidences the power as well as the universality of the gospel.[53] After the disciples are "filled with the Holy Spirit" (Acts 2:4), "they began to speak in different languages as the Spirit gave them to speak" (Acts 2:4). The "crowd" (Acts 2:6) is not a haphazard gathering of people.[54] Rather, Luke explicitly indicates that the crowd represents Jews from the "scattered" (Gn 11:8) nations of the diaspora and from their respective linguistic groups (Acts 2:9-11). They are given the gift to hear of "the great deeds of God" (Acts 2:11) in their innate languages (Acts 2:11). The connection is thus made between the gift of the Spirit, the tongues of fire, and the preaching of the gospel to all nations in their particular languages. The witness the disciples bear is speaking the good news through the gift of tongues. The different languages are no longer a curse, as in Babel, but a gift, a locus of revelation, a medium of evangelization. In the Pentecost narrative Luke employs the same verb as that used in the Septuagint account of Babel to indicate the confusion caused by the many languages. In Acts 2:6, however, "confused" (*syncheō*) no longer has the negative meaning of Genesis 11:9, but is a manifestation of the wonder of understanding in different languages the marvelous deeds of God in humanity's behalf.

Two images in the Pentecost account are paradigmatic for ministry in a multicultural setting. These images are that of the disciples "gathered together in one place" (Acts 2:1, 46) and "tongues as of fire" (Acts 2:3).

"Gathered together in one place" is found at the beginning (Acts 2:1) and at the conclusion (Acts 2:46) of the second chapter, indicating the unity of heart and mind of the first Christian community. Unity is both the condition for and the result of the outpouring of the Spirit.[55] Montague points out that though translated "in one place," the Greek expression indicates more than locality. It is frequently found in the Septuagint as rendering the Hebrew *yahad*, meaning "unity of mind and heart."[56] This image of unity in the Christian community that opens the Pentecost account reaches over to the concluding words of the chapter: "Every day they devoted themselves to gathering together in the temple . . ."(Acts 2:46). By his choice of words, Luke indicates that the scattering of Babel has been overcome in the gathering of people "in one place" who are made "one in heart and mind" by the Spirit, the source of unity.[57] This unity does not mean a systemic uniformity or, as someone once told me, "They are always welcome at our church—as long as they do it our way." This unity means the full manifestation of the theology of catholicity expressed in *Lumen Gentium* 13 where each individual part contributes to the fullness of the church so that both the whole and individuals are built up into the one Body of Christ.[58]

Ministerial experience reveals that the local church where people come together often becomes a space where cultural differences are radicalized and, though "together in one place," we find ourselves still "scattered" as in Babel. The Pentecost account invites us to transform this "one place" of the local church into the gathering of the people of God united in witnessing to the unity of the Spirit. For "the Spirit is the one who enables all to be one and unity to be a multitude."[59] In the true gathering of the many in the one place of the church, the sectarian city of Babel becomes the new Jerusalem, brought into harmony by the Spirit.

The last and central image to be considered reflects the universality of the covenant and underlines the role of language in salvation history. "There appeared to them tongues as of fire, dividing (as from a single source) and they settled on each of them" (Acts 2:3). Tongues are a symbol of the gift of the Spirit and of the heterogeneity of lan-

guages that will be spoken by the apostles. Montague points out that
Luke uses the word "tongue" as a bridge from "fire" in Acts 2:3 to
"language" in 2:4.[60] At Pentecost, the Spirit descends on the disciples
in "tongues as of fire" and the first sign of this outpouring of the Spirit
is speaking in different tongues (Acts 2:4). As at Sinai, the word of the
covenant has been manifested into all the languages of the world, and
Luke indicates that a communication to the different linguistic groups
has taken place. Translated into specific multicultural situations within
the local church, the words of fire impel us to communicate with "the
other," even when we do not speak or understand each other's language. For the essence of speech is communication (1 Cor 12:7) and
the essence of that communication, as Montague states, is the manifestation of the Spirit in unity and understanding.[61] "The Spirit of the
Lord," who dwells in each of us and "holds everything together . . .
knows every word said" (Wis 1:7). In that one Spirit, we also will
know what is said by the other and will be able to gather, not in divi-
siveness or suspicion, but in communion with one another in the one
Spirit. In this way, the local church will truly reflect the catholicity of
witness of which Augustine and Congar so eloquently speak.[62]

A Place for the Spirit

Because the local church is the space where the catholicity of the
church becomes manifested, I would like to consider two examples of
how a Catholic parish and an Episcopal parish are striving to live the
paradigm of Pentecost. The pastors of these two parishes responded to
several inquiries I made while researching this paper.

The diversity in the Catholic parish was a source of cultural polarization and rifts. Yet during the past two years, the focus has shifted
and cultural diversity is emerging as gift rather than as impediment to
unity, as wealth rather than impoverishment. The parish includes 37
nationalities of first-generation immigrants. The parish census reveals
the following linguistic preferences: 2,742 families speak English and
Spanish, 1,836 families speak English only, 1,652 families speak only
Spanish, 123 families speak English and French, 28 families speak
French only, 25 families speak English and Portuguese, 10 families
speak only Portuguese, 9 families speak English and Creole, 7 families speak English and Italian, 5 families speak English and Chinese, 3
families speak English and German, and 2 families speak Tagalog.

The new pastor is employing diverse means for the building of community. The strategies consist of three elements: communication, collaboration, and celebration. The first goal, communication, is accomplished through availability and listening. He was apologetic about the numerous interruptions during our interview but said he is making a concerted effort to be approachable and not to build walls between himself and the community. Because of his native identification with the most numerous cultural minority in south Florida, Cuban Americans, his availability to all groups is especially important so as not to give the impression of favoritism.

Collaboration is fostered by granting equal time and opportunities to each cultural group, being careful that one group does not impose its culture on another, and by promoting an atmosphere of *koinonia* and respect for diversity. Collaboration and communication are also encouraged among the cultural groups through engagement in the parish council and in cultural events.

Celebration takes place in the Eucharist, celebrated in English, Spanish, and French. It is also accomplished by monthly social festivities, where different cultural heritages are hosted, with music and ethnic foods playing an important part. Some bilingual services, such as the stations of the cross and the rosary, have been attempted, although the pastor noted that these have to be approached with caution and sensitivity. Resistance to and criticism of bilingual services have been expressed by the English-speaking group of the parish. I have observed that on Sunday the Eucharist becomes a space where all are welcome as the diversity of cultures gathers to celebrate and remember. Catholicity is striving to become a practiced and practical reality.

The second example comes from an Episcopal parish where I have occasionally been invited to minister. As the neighborhood changed, this church saw the need to reach out to Hispanics. While the Spanish-speaking congregation grew, the English-speaking congregation diminished. Last year, an interesting reversal took place. An affluent, predominantly Anglo-Episcopal parish entered into a partnership with this working-class predominantly Hispanic parish. The "companion relationship" calls for assistance in strategic resource planning from the affluent parish in exchange for support from the working-class parish in developing a Hispanic ministry, in multicultural sensitization, and in sharing the expertise gained from twenty years of serving the Spanish-speaking community. The project is at the beginning stages and its success remains to be seen, but both parishes have taken a prophetic stance and are striving to respond to the multicultural challenge by a faith that models inclusivity and cooperation.

Conclusion

The life of the church today takes place within a multicultural structure. This awareness calls the members of the church to be present to the diversity weaving through the fabric of the church's experience. This mutual presence excludes any ethnocentric imposition but is rather the expression of a faith lived and witnessed in a context where other cultures are affirmed and validated.[63]

The great ecclesiologist of our times, Yves Congar, reflected on this vocation to live the gospel in multicultural terms when he said that "the Church today is called to be the Church of the peoples in a new way."[64] The vocation to universality that the church received at Pentecost does not demand uniformity, but is understood in terms of "uniplurality" where all persons understand and express in their own languages the marvels that God has done.[65] It is in this diversity that the full splendor of the church's catholicity is manifested. For, as Congar says, "The Church is catholic because it is particular, and it has the fullness of gifts because each has particular gifts."[66] It is in the Spirit, the One who makes the church catholic,[67] that the church can overcome Babel, "not by a return to a uniformity that existed before Babel, but by proclaiming an implantation of the same gospel and the same faith in varied and diverse cultural soils and human spaces."[68]

Pentecost continues to call us to be together in one place awaiting the sound of a strong driving wind that fills the house of the church with a multitude of languages. The witness of being of "one heart and mind" does not mean we will speak or understand each other's languages,[69] but it means we may speak and hear across the words at a different level and find joy in diversity and in each other's experiences.

The very life of God is constituted by expression,[70] by unity in difference.[71] Professing belief in this one God who is not solitary but One and yet diverse is what makes us Christian. In the mystery of God's self-giving, the Holy Spirit is named as the power of newness, "in a time and space that has been opened by the Word,"[72] in the beautiful words of Congar. In the Trinity, it is the Spirit who opens the way to recognize the other.[73] This same Spirit calls us forward to acknowledge and value "the other" in our midst. Whether the power of the Spirit comes as "one, still, small voice" (1 Kgs 19:12) or whether this power breaks out in prophetic language diversified within our multicultural setting, the "tongues as of fire" are upon us giving and eliciting from us the words and the gift of hearing (Is 50:4, 5).

Notes

[1]St. Augustine, *Sermons* 266, 267, 268, 269 (*PL* 38, 1225-1227), cited in *Ad Gentes*, 4.

[2]Bradford E. Hinze in "Releasing the Power of the Spirit in a Trinitarian Ecclesiology," *Advents of the Spirit: An Introduction to the Current Study of Pneumatology*, ed. Bradford E. Hinze and D. Lyle Dabney (Milwaukee: Marquette University Press, 2001) elaborates on the place of pneumatology in trinitarian ecclesiology. Of particular relevance is his elucidation of the role of the Spirit in the drive toward a more genuine catholicity through the recognition of diversity of cultures and peoples in the church.

[3]Virgilio Elizondo, "Diversity Is Church's Challenge," *National Catholic Reporter*, 20 January 1995, 19.

[4]Gilbert C. Romero, *Hispanic Devotional Piety: Tracing the Biblical Roots* (New York: Orbis Books, 1991), 52.

[5]George Montague, *The Holy Spirit: Growth of a Biblical Tradition* (New York: Paulist Press, 1976), 279-80. Throughout this essay I will be drawing from Montague's insights in this book.

[6]Numerous patristic writings present Pentecost as a reversal of Babel: Origen, *in Genesim*, c. 1 (*PG* 12, 112); St. Gregory Nazianzen, *Oratio* 41, 16 (*PG* 36, 449); St. John Chrysostom, *Hom. in Pentec.*, 2 (*PG* 50, 467); St. Augustine, *Enn. in Ps* 46, 11 (*PL* 36, 636; CChr. 39, 664 ff.); *Sermon* 271 (*PL* 38, 1245); St. Cyril of Alexandria, *Glaphyra in Genesim* II (*PG* 69, 79); St. Gregory the Great, *Hom. in Evang.*, Lib. II, Hom. 30, 4 (*PL* 76, 1222); St. Bede, *in Hexaem.*, lib. III (*PL* 91, 125). See *Ad Gentes*, 4.

[7]Yves Congar, *I Believe in the Holy Spirit*, vol. 1, *The Holy Spirit in the 'Economy': Revelation and Experience of the Spirit*, trans. David Smith (New York: Crossroad, 2003), 172.

[8]Marcello Azevedo, *Vivir la Fe en un Mundo Plural: Discrepancias y Convergencias* (Navarra: Verbo Divino, 1993), 135.

[9]Milton Gordon, *Assimilation in American Life* (New York: Oxford, 1964), cited in *Hispanics in the United States: The Current Crisis of Inculturation, Faith and Culture. A Multicultural Catechetical Resource* (Washington: USCC, 1987), 51.

[10]Azevedo, *Vivir la Fe en un Mundo Plural*, 137-38.

[11]Mary Ann Tolbert, "The Politics and Poetics of Location," *Reading from This Place. Social Location and Biblical Interpretation in the United States,* vol.

1, ed. Fernando F. Segovia and Mary Ann Tolbert (Minneapolis: Fortress Press, 1995), 315.

[12]The statistics and the poll results in the following two pages were taken from Robin Benedick and Antonio Fins, "A Failure to Communicate: Languages Generate Jobs, But Also Lead to Alienation," *Broward Sun-Sentinel,* 11 May 2003, accessed 13 May 2003, [newsbank on-line]; available from Infoweb, http://infoweb.newsbank.com/iw-search/we/InfoWeb; Internet.

[13]In 1993, the Miami Metro Commission, composed of four black commissioners, three white non-Hispanics and six Hispanics, voted unanimously to overturn the county's English-only law that had been in effect for ten years. It is commonly believed that the law deepened the ethnic divisions in Dade County. "Today in Herald History," *Miami Herald,* 30 May 2003, A-3.

[14]I use "Babelian paradigm" to indicate the fragmentation of the human community caused by and evidenced in the multiple languages spoken by people from diverse nationalities. This negative model is the one evidenced in the Genesis story of the Tower of Babel.

[15]Benedick and Fins, "A Failure to Communicate," 1-7.

[16]Robert J. Schreiter, "Faith and Cultures: Challenges to a World Church," *Theological Studies* 50 (1989): 746.

[17]Ibid.

[18]Bernard Lonergan, *Method in Theology* (London: Darton, Longman and Todd, 1972), xi, cited in Schreiter, "Faith and Cultures," 746.

[19]Schreiter, "Faith and Cultures," 746.

[20]See also Congar, *The Holy Spirit in the 'Economy,'* 170-77; Casiano Floristan, *La Iglesia: Comunidad de Creyentes* (Salamanca: Ediciones Sígueme, 1999), 408.

[21]The whole of *Lumen Gentium* reflects this ecclesiology of *koinonia*. See Michael G. Lawler and Thomas J. Shanahan, *Church: A Spirited Communion* (Collegeville: Liturgical Press, 1995).

[22]Congar, *The Holy Spirit in the 'Economy,'* 171.

[23]Azevedo, *Vivir la Fe en un Mundo Plural,* 40-54.

[24]Schreiter, "Faith and Cultures," 747.

[25]The classical meaning of "drama" refers to a tragedy played out by diverse actors. In *Evangelii Nuntiandi,* the actors are the bearers and the recipients of the gospel. The tragedy is "the split between the Gospel and culture" of the recipients (*Evangelii Nuntiandi,* 20).

[26]A. A. Roest Crollius, "What Is So New about Inculturation? A Concept and Its Implications," *Gregorianum* 59 (1978): 721-38, cited by Schreiter, "Faith and Cultures," 753.

[27]Minority people are classified not in terms of their numbers but in terms of their relationship to the dominant culture. Thus, in Dade County, even though native English speakers of European descent are a numerical minority and Latinos/as are a numerical majority, the latter are still considered a minority because the Anglo-European culture is dominant.

[28]For the important role continuity of language has played in the continuity of faith for Catholic immigrants in the United States, see Joseph P. Fitzpatrick, *One*

Church Many Cultures: Challenge of Diversity (New York: Sheed & Ward, 1987), 32.

[29]On Johann Baptist Metz's category of the "dangerous memory" of the suffering, death, and resurrection of Christ, see *Faith in History and Society: Towards a Practical Fundamental Theology* (New York: Seabury Press, 1980). I propose my autobiographical data as source for this reflection. As a child, I remember my grandparents reverting occasionally to Galician (paternal) and Valencian (maternal). I still wonder why four and a half centuries of Castilian Spanish had not been able to eradicate their native language. I also heard Basque émigrés who were friends of my family remark that Franco forbade the Basque to speak Euskara during his rule. An old Irish nun, while explaining to me the lyrics of "Danny Boy," told me that the Irish were forbidden to speak Gaelic by the English during England's rule. When visiting western Ireland four years ago, we experienced the mass celebrated in Gaelic and were told Ireland has reclaimed Gaelic as a sign of its sovereignty.

[30]For an insightful consideration of the role and function of the Spirit as the divine source of reconciliation and communion in contemporary society, see Anselm Kyongsuk Min, "Solidarity of Others in the Power of the Holy Spirit: Pneumatology in a Divided World," *Advents of the Spirit,* 416-43.

[31]See Fernando Segovia, "Toward a Hermeneutics of the Diaspora: A Hermeneutics of Otherness and Engagement," *Reading from This Place,* 65, 67, 69, 73.

[32]Clyde T. Francisco notes that the Genesis passage indicates a motivation to live in a privileged society that shuts out the less fortunate inhabitants of the world. *The Broadman Bible Commentary,* vol. 1, rev. ed., ed. Clifton J. Allen (Nashville: Broadman Press, 1969), 152.

[33]Floristan, *La Iglesia,* 169-70.

[34]Congar, *The Holy Spirit in the 'Economy,'* 44.

[35]I purposefully use the word "through" because the patristic interpretation of the reversal of Babel at Pentecost implies that the curse of multiple languages has been transmuted into a blessing. It is after being filled by the Spirit that the disciples began to speak in languages so that "God's deeds of power" (Acts 2:11) may be proclaimed in and through diverse languages.

[36]*Mekilta* II, 234f. Cited in Brevard S. Childs, *The Book of Exodus: A Critical, Theological Commentary* (Philadelphia: Westminster Press, 1976), 380.

[37]Carroll Stuhlmueller, *Biblical Meditations for the Easter Season* (New York: Paulist Press, 1980), 224.

[38]On this image, see George Montague, "The Fire in the Word: The Holy Spirit in Scripture," in *Advents of the Spirit,* 35-65.

[39]Montague, *The Holy Spirit,* 276. See also Congar, *The Holy Spirit in the 'Economy,'* 48.

[40]*The Book of Jubilees 6:17-21,* cited in Luke Timothy Johnson, *The Acts of the Apostles, Sacra Pagina,* vol. 5, ed. Daniel J. Harrington (Collegeville: Liturgical Press, 1992), 44.

[41]Justin Taylor, *Hechos de los Apóstoles, Comentario Bíblico Internacional,*

ed. William R. Farmer and Armando J. Levoratti, Sean McEvenue, David L. Dungan (Navarra: Verbo Divino, 1999), 1378.

[42]Montague, "The Fire in the Word," 35.

[43]See Johnson, *The Acts of the Apostles*, 46.

[44]Moshe Weinfeld, *The Anchor Bible. Deuteronomy 1-11. A New Translation with Introduction and Commentary,* vol. 5 (New York: Doubleday, 1991), 213.

[45]John R. Levison, "The Pluriform Foundation of Christian Pneumatology," *Advents of the Spirit*, 75.

[46]Congar, *The Holy Spirit in the 'Economy,'* 44.

[47]Philo Judaeus, *De Decalogo*, 33-35, 46, cited in Johnson, *The Acts of the Apostles*, 46. See also Montague, *The Holy Spirit*, 278-79.

[48]*Midrash Tanchuma 26C*, cited in F. F. Bruce, "Commentary on The Book of the Acts," *The New International Commentary on the New Testament*, ed. F. F. Bruce (Grand Rapids: Eerdmans, 1979), 60.

[49]Ibid.

[50]Bruce, "Commentary on The Book of the Acts," 59.

[51]Stuhlmueller, *Biblical Meditations for the Easter Season*, 224.

[52]Montague, *The Holy Spirit*, 279-80.

[53]Congar, *The Holy Spirit in the 'Economy,'* 44.

[54]Johnson, *The Acts of the Apostles*, 46.

[55]Congar, *I Believe in the Holy Spirit*, vol. 2, *He Is Lord and Giver of Life* (New York: Seabury Press; London: Geoffrey Chapman, 1983), 15.

[56]Montague, *The Holy Spirit*, 277.

[57]J. A. Möhler, *Symbolik* ([1]1832, critical edition, Cologne: Jakob Hegner, 1960-1), §37. Cited in Congar, *He Is Lord and Giver of Life*, 15.

[58]Congar, *The Holy Spirit in the 'Economy,'* 171; idem, *He Is Lord and Giver of Life*, 16-17.

[59]Congar, *He Is Lord and Giver of Life*, 18.

[60]Montague, *The Holy Spirit*, 277.

[61]Ibid., 279.

[62]St. Augustine, *Sermons* 266, 267, 268, 269 (*PL* 38, 1225-1227). Cited in *Ad Gentes*, 4. See also Congar, "The Holy Spirit Is the Principle of Catholicity," in *He Is Lord and Giver of Life*, 24-25.

[63]Azevedo, *Vivir la Fe*, 149.

[64]Congar, *He Is Lord and Giver of Life*, 25.

[65]Ibid., 17.

[66]Ibid., 26.

[67]Ibid., 27.

[68]Ibid., 25.

[69]On several occasions I have heard fear of other language groups expressed as "What do they expect? That we learn Spanish?" This, of course, is an unrealistic goal. Multicultural engagement can happen through other means as the following anecdote indicates. Some years ago I was involved in a ministry training program at a Haitian mission. One evening I was asked by a group of teenage boys in the

neighborhood whether I was a "white Haitian." Startled by their question, I asked what they meant. They said they had seen me coming to "the church" for three years and thought I was a "white Haitian." My Creole is rudimentary, but the fact that they identified me with their culture taught me that "speaking in tongues" can be done at many levels and communication can take many forms, such as collaboration in ministry and sharing with others in the music, food, and dance of their cultures. In the beautiful image presented by Bradford Hinze, this sharing exemplifies the eschatological banquet, where the richness of ethnic foods, beverages, and rejoicing will fill the house of God and bring to fullness the manifestation of communion and catholicity. See Bradford E. Hinze, "Ethnic and Racial Diversity and the Catholicity of the Church," *Theology: Expanding the Borders*, The Annual of the College Theology Society, vol. 43, ed. María Pilar Aquino and Roberto S. Goizueta (Mystic, Conn.: Twenty-Third Publications, 1998), 189.

[70]The Word is the expression of the Father. The Spirit is the expression of their mutual love.

[71]Congar, *He Is Lord and Giver of Life,* 33.

[72]Ibid.

[73]Ibid.

Part III

ADVANCING THE SPIRIT'S WORK
OF COMMUNION AND JUSTICE

Liberation for Communion:
The Church's Justice Mission
in an Unjust Society

Jamie T. Phelps

Let love be sincere; hate what is evil, hold on to what is good; love one another with mutual affection; anticipate one another in showing honor. Do not grow slack in zeal, be fervent in spirit, serve the Lord. Rejoice in hope, endure in affliction, persevere in prayer. Contribute to the needs of the holy ones, exercise hospitality. Bless those who persecute [you], bless and do not curse them. Rejoice with those who rejoice, weep with those who weep. Have the same regard for one another; do not be haughty but associate with the lowly; do not be wise in your own estimation. (Romans 12:9-16 NAB)

As we begin our exploration of the church's mission in an unjust society as a process of liberation for communion, the text of Romans seems an appropriate place to start. To seek justice is to seek the mutuality of love made possible by the power of the Holy Spirit. The Romans text provides one set of indicators of those who have embraced a way of love embodied and proclaimed by Jesus.

Context, Thesis, Assumptions, and Organizing Questions

As a starting locus for my theological work, I have chosen to be attentive to the questions arising from the context and perspective of those whose lives are negatively conditioned by unjust social systems of domination and control. From the perspective of the marginalized and excluded, the world constructed by human beings is a world fragmented by negative forces of nationalism, neo-colonialism, racism, sexism, classism, and religious-cultural imperialism. In such a world the non-privileged "other" is distinguishable from the dominating modern self and is ordinarily denied the recognition of his or her full humanity and equality. Oppressed and marginalized peoples are excluded from full and constructive decision-making and participation as subjects in both church and society. In such unjust situations, the church's justice mission, consistent with Jesus' preaching and embodiment of the kingdom, is to liberate individuals, groups and nations from "sin and all that oppresses" and to enable them to participate in the social construction of ecclesial and social institutions characterized by patterns of inclusive communion.

Several assumptions underlie my thinking. First, the church's mission is the continuance of the mission of Jesus as he preached and embodied the coming of the kingdom. Second, Jesus' incarnation, life, death, and resurrection compel us to recognize that God works through and in history. Third, the church's mission of evangelization involves preaching the good news of the kingdom in such a way that it reveals to us that our way of thinking and viewing the world must be brought into conformity with the way of Jesus. Fourth, only by the power of the Holy Spirit, activated by our positive response to God's presence in us, can human beings follow the way of God's universal love.

In the following essay, I will focus on four questions: What are the dominative power dynamics in socially unjust interpersonal and institutionalized human encounters? Does God choose some and abandon others within the human community? What is the relationship between liberation and conversion for the oppressed and the liberation and conversion for the oppressed and for the oppressors? What are some aspects of the concept of church as communion and how do they relate to the pursuit of justice?

Question 1. What are the dominative power dynamics in socially unjust interpersonal and institutionalized human encounters?

In too many instances, those who hold dominative power within the social and ecclesial institutions of our society do not see the "other" as a full human being who has the rights and responsibility to act as the subject of his or her own human development and social and ecclesial transformation. Joerg Rieger's *Remember the Poor* describes accurately the relational dynamic between the modern self and the so-called "other." Most often this non-privileged "other" is perceived as an extension of the dominating modern self who perceives itself in the imaginary idealized shadow-free self-image.[1] The "other" is subjected to the power and authority of the modern dominating self as it "assigns to himself the center of the universe."[2] The modern self sees the "other" simply as an extension of his or her modern narcissistic self used only for her own self-interest and purposes.[3] As Gustavo Gutiérrez has observed, this modern self is "myopic when it comes to the claims of others in both social and economic areas."[4]

While Rieger's analysis provides an insightful description of the interpersonal dynamic of the individual modern self's encounter with the other, Iris Marion Young develops a language and theory of justice that speaks of both interpersonal and social justice as applied to relationships within a community. Her *Justice and the Politics of Difference* describes what she has termed the "five faces of oppression": class, race and gender exploitation; marginalization; powerlessness; cultural imperialism; and systemic violence.[5] Class, race, and gender exploitation is the method by which the modern self uses the talents, skills, and labor of one group to benefit the dominant group. Marginalization is the process by which the non-dominant group is excluded and rendered "invisible" within society. Marginal people are largely racially identifiable, isolated, and subjected to material deprivation. In extreme instances "marginals" are subjected to extermination. Powerlessness is described as a process by which select persons or groups are denied authority, status, and a sense of full human identity. Cultural imperialism renders some groups powerless as the "dominant meanings" make the experience and perspective of non-dominant groups meaningless. The true reality of non-dominant groups is rendered invisible by stereotyping and the designation of their experiences as lacking any positive cultural value for the whole community.

Systemic violence is suffered by select groups of "Blacks, Asians, Arab, gay men and lesbians" who suffer random but targeted attacks, exclusion or humiliation, simply because they are members of a particular group.[6] Racial profiling of Arabs has increased since the September 11, 2001, terrorist attack on the symbols of U.S. economic, military, and political power. Black men and women and dark-skinned Latino/a Hispanics have been subjected to racial profiling by police agents and teachers. Many people accept the erroneous, yet common assumption that Blacks are more prone to violence and are less intelligent than other human beings.

Members of select cultural groups and nations both within and beyond the United States are considered inferior and incapable of self-governance. They are deemed incapable of participation as subjects of their own future or of contributing to the global community in any way other than as extensions or tools for the global economic corporate institution. Thus the skills and resources of dominated "third world" nations and peoples are exploited for the benefit of the dominant "first world" nations and peoples.

Two examples come to mind: South Africa and Iraq. Not so long ago apartheid was a social system that denied Black South Africans a role as participating subjects within South Africa and the international community. Colonial peoples settled in South Africa and established first English and then Dutch domination and control. Using the labor of Black Africans and relegating them to the infertile areas of the nation, Afrikaners exploited the labor of the native Africans to retrieve diamonds and other natural resources of the land for the benefit of the English and Afrikaners and also world markets, including the United States, with little or no benefit for the indigenous African tribes of South Africa. Currently the nation of Iraq, whose religious majority is composed of diverse Arab Muslim communities, is in danger of being subject to post-war neo-colonialism as it is exploited for its oil and other natural resources. Eurocentric educational systems have taught most students little about the culture, history, and religious customs of the African or Islamic peoples. As a consequence they are often judged through the lens of our own social or cultural biases.

We export our ideal of a democratic participatory nation without ever considering whether or not these processes are compatible with positive aspects of the existing social, cultural, and religious customs of other nations. We assume that our way of life is superior to theirs without examining the particularities of the region that might reveal a distinct and equally valuable worldview with its distinct norms and customs.

This statement should not be construed to be supportive of the clear dynamics of religious and cultural oppression that have been characteristic of the Saddam Hussein regime in Iraq. There is no doubt that Hussein was a dictator guilty of enormous destruction inflicted on his own people. Many Iraqi citizens themselves have decried the injustices of his regime and have fled the country for asylum. The victims of oppression and Hussein's exploitative regime need to be the primary subjects of the reconstruction efforts in post-war Iraq, but it is not clear at this point that the U.S. government considers the native peoples of Iraq capable of self-governance. A question still lingers about the morality of a pre-emptive strike. Many do agree with the moral statements against the war by many religious leaders throughout the world.[7] Mindful that "the end does not justify the means" we are urged to support efforts at peacemaking.

The situations in Africa and the Middle East are only two modern instances of neo-colonial exploitation. Turning to the United States we can see a historic pattern of oppression that continues to the present day. Within the United States the descendants of African slaves, the indigenous Native Americans, Mexicans, Puerto Ricans, and Japanese embody the consequence of historical colonization, conquest, and enslavement. The dehumanization and devaluation of the past has lingering effects on the contemporary lives of some members of these cultural groups. Many continue to be marginalized, rendered invisible, or manipulated. Many are relegated to positions of powerlessness or subjected to manipulation because of their economic poverty or cultural identity. White racial and cultural superiority perpetuates negative stereotypes of people of color while their cultural gifts and skills are appropriated or absorbed by the dominant culture. The majority of people of color continue to be excluded from full participation in dominant cultural, social, economic, and ecclesial institutions.[8]

Charles Mills addresses the question of the persistent oppression of the "racialized other." He constructed the epistemological concept of "racial contract" to describe the paradigmatic dynamic of social oppression, devaluation, marginalization, and violence that dehumanizes and seeks to render oppressed members of the U.S. and the global society invisible and powerless.[9]

According to Mills, the racial contract was a hidden clause within the assumption of the political theorist who articulated the concept of social contract. The social contract, the idea that the establishment of civil society and government was established by the popular consent of equal individuals, was considered foundational to our founding documents, the Declaration of Independence and the Constitution of the United States, and later to Abraham Lincoln's vision of the nation.

The Preamble to the Constitution affirms that the U.S. government was being established for the common good of "the people of the United States."

> We the people of the United States, in order to form a more perfect union, establish justice, insure domestic tranquility, provide for the common defense, promote the general welfare, and secure the blessings of liberty to ourselves and our prosperity, do ordain and establish this Constitution for the United States of America.[10]

The Declaration asserted "all men are created equal, that they are endowed by their Creator with certain unalienable Rights of Life, Liberty and the pursuit of Happiness."[11] Lincoln affirmed these sentiments in his Gettysburg Address: "this nation, under God, shall have a new birth of freedom—and that government of the people, by the people and for the people, shall not perish from the earth."[12] These documents are articulations of the social contract philosophy of our nation. Our "founding fathers" ideally envisioned political processes by which all individuals would entrust "in a relationship of trust" their natural rights and powers to a governing entity, which would rule according to a moral contract and thereby help the "citizens . . . regulate their behavior."[13]

The racial contract contradicts the ideological vision proclaimed by the social contract theorists such as Hobbes, Rousseau, and other political philosophers. It reveals the real story of how the U.S. society was created. Europeans conquered Native peoples, enslaved African peoples, and created a state that privileged "whites as a group with respect to the nonwhites as a group"[14] and established a moral code that legitimized the "exploitation of their [non-white] bodies, land, and resources, and the denial of equal socioeconomic opportunities to them."[15] Mills underscores the reality that "all whites are beneficiaries of the [racial] Contract, though some whites are not signatories of it."[16]

The social contract that undergirded the governance of the United States in reality was an exclusive contract "which has been foundationally shaped for the last five hundred years by the realities of European domination and the gradual consolidation of global white supremacy."[17] It benefits or privileges all whites while rendering Blacks and other people of color as "non-human" or "subhuman" and "non-persons."

The legal majority opinion drafted by Chief Justice Roger Taney underscored this perception. The justices ruled 9-2 against Dred Scott, who had escaped slavery and was living in a free state. Scott's claim to freedom was rejected in Taney's written opinion, which stated that neither the Constitution nor the Declaration of Independence had Africans or the descendents of Africans in mind when these documents were shaped and signed. Taney further stipulated:

> They [Africans] had for more than a century before been regarded as beings of an inferior order, and altogether unfit to associate with the white race, either in social or political relations; and so far inferior, that they had no rights which the white man was bound to respect; and that the negro might justly and lawfully be reduced to slavery for his benefit.[18]

While constitutional amendments of the nineteenth century and civil rights legislation of the twentieth century sought to alter this vitiation of Black humanity, the constant surfacing of anti-Black violence manifested by our persistent marginalization, devaluation, exploitation, and legal dehumanization suggests that the denial of the full humanity of Blacks still lies within the collective unconscious of much of the human community, with its deep roots in the history of colonial expansion and modern scientific development.[19]

During European colonial expansion, the world of human beings was divided between "men" and "natives."[20] Historically, the Western legal tradition legitimized cultural imperialism by asserting "the rightness and necessity of subjugating and assimilating other peoples to [the European] worldview."[21]

Throughout the nineteenth and twentieth centuries, David Walker, W. E. B. Dubois, and other Black intellectuals and social transformers sought to unmask the complicity of scholars from the dominant culture to conceal, overlook, and otherwise deny the existence and prevalence of the racial contract. Mills's exposition does not leave us without hope. The very intent of his work is to help intellectuals and others acknowledge truthfully the existence of a "racial contract" so steps can be taken to eliminate it.[22]

While we must admit that there has been some progress in the inclusion of some Blacks, Hispanics, Asians, and Native Americans in our social, political, and ecclesial institutions, Mills's racial contract theory enables us to see more clearly how the patterns of domination, devaluations, marginalization, and systemic violence against oppressed groups are still prevalent in the United States and throughout the world. From a Christian moral perspective it should be self-evident that such patterns of relationships are sinful and contradict the heart of the gospel, Jesus' mission, and the universal mission of the church.

Failing their human calling to mediate God's unconditional and universal love in our concrete historical situations, dominant human beings and cultural groups have constructed ecclesial and social institutions and processes that embody and nurture their self-centered individualism, their will to power and control, and their false claims of superiority. The narcissism of the modern self in all too many situations embodies a message to dominated and oppressed "others" that what they think, do, and say is inferior. Many of the privileged members of the dominant group who exercise power have perpetuated or allowed the perpetuation of a false image of a God who favors rich people over poor people, white people over non-white people, men over women, and people from Europe and North America over people from Africa, Asia, and Latin America. Too many of our social and ecclesial institutional actions mediate a portrait of God who loves *selectively and exclusively.*[23] We have no money for social services and education of the poor, but we have an abundance of resources for corporate adventures and war. Churches and schools that serve poor people of color are being closed because of lack of economic resources, yet churches and schools flourish in communities of the middle class and wealthy white America.

Sadly, I must acknowledge that I have not seen or heard of any cultural, gender, class, or national groups that have totally escaped the temptation of using their power for domination and for gaining absolute power and control because of a false sense of superiority. Almost every nation and culture includes people who are treated as non-peoples or inferior beings. Within almost every nation and culture there are people whose humanity is subtly denied and repressed by violent ideological and social patterns of control. The Dalits in India, the Negritos in the Philippines, Koreans in Japan, Eastern Europeans in Europe, Eritreans in Ethiopia, and so on, all are subjected to institutionalized dynamics of oppression as the "other" in the dominant cultures of their nations. Women and men of different cultures, religions, and economic status suffer humiliation, isolation, and marginalization at the hands of those who fail to see them for who they truly are.

These oppressed peoples and cultures, which have been objectified, dehumanized, and marginalized, cry out, "Is our God a God of all the people or does God really have favorites, choosing some creatures over others?" We, the church, must respond with a resolute "No! The one true God is a God of universal love and inclusion. The one true God is a God who calls us to universal communion of interactive love."

Question 2. Does God choose some and abandon others within the human community?

Our religious traditions give evidence that God shows no partiality. All are called to communion with the Divine and each other. The questions of human racial-cultural, gender, and intra-group divisions posed by our concrete reality have a historical precedent in the early Christian tradition in the question of the relationship of the Jews to the Gentiles. The biblical question of the relationship between Jew and Gentile explored in the Acts of the Apostles translates into the question of the relationship of the rich and powerful dominant racial-cultural, gender, and social group to the poor and marginalized racial-cultural, gender, and social groups within the world today. Peter's response to Cornelius in Acts 10 is relevant for our contemporary question of human division, social privileging, and patterns of exclusion: "In truth, I see that God shows no partiality. Rather, in every nation whoever fears him and acts uprightly is acceptable to him" (Acts 10:34b-35).[24]

God accepts all who acknowledge and live in accord with the divine will. This acceptance is in fact a call to communion—a communion realized most fully within the Trinity. While one cannot exhaustively explore the trinitarian theology of communion in a brief essay such as this, one can, however, point briefly to evidence of the Trinity as an appropriate model of and embodiment of God's call for us to embrace human unity in diversity as a divine mandate. We turn to four sources for evidence of this reality: the prayer of Jesus, the trinitarian expositions of the Cappadocians, the contemporary theological work of John Zizioulas, and finally Christian theological anthropology that affirms that all are made in the image and likeness of God.

If it is true that God's salvific will is universal, to mitigate this universality is to contradict God's will as made manifest through the mission of Jesus and the early Christian community. Jesus' mission was to the world. According to the Gospel of John, Jesus prayed that his disciples might know a unity among themselves that paralleled the unity he had with his Father. "[I pray] . . . so that all may be one as you, Father, are in me and I in you, that they also may be in us, that the world may believe that you sent me. And I have given them the glory you gave me, so that they may be one, as we are one" (Jn 17:21-22). What does "that all may be one as you, Father, are in me and I in you" mean? How were Jesus and the Father one?

The church Fathers wrestled with this question by exploring their diverse experiences of the one God and searching for a language that made such unity in diversity understandable. Patricia Fox's *God as Communion* summarizes the patristic development well.[25] Sabellianism (persons as modes of the one God), tritheism (there are three Gods!), and subordinationism (the Son is less than the Father and the Spirit is less than the Son) were failed attempts to explain their contemporary experience of God.[26] The Cappadocians challenged the understanding of person within the theology of Sabellius by asserting that "each person of the trinity was a full and complete being (*hypostasis*)" who shared a common substance (*ousia*). Basil of Caesarea asserted "that the oneness of God is to be found in the *koinonia* or community of the three persons." His doxology, "Glory be to the Father, with the Son, and with the Holy Spirit," reinforced in prayer the understanding that Father, Son, and Spirit were equal.[27] Basil further argued that the source of God's being was a person (classically identified as the Father) who out of love begot the Son and brought forth the Spirit. Furthermore the ground for God's ontological freedom is in his personal existence.[28]

The contemporary Eastern Orthodox theologian Zizioulas teaches that the tri-unity of God reveals that God is free person who "freely wills communion with the Spirit and the Son."[29] Essentially God's act of love constitutes the very person of the Divine One who "subsists" as Trinity or a community of persons.

The Christian understanding of the personhood of God helps shape our theological anthropology and reveals the falseness of our human divisions. Zizioulas, following the lead of the Cappadocians, teaches us that it is our relationship of loving "the other" freely that constitutes our human person. He asserts, "by being an inseparable part of a relationship that matters ontologically we emerge as unique and irreplaceable entities."[30] To be human beings made in the image and likeness of God means that our unique personhood is constituted and made manifest in loving relationships that parallel God's self-constitutive act of love that flows over into the acts of creation.

As persons made in the image and likeness of God, we too engage in patterns of relationship that are analogous to the perichoretic dance of communion that characterizes the relationships of the persons in the Trinity. We, like the persons who constitute the trinitarian God, must form a communion of persons, cultures, religions, and nations that maintains the basic unity of the human community and the particularity and distinctiveness of personal, cultural, religious, and national identity. Our oneness with each other must embrace the whole human and natural universe without attempting to homogenize the diversity with which God has embedded creation.

Jesus' prayer for unity is nothing less than his expressed desire that we come to a fuller understanding of who we are as human beings, that is, creatures whose lives originate and are sustained by maintaining communion with God, with all human beings, and the whole of creation. Growth in our human identity requires that we expand our community of love beyond our communities of origin and cultural, national, and religious identity until it embraces the whole human community and all creation.

Question 3. What is the relationship between liberation and conversion for the oppressed and for the oppressors?

To realize their full humanity within a context of all pervasive domination that denied it, it has been necessary for oppressed peoples to come to a consciousness of their true identity apart from those definitions and concepts ascribed to them by the dominating culture. Oppressed Blacks and other oppressed peoples have had to engage in a process of liberation, which involves conversion and community building. Thus, Christian liberation is a matter of reclaiming human personhood as prelude to communion. Such liberation involves conversion from unjust sinful patterns of human exclusion and domination to grace-filled and just patterns of human inclusion.

Conversion requires a three-fold process of separation, liberation, and integration. First, dominated persons and cultural groups must separate themselves from the false understandings, identity, and patterns of relationship that have been forged by the sinful behavior of their oppressors. Second, dominated persons and cultural groups must discover and reclaim a self-identity through a process of liberation that affirms their divinely given and graced human dignity. Finally, they must establish communities of inclusion characterized by new patterns of relationship of communion with one another and their estranged brothers and sisters who formerly dominated and oppressed them.

Historically, oppressed and marginalized groups have resisted their dehumanization by creating alternative communities in which they were able to preserve their sense of human dignity and purpose. African American slave narratives reveal how slaves built a world within a world. The emergence of separate racial-cultural groups and conferences within our churches and social institutions has been in almost every case a response of men and women of faith who rejected the false image of a God who had relegated them to a life of subjugation and marginalization. These men and women claimed their identity as children of God and began to use the power of the Spirit within them to forge communities of hope and trust in the God who showed no partiality.

In the United States, for example, during the nineteenth century Black Roman Catholics and Black Protestants created separate ecclesial and civic conferences or organizations to provide spaces to nurture and sustain their faith and create spaces in which they could engage the particular issues and questions of culture and life, create institutions to address their social needs, and develop rituals of healing and hope. Both Black and white women created separate spaces in their women's clubs and the suffragette movements. The twentieth century saw the emergence of similar groups among Hispanics, Asians, and Native Americans in both church and society.[31]

For those who have had their humanity and subjectivity denied by objectification, class, race, and gender exploitation, marginalization, powerlessness, cultural imperialism, and/or systemic violence, the first step toward realizing their full humanity is to claim and maintain the fullness of their human dignity and to live authentically human lives regardless of their social or economic condition. For some this requires a rejection of their internalized self-hate and dependency and a reclamation of their true identity as fully capable and responsible collaborating subjects in church and society.

The process of reintegration requires the establishment of new patterns of relationship with those who previously rejected the possibility of full communion. The re-integration of white and Protestant denominations from the same religious tradition that separated during the nineteenth century because of racism represents an attempt to reclaim the communion that was broken first by the marginalization and devaluation of Blacks within the predominantly white churches.

Within Roman Catholicism events like the *Encuentro* held in Los Angeles in the summer of 2000 was one effort to integrate the Hispanic, Black, Asian, Native American, and European-American Catholics and their issues within the dominant dynamics of the local church in the United States. Unfortunately, the closing of Black schools and parishes across the nation and the denial of the significance of the Black Catholic presence within the church leave many Black Catholics on the margins of Catholicism. The particular social and religious concerns and contributions of Black Catholics often are overlooked and their cause goes unheeded by the dominant culture even though individual Black Catholics assume leadership roles in the broader church. Anti-Black racism is still alive in church and society.

During the last half of the twentieth century and the first years of the twenty-first century Blacks, Hispanics, Asians, and Native Americans have experienced intellectual, spiritual, and moral conversion as they rejected their dehumanization and claimed their full humanity as children of God. Similar processes are evident in the just struggles against domination and colonialism by Eastern Europeans, Africans, and Latin American peoples. Such struggles entail much pain, suffering, and even death as people seek to dislodge the old social patterns of domination and embrace patterns of self-determination and the building of new nations. These struggles were and remain fraught with ambiguity. New nations must face their previous complicity with oppression. They must also examine how the continuance of unjust systems of privilege and domination persists because internalized patterns of domination are manifested anew in the absence of a creative vision of alternative patterns of relationship.

Christian liberation not only frees the dominated and oppressed but also the oppressors, that is, those who use racial, class, and gender

privilege to exercise their power in a dominating and oppressive manner. Those who oppress or benefit from the social arrangements constructed by oppressors must undergo a similar conversion. Liberation
of the dominating oppressor also requires a three-fold process of separation, liberation, and integration. Those who have used a false ideology of personal or social superiority to legitimize their domination
and control must undergo a radical conversion. The first step involves
a separation from the false self-image spawned by their assumptions
of moral and intellectual superiority. They must separate themselves
from the false understandings, identity, and sinful patterns of relationship forged in the context of the fundamental sin of white supremacist
ideology and manifest in the interpersonal and social sins of racism,
sexism, and classism. Second, the oppressor must experience an intellectual, spiritual, and moral conversion through which they come to a
new understanding of themselves in relationship to the "dominated
other." They must come to a realization that the God who gifted them
has also gifted other individuals, nations, religious, and cultural groups.
One is thus liberated from a false sense of self to a realistic understanding of one's gifts and shadows. Finally, the converted oppressors must establish new patterns of relationship. They must overcome
their estrangement from their brothers and sisters whom they formally
oppressed and dominated and collaborate with them to create new
communities of inclusion and communion.

As ecclesial and social institutions controlled by the dominant culture initiate attempts to become more attentive to their racial-cultural
diversity, they are led into the processes of personal, interpersonal,
and social liberation I have described above. These processes cannot
be accomplished by human will alone but are made possible by the
power of the Holy Spirit. As we sinful persons say "yes" to the power
and way of the God of Jesus Christ we begin to experience interior
conversion as a necessary aspect of ecclesial and social transformation. We enter anew into processes of intellectual, spiritual, and moral
conversion, but not without pain and suffering.

The liberation of the oppressed and oppressor "in all strata of humanity" is one aspect of contemporary evangelization. As *Evangelii
Nuntiandi* clearly states,

> At the kernel and center of his Good News, Christ proclaims
> salvation, this great gift of God which is liberation from every-

thing that oppresses man but which is above all liberation from sin and the Evil One, in the joy of knowing God and being known by him, of seeing him, and of being given over to him (EN, 9).

[And again, the Church] seeks to convert, solely through the divine power of the Message she proclaims, both the personal and collective consciences of people, the activities in which they engage, and the lives and concrete milieux, which are theirs (EN, 18).

Question 4. What are some aspects of the concept of church as communion and how do they relate to the pursuit of justice?

God's universal call to communion proclaimed and made possible by the redemptive act of Jesus is an essential aspect of a multi-faceted mission of the church. The church, as the communion of Christian believers and disciples of Christ, is called to continue the fundamental mission of Jesus by preparing the human community for the full realization of gift of the kingdom inaugurated but only partially realized during Jesus' sojourn on earth. This essential view of the unity of humankind with God was the primary focus of two documents that addressed the ecclesiology of the Second Vatican Council: *The Final Report of the 1985 Synod of Bishops* and *Some Aspects of the Church Understood as Communion* issued by the Congregation for the Doctrine of the Faith. While legitimate criticisms have been raised regarding both documents, for the purpose of this essay I wish to underscore their constructive insights.[32]

The *Final Report of the 1985 Synod of Bishops* identified the "ecclesiology of communion" as the "central and fundamental idea of the council's documents."[33] The report continued by articulating a sacramental definition of communion as "a matter of communion with God through Jesus Christ, in the Holy Spirit. This communion is had in the Word of God and in the sacraments."[34] The report describes baptism as the door to the "intimate communion of the faithful in the Body of Christ which is the Church" and the Eucharist as "the source and the culmination of the whole Christian life."[35] Clearly the document is affirming *koinonia* or communion-formation. At the same time it affirms the social transformation aspect of church mission as a process of inculturation. The mission of social transformation requires

mission in the service of the poor, the oppressed and the outcast.
. . . Besides material poverty there is a lack of liberty and of
spiritual forms of poverty, and it is particularly grace when
religious liberty is suppressed by force. . . . The Church must
prophetically denounce every form of poverty and oppression,
and everywhere defend and promote the fundamental and inalienable rights of the human person.[36]

According to the *Final Report*, the church is obliged to defend three
specific groups: the human life of those whose life is threatened from
its beginning (referencing the church's anti-abortion stance), those who
suffer persecution because of their faith, and finally, those who suffer
for "the promotion of justice."[37]

Inculturation from the perspective of communion requires an integration within the church of all those elements "of positive value"
from each culture. Inculturation involves "the intimate transformation
of authentic cultural values through their integration in Christianity in
the various human cultures."[38] Thus it is more than "external adapta-
tion."

Historically, enslaved Africans, either purchased in Africa or born
and raised in America, were considered chattel slaves who could be
bred, bought, and sold like any other animal. They were considered
not fully human and as such were incapable of developing any distinct
culture.[39] The hundred years following the Civil War saw a gradual
modification of the overt disregard for Black humanity, and by the
middle of the twentieth-century Civil Rights Movement the presence
and condition of Black people gained the concerted attention of many
Catholics and Protestants. Inspired by the eloquence of Dr. Martin
Luther King, Jr., and moved to compassion by the bloody confrontations of Blacks seeking full equality and civil rights, some courageous
priests, religious women and men, and lay Catholics began to labor
for the rights of Blacks and participated in the education and evangelization of Blacks as a matter of justice. Sadly, these efforts have largely
waned as the church and society have turned their attention to the
large number of Hispanic immigrants who have expanded the U.S.
Hispanic/Latino population.[40]

While some religious congregations, individual lay persons, priests,
women and men religious, and bishops continue to be sensitive and
constructively attentive to the experience of Black people within our

church and society, many U.S. Catholics seem to be indifferent or hostile to the approximately two to three million Black Catholics (African American, Africans, and Afro-Caribbean peoples) in their midst. The separation of U.S. parish communities according to the racial cultural identification of its members prevents an "intimate communion" of the Catholics of diverse cultural-racial backgrounds who belong to the one Body of Christ. To complicate the matter further, in many parishes with a multicultural membership, one witnesses one of three patterns: 1) the domination or cultural hegemony of one Euro-American cultural sensibility or consciousness (such as Irish, Polish, German, Italian) and the marginalization of other cultures within the parish; 2) racial-cultural struggles for parish power and recognition; or 3) some attempt to celebrate the cultural diversity within the parish.

Too often, many U.S. Catholics simply assume that most African Americans are "naturally" Protestant without ever questioning why or exploring the history of the U.S. Catholic Church in the Black community and other communities of color.[41] This assumption, combined with their conscious or unconscious conformity to the prevailing racist ideology of the dominant culture, marginalizes and renders Black Catholics and other Catholics of color invisible to the majority Euro-American Catholics.

Most Euro-American Catholic priests, sisters, and lay ecclesial leaders are not formally educated to engage in cross-cultural collaborative ministry, in evangelization within the Black community, or in the struggles for social justice as these relate specifically to the situation of Black people. U.S. Catholic theologians who prepare Catholics for ministry have not studied the history or theology of Blacks in general or Black Catholics in particular. This lack of accurate knowledge of Black history and Black Catholic history, theology, and spirituality militates against preparation for effective cross-cultural ministry within the Black community.

The historic exclusion of Black Catholic women and men from priesthood and/or membership in religious congregations[42] compounds the problem of providing Catholic priests and religious to carry on effective inculturated church ministry within the Black community. Black Catholic lay ministers are emerging in the contemporary U.S. Catholic community. However, it remains to be seen if their efforts, combined with clergy and religious both Black and white, are sufficient to maintain and expand a vibrant sacramental and social justice ministry to address the spiritual development and evangelization and social transformation of Black Catholics. Such efforts should be focused specifically on the eradication of "poverty and oppression" and the promotion of the fundamental and inalienable rights of Black people within church and society in accord with the teachings of the *Final Report*.[43]

Continuing a critical reflection on the themes and interpretations of communion identified in the *Final Report*, the Congregation for the Doctrine of the Faith's letter, *Some Aspects of the Faith Understood as Communion*, clarifies, elaborates, and expands the church's understanding of ecclesial communion. The letter describes the concept of communion as "the Mystery of the personal union of each human being with the divine Trinity and with the rest of mankind, initiated with the faith, and, having begun as a reality in the Church on earth, is directed towards its eschatological fulfillment in the heavenly Church."[44]

It further identifies the vertical (communion with God) and horizontal (communion among humankind) dimensions of communion as two essential aspects that are a "gift [as well as] a fruit of God's initiative carried out in the paschal mystery." On one hand, the vertical dimension is the invisible communion "of each human being with the Father through Christ in the Holy Spirit, and with the others who are fellow sharers in the divine nature, in the passion of Christ, in the same faith, in the same Spirit."[45] On the other hand, the horizontal dimension is "made visible through the teachings of the apostles, the sacraments, and the hierarchical order in the church on earth."[46]

Finally, it applies the concept of communion as it clarifies 1) the relationship between the universal and particular churches; 2) unity and diversity; nd 3) ecumenical relationships. The document asserts clearly that "the universal *communion of the faithful* and the *communion of the Churches* . . . constitute the same reality seen from different viewpoints. . . . [W]hoever belongs to one particular Church belongs to all the Churches; since belonging to the *Communion*, like belonging to the Church, is never simply particular, but by its very nature is always universal."[47]

Given these teachings, one looks for visible manifestations of the invisible communion of diverse racial-cultural groups within the contemporary church. The church clearly teaches that all human beings form one human community by virtue of their creation by the same

Creator and biological generation.[48] Yet human choice, history, and culture have spawned division rather than a recognition of unity of the human community expressed through diverse cultures and historical interpretations.

Stirred to explore the notion of communion ecclesiology as a lens through which to revisit the documents of Vatican II and subsequent theological interpretations of many of them by the *Final Report*, Dennis Doyle has written a foundational text to clarify the understanding and experience of church as a communion.[49] After describing five reductionistic tendencies evident in contemporary understandings of church, Doyle identifies five dimensions and images of the church understood as communion along with six versions of communion ecclesiology that emerged in twentieth-century Catholicism. He insists that we resist the temptation to engage these diverse approaches polemically to ascertain the "correct interpretation." Communion ecclesiology by its very nature is multifaceted.[50]

Five reductionistic tendencies are evident in our understandings of church: individualism, the church as merely human, juridicism, mystification, and exclusivism. Inividualism insists that the individual is the basis of human reality rather than community. Viewing the church as merely human denies the vertical dimension of the church by which the church experiences the mystical and transcendent presence of the triune God as a constitutive reality. Juridicism involves a distortive overemphasis on the legal and juridical aspect of church at the expense of the sacramental by which the church is understood as the horizontal and visible element, mediating and interpreting the presence of God in our midst. Mystification focuses on the spiritual element of the mystery of God in our midst while it de-emphasizes the human and historical aspects of the church signaled by the image of the church as the people of God engaged in an historical journey toward full communion with God and one another because of God. Exclusivism embraces a view of the church that denies the presence of "grace and goodness outside the visible confines of the church."[51]

The church as communion, for Doyle, encompasses five dimensions: divine, mystical, sacramental, historical, and social. Referencing Henri de Lubac's accomplishments in addressing all five dimensions, Doyle comments on their meanings. The divine dimension emphasizes the church as a response to the call to enter into communion with the triune God. The mystical dimension acknowledges the reality and mystery of the church as the body of Christ that "represents the spiritual and social reunification of the unity of humankind."[52] The sacramental dimension asserts the integral relationship between the invisible and visible realities of the church underscored in *Lumen Gentium*, and affirms the sacraments as a visible means by which God's grace is made effective in the minds, hearts, and actions of the faithful as they move toward unity with God and one another.[53] Without both elements there is no church. The historical dimension focuses on the church's historic journey as a development within Judaism and its emergence as the concrete experience of the people of God whose salvific journey has been one marred by human weakness and sin. The social dimension refers to the church's identity as those who gather as believers to form a community that will engage in embodying and proclaiming to the world the good news of God's call to salvation and the possibility of the full realization of the kingdom through the power of the Spirit.[54]

Conclusion

Reviewing the church's teachings on communion and Doyle's exploration of diverse theological interpretations makes it clear that the church as a community of believers and its leadership empowered by the Holy Spirit can realize the call to ecclesial and social unity that Jesus proclaimed under the rubric of the coming of the kingdom or reign of God. Situations of oppression and domination contradict this call to unity and communion. Processes of liberation that conform to the way of Christ are directed toward overcoming our personal and social sins and enable the emergence of ever widening communities of inclusion characterized by love and justice. These communities are maintained as grace-filled spaces of hope rooted in an interior change brought about by our participation in the sacramental life of the community. The emphasis on the Eucharist is central. It is there that we sinful, holy human beings sacramentally transcend the boundaries of our human frailties and encounter the transcendent triune God. Through our communion with God we discover our *own and others'* true human identity as children of God made in the divine image and likeness. As a consequence, called to replicate the perichoretic dance of creation, redemptive suffering, and sanctification, we continue the mission of Jesus Christ that is and was the continuance of the mission of God made possible by the divine presence in the midst of our ordinary historical life experiences.

Notes

[1] Joerg Rieger, *Remember the Poor: The Challenge to Theology in the Twenty-First Century* (Harrisburg, Pa.: Trinity Press International, 1998), 26-27. This fascinating text analyzes theology's inability to see or acknowledge those on the underside because of the distorted self-image the dominant modern self constructs of itself. The modern self and its corruptive use of power and authority is a product of its objectification of "the other."

[2] Ibid., 28.

[3] Ibid., 61.

[4] Gustavo Gutiérrez, "The Truth Shall Make You Free," in *The Truth Shall Make You Free: Confrontations* (Maryknoll, N.Y.: Orbis Books, 1990), 113, as quoted in Rieger, *Remember the Poor*, 61.

[5] Iris Marion Young, *Justice and the Politics of Difference* (Princeton, N.J.: Princeton University Press, 1990), 53-65.

[6] Ibid., 61.

[7] See the ecumenical statement of "100 Leading Christian Ethicists Oppose the Iraqi War," http://.sojo.net/index.cfm?action=action.ethicists_statement: "as Christian Ethicists we share a common moral presumption against a preemptive war on Iraq by the United States." See also the statements by Bishop Wilton Gregory, President of the United States Catholic Conference of Bishops, "Statement on the War with Iraq" (March 19, 2003), http://www.nccbuscc.org/sdwp/peace/stm31903.htm; Cardinal Pio Laghi's Statement (March 5, 2003), http://www.nccbuscc.org/comm/archives/2003/03-051.htm; and the statements of the pope and other "Church Leaders on the Threat of War in Iraq," http://ww.usccb.org/sdwppeace/quotes/htm.

[8] One of the consistent methods of systemic oppression is the socialization of members of oppressed nations and cultures into the worldview and values of the dominant culture and the manipulation of these persons who have internalized their oppressive identities and participate in the on-going oppression and devaluation of their own culture. In most colonial systems indigenous persons were trained and used as the intermediary personnel to restrain and enforce compliance with the ruling power. This pattern of the misuse of indigenous or cultural leaders was evident during slavery, during apartheid in South Africa, and even in the contemporary political arena of political parties, ward committeemen, alderpersons in city councils, and so on. Those who enforce the ideology of the dominant culture or party are rewarded for their compliance even if such compliance betrays the human dignity and rights of their cultural family, those they have been elected to represent or, in the case of the church, those to whom they minister.

[9] Charles Mills, *The Racial Contract* (Ithaca, N.Y.: Cornell University Press, 1997), 1-2.

[10]"The Constitution of the United States," http://memory.loc.bov/const/const.htm, page 1 of 10.

[11]"Declaration of Independence," http://independenceroadtrip.org/Declaration/index.html, page 1 of 4.

[12]"Gettysburg Address," http://www.loc.gov/exhibits/gadd/4403.html.

[13]Mills, *The Racial Contract*, 10.

[14]Ibid., 11.

[15]Ibid.

[16]Ibid.

[17]Jean-Paul Sartre, Preface to Frantz Fanon, *Wretched of the Earth*, trans. Constance Farrington (New York: Grove Weidenfeld, 1991), as quoted in Mills, *The Racial Contract*, 20.

[18]See Dred Scott vs. Sanford: 1857 United States Supreme Court, http://www.demog.berkeley.edu/145/documents, page 7 of 47; Mills, *The Racial Contract*, 24.

[19]See Yehudi O. Webster, *The Racialization of America* (New York: St. Martin's Press, 1992) for a historical, cultural, and social-political analysis of the vocabulary and use of terms relative to this social construction.

[20]Mills, *The Racial Contract*, 20.

[21]Lumbee Indian legal scholar Robert A. Williams, Jr., "The Algebra of Federal Indian Law: The Hard Trail of Decolonizing and Americanizing the White Man's Indian Jurisprudence," *Wisconsin Law Review 1986* (1986): 229, cited in Mills, *The Racial Contract*, 21.

[22]Mills, *The Racial Contract*, 133.

[23]See William R. Jones, *Is God a White Racist?* (Boston: Beacon Press, 1998). This text suggests the seriousness of examining the *a priori* assumptions of "divine racism" found in selected literature and the records of religious and theological writings and preaching. Jones critically examines the assumptions of God's omnipotence and universal love and call to salvation from the perspective of the historical fact of the innocent collective and individual suffering of Black people because of their Blackness. This is the central theodicy question that arises during a critical examination of the historical experience of Black people in the context of a world constructed to nurture and maintain white people's exclusive domination and control of human cultures, churches, and social institutions.

[24]The Acts of the Apostles gives us St. Luke's theological interpretation of the events and concerns that preoccupied some of the early Christians. Acts emphasizes the role of the Holy Spirit in the lives of those men and women called to spread the gospel and form the Christian community among the gentile community.

[25]Patricia Fox, *God as Communion* (Collegeville, Minn.: Liturgical Press, 2001).

[26]Ibid., 38.

[27]Ibid., 39.

[28]Ibid., 40.

[29]Ibid.

[30]Ibid.

[31]In most cases these institutions were created when the dominant-culture Christians could not or would not acknowledge "the racial-cultural or other's" full humanity and dignity as a God-given reality. Though the impulse to community was deep within their cultural traditions, the barriers to inclusion in dominant-cultured churches and social institutions necessitated the creation of alternate churches and congregations to claim their authentic identity. Having their full humanity denied, they had to find ways to reject their enslaved persons and create their true personhood. These processes were imbued by the presence of God deep within them. An interior spiritual change grounded the exterior one.

[32]See Walter Kasper, "Church as Communio" in *New Blackfriars* 74 (1993): 232-244; Avery Dulles, "The Extraordinary Synod of 1985," in the *Reshaping of Catholicism: Current Challenges in the Theology of Church* (San Francisco, Harper & Row, 1988), 184-207; Kilian McDonnell, "Vatican II (1962-1965); Puebla (1979); Synod (1985); Koinonia/Communion as an Integral Ecclesiology," *Journal of Ecumenical Studies* 25 (1988): 399-427.

[33]In the section on "The Church as Communion" in the Synod of Bishops, "The Final Report of the 1985 Synod," *Origins* 15 (December 19, 1985): 444-450, at 448; also at http://library.saint-mike.org/Synod_Bishops/Final_Report1985.html at Part II, see B.b.C.I.

[34]Ibid.

[35]Ibid.

[36]Ibid., 450, "Preferential option for the poor and human promotion," in Part II, b.B.D.6.

[37]Ibid.

[38]Ibid., "Inculturation," Part II, C.4, 13.

[39]Jamie T. Phelps, O.P., "African American Culture as Source and Context of Black Catholic Theology and Church Mission," in *Journal of Hispanic and Latin American Theology* 3 (1996): 47.

[40]Recent Catholic statistics seem pertinent here. The trend report in the March 4, 2002 edition of *Newsweek* noted that there was a total of 63 million U.S. Roman Catholics of which 64% were White non-Hispanic, 29% Hispanic, 3% Black, 3% Asian and 2% Other. The 2000 census reported a total U.S. population of all races as 274,595,678, of which 216,930,975 or 71% were White; 36,429,434 or 12.9% were Black; 35,305,818 or 12.5% were Hispanic; 4,118,435 or 1.5% were Eskimo; and 11,898,828 or 4.2% were Asian Pacific. If the Black population in the United States according to the U.S. 2000 census was 12.9% and the Hispanic population 12.5%, then the question must be asked: Why is there such a large disparity between the Black and Hispanic presence in the U.S. Catholic Church in which 29% of U.S. Catholics are Hispanic and only 3% are Black?

[41]See Cyprian Davis, *The History of Black Catholics* (New York: Crossroad, 1991); Marilyn Wenze Nickels, *Black Catholic Protest and the Federated Colored Catholics, 1917-33* (New York: Garland Publishing, 1988); Morris J. MacGregor, *The Emergence of a Black Catholic Community: St Augustine's in Washington* (Washington, D.C.: Catholic University Press, 1999); John T. McGreevy, *Parish Boundaries* (Chicago: University of Chicago Press, 1996).

[42]Stephen J. Ochs, *Desegregating the Altar* (Baton Rouge: Louisiana State University Press, 1991); Sister Mary Bernard Deggs, *No Cross, No Crown*, ed. Virginia Meacham Gould and Charles E. Nolan (Indianapolis: Indiana University Press, 2001); Diane Batts Morrow, *Persons of Color and Religious at the Same Time: The Oblate Sisters of Providence, 1828-1860* (Chapel Hill: University of North Carolina, 2002).

[43]Two major graduate theology programs have been established by Black Catholic initiative to provide the theological and spiritual formation of ministers serving in the Black Catholic Community. The first, The Institute for Black Catholic Studies of Xavier University of Louisiana, was founded in 1980 to prepare indigenous and cross-cultural ministers for their work in the U.S. Black Catholic Community. The second, The Augustus Tolton Program for Pastoral Ministry, founded in 1990 at the Catholic Theological Union in Chicago, focuses on the formation of Black Catholic laywomen and men for professional ministry within the Chicago archdiocese. In addition, The Black Secretariate at the United States Catholic Congress and the National Black Catholic Congress are two national bodies that are making an effort to network and provide programs to assist the further development of the U.S. Catholic Church's mission. The Black Catholic Theological Symposium gathers Black Catholic theologians and scholars from related fields to discuss issues pertinent to the Black community and Black Catholic theology and provide consultation to interested parties. The Black Theology Group of the Catholic Theological Society engages other Catholic theologians in discussion of Black Catholic theological concerns. Black Catholic priests, religious women, seminarians, and deacons have developed national organizations for personal support and to address the needs of the Black community. See *Black and Catholic: The Challenge and Gift of Black Folk: Contributions of African American Experience and World View to Catholic Theology*, ed. Jamie T. Phelps (Milwaukee: Marquette University Press, 2002). For a fuller discussion of these national Black Catholic organizations and initiatives, see Jamie T. Phelps, "American Catholics: The Struggles, Contributions and Gifts of a Marginalized Community," ibid., 19-42.

[44]Congregation for the Doctrine of the Faith, "Some Aspects of the Church Understood as Communion" no. 3 http://www.vatican.va/roman_curia/congregations'cfaith/documents/re_con_cfaith_doc28051992_communionis-notio_en.html.

[45]Ibid., 4.

[46]Ibid., 4.

[47]Ibid., 10.

[48]Recent documented DNA evidence suggests that the entire human race arose from a single African genetic origin. This biological evidence can be interpreted to support the theological faith position of creationists who attribute the creation of human beings and all living creatures to an act of God. It also supports the position of scientific evolutionists who insist that creation involved the evolution of all creatures from a single organism. Some creationists believe that the first created beings, including the human species, were made by God in a manner that allowed future development through biological mutation.

⁴⁹Dennis Doyle, *Communion Ecclesiology* (Maryknoll, N.Y.: Orbis Books, 2000). This work resembles Avery Dulles's *Models of the Church* (Garden City, N.Y.: Image Books, 1974), which has become a classical text for interpreting the multiple understandings of the church. While Dulles speaks of distinct models, Doyle prefers the term "dimension" since this makes it clear that all dimensions of communion ecclesiology are essential to the meaning.

⁵⁰Doyle, *Communion Ecclesiology*, 20.

⁵¹Ibid., 14-16.

⁵²Ibid., 63-64.

⁵³*Lumen Gentium*, 8.

⁵⁴Doyle, *Communion Ecclesiology*, 62-70.

Toward a Theology of Spirit
That Builds Up the Just Community

Mary Elsbernd

And the Spirit of the Lord descended upon them,
they began to decry unjust practices in the city gates,
the market place, and the sanctuary.

As the above midrashic interpretation suggests, the link between the Spirit and the works of justice is a significant thread in the Hebrew and Christian scriptures.[1] This investigation explores this thread in the documents of Catholic social teaching and the theological reflection of justice practitioners. On the basis of this exploration, four building blocks toward a theology of the Spirit are highlighted, along with their implications for the doing of justice. These building blocks are rooted in the scriptures and can be traced in Catholic social teaching as well as in the lived experience of ministers of justice.[2] This work proposes that a theology of the Spirit based on these building blocks will provide strong foundations for the formation of a just community and the practice of justice.

The Holy Spirit in Catholic Social Teaching

The Roman Catholic tradition of social teaching is widely understood to have begun with *Rerum Novarum* (RN 1891) and to continue through *Centesimus Annus* (1991). When one examines the place of the Holy Spirit within these eleven documents, one notes that the first four chapters of *Gaudium et Spes* (1-45) and its conclusion (91-93) account for one half of the references to the Spirit in the eleven documents of Catholic social teaching.[3] The documents *Populorum*

Progressio (PP, 1967), *Octogesimo Adveniens* (OA, 1971), and *Justice in the World* (JW, 1971), written in the six years immediately following Vatican Council II, account for another quarter of the references. The final 25 percent of references to the Spirit occur in documents written in the seventy-four years of Catholic social teaching between *Rerum Novarum* and *Gaudium et Spes* (GS, 1965) and during the years between 1971 and 1991.

The above numerical overview suggests a link between the Spirit and renewal or transformative action, which is supported by further study of the content of the references. None of the references to the Spirit in the documents of Catholic social teaching, however, provides a developed theology of the Holy Spirit. Rather the Spirit is mentioned in the treatment of another point, most frequently the end times or Christian activity in the world, which provides a context for a transformational image of the Spirit. The trinitarian and institutional church contexts that co-exist in the documents describe a different understanding of the Spirit.

Spirit as Transformative Action in the World and in Eschatological Vision

The Spirit is mentioned in connection with the kingdom of God (GS 39), human destiny (GS 10, PP 42), the age to come (GS 38), and the eschatological era (GS 40). The Spirit is the first fruits and pledge of full inheritance that is the renewal of humanity already begun in Jesus. Through the action of Christians (OA 51), the Spirit is at work transforming this world into the city of God by nurturing the values of dignity, community, freedom, justice, and peace (GS 39). In the power of the Spirit, Christian initiative in the service of humanity testifies to "those things which are decisive for the existence and future of humanity" (JW 38). In the Spirit, human work and earthly goods embody and proclaim the city of God (*Sollicitudo Rei Socialis* [SRS] 48) as well as advance the work of Christ (GS 3, 11, 43). These passages describe a Spirit who leads, pulls, and attracts humanity into a future that is the Spirit's domain.

Octogesimo Adveniens 37 specifically develops the similarities and differences between utopian futures and the eschatological future heralded by the Spirit. At their worst, utopian dreams are escapes from concrete efforts to create a better world. At their best, utopian intuitions use human imagination "to perceive in the present the disregarded possibility hidden within it, and to direct itself toward a fresh future." The power of persuasion serves to mobilize persons and resources toward that hidden possibility. *Octogesimo Adveniens* concludes that in the extent to which the insights of utopian programs retain a social dimension and reject ideology, there are no inherent contradictions between utopian visions and the city of God.

The eschatological vision of Christianity, however, differs from a utopian future with respect to position, openness, and power. Regarding position, the eschatological vision reaches into the present from the future and begs for creative embodiment, while utopias move into the future from the present. Regarding openness, the eschatological vision requires a personal and communal readiness to allow the Spirit to shatter constrictive limits, to crack apart comfortable patterns, and to stretch beyond vested interests.[4] Finally, with regard to power, the Spirit is not only the desire for the eschatological future but also the power to enflesh that future in every time and place; human freedom converts possibility into transformative action that embodies the city of God (OA 41). The Spirit then comes from the future, transforms barriers into open spaces, and concretizes the eschatological vision.

Four specific activities of the Spirit are associated with the movement of the human community toward the city of God. First, actions that gather people together are a primary activity of the Spirit. The Spirit unifies diverse Christian communities (GS 92, OA 2), the church as institution (GS 40), social movements (GS 42), and the whole world (GS 92). Second, the Spirit acts to renew the Roman Catholic Church (GS 21), Christians (GS 37), and the earth through the process of development (GS 26).

Third, the Spirit activates Christians and arouses humanity (GS 45, 93) to build up the human community into God's own city of peace, justice, and community (OA 37). The Spirit's action begins in the heart (OA 2), animating desires (SR 38), actuating longings (GS 38), and stimulating receptivity (JW 1). Then the Spirit enables the embodiment of those very longings through transformative action.[5] As we read in *Gaudium et Spes*, the Spirit is an energy that "arouses not only a desire for the age to come, but, by that very fact, he animates, purifies, and strengthens those noble longings too by which the human family strives to make its life more human" (GS 38). *Gaudium et Spes* adds that the acknowledgment of God "compel[s] us all to receive the impulses of the Spirit faithfully and to measure up to them energetically" (GS 92).

Fourth, the Spirit works among Christian and human communities "to discern the options and commitments which are called for in order to bring about the social, political, and economic changes seen in many cases to be urgently needed" (OA 4). The discerning Spirit works particularly among communities conscious of their responsibilities in society (OA 2) and seeking a more just world (GS 44). *Gaudium et Spes* adds that the discerning Spirit is present in socio-political events as well as in the community (GS 4).[6]

These passages in Catholic social teaching describe the Spirit as the desires and longings of the human heart for the eschatological vision of justice, community, and peace. This Spirit also affects human and Christian initiatives toward the building up of the city of God. Thus, the Spirit is leaven in the human community, both raising up a vision and enabling its embodiment. Human and Christian communities take initiative because these communities are created by God, liberated by Jesus Christ, and enlivened by the Spirit.

The Trinitarian God in Catholic Social Teaching

In a few documents of Catholic social teaching, the Spirit is mentioned in a trinitarian context. Already *Gaudium et Spes* recognized that trinitarian unity was reflected in the unity of all the children of God: "Our hearts embrace also those brothers and communities not yet living with us in full communion. To them we are linked nonetheless by our profession of the Father and the Son and the Holy Spirit, and by the bond of charity" (GS 92). The ethical implications of this remark are not developed until nearly twenty-five years later in *Sollicitudo Rei Socialis*. The document's discussion of human interdependence presents the intimate life of the Trinity as a model for solidarity, that is, the Christian virtue that embraces the human reality of interdependence.

Relying on the masculine family imagery, *Sollicitudo Rei Socialis* asserts that the "common fatherhood of God," "brotherhood of all in Christ," and "presence and life-giving action of the Holy Spirit" provide both a vision and new criteria with which to interpret the world (SR 40). These criteria include forgiveness, reconciliation, the possibility of dignified lives (cf. SR 47), and love of enemy to the point of death if necessary. Since creation, redemption, and life-giving action recognize every other person as a member of God's family, these criteria provide standards to measure the progress of the human communities toward becoming the city of God. Thus the city of God is embodied in today's world wherever forgiveness and lives lived in dignity are present. Wherever structures that facilitate reconciliation and love of enemy are part of the social fabric, the new heavens and the new earth are breaking into this age.

Sollicitudo Rei Socialis 40 speaks of "the presence and life-giving action of the Holy Spirit." When read in conjunction with the previous section, we can conclude that the longings for forgiveness, reconciliation, human dignity, love, and community are Spirit-caused desires that also activate persons toward the realizations of these longings.

However both *Gaudium et Spes* and *Sollicitudo Rei Socialis* accent trinitarian unity rather than fundamental equality and relationships constituted in diversity. These latter points may actually provide richer understandings for community life today than a simplistic stress on unity.

The Spirit as "Spiritual Presence" in the Church

Alongside the references to the Spirit as transformative action in the world and trinitarian person, a final constellation in Catholic social teaching associates the Spirit with Christ, with the institutional church,[7] and with the transformation of this world into specifically spiritual or Christian realities. This perspective on the Spirit occurs already in *Gaudium et Spes*, but is more pronounced in the documents after 1971.

In these passages the Spirit is associated in a special way with the church as an institution (GS 43). The bishops rule the church with the pope under the mandate of the Holy Spirit (*Quadragesimo Anno* 138). Similarly, the Spirit assists the magisterium to set forth its teachings via the texts of Vatican Council II (GS 93) and in the development of Catholic social teaching (SR 1) by guaranteeing continuity with past teachings. At times the Spirit seems to be conjoined with Christ (*Laborem Exercens* [LE] 27, SR 48) or the priest (SR 48), rather than a separate, dynamic person. Taken together, these texts link the Spirit to institutional functions of the church.

In other passages the Spirit functions to change worldly realities into something holy. For example, the Spirit makes human dignity holy (SR 47), frees from sin (JW 5), turns development into the reign of God (LE 27), and makes human work (LE 27, SR 48) part of the paschal mystery of Jesus (GS 22). A certain distrust of human action and the goodness of God's creation lurks behind these passages. These world realities become holy explicitly through the Spirit's action.

Sollicitudo Rei Socialis 48 describes the role of the Spirit in relationship to the Eucharist. The once and for all sacrifice of Jesus Christ on the cross is made present again in the Eucharist. The "power of the Spirit and the words of the minister" mysteriously transform the bread and wine, the fruits of the earth and the work of human hands, into the body and blood of Christ. The action of the gathered community is not mentioned. Through the Spirit, Christ subsumes material bread and wine into the one sacrifice on the cross that already inaugurated, proclaimed, and anticipated the kingdom of God. In this perspective, Christian communities unite themselves in the Spirit with what was already completed in the past.[8]

In these documents of Catholic social teaching the Spirit comes from the past into the present and is closely associated with the spiritual and institutional arenas. This alternative portrayal of the Spirit restrains the understanding of the Spirit as one who roams the whole world—not only the Christian communities—and as an eschatological desire that initiates transformation on behalf of justice.

The Holy Spirit in the Lives of Practitioners of Justice

An informal survey of fifty-one practitioners and ministers of justice in the greater Chicago area explored their operative understandings of God, the human person, and justice.[9] Just over 90 percent of the respondents were ethnically Euro-Americans, Roman Catholic, and socio-economically middle class. An almost equal number of men (twenty-four) and women (twenty-seven), who ranged in age from the mid-twenties to the early seventies, participated in the survey.[10]

Some survey respondents explicitly mentioned an indwelling Spirit (18 percent) who directed, guided, and gave them courage (cf. OA 4, GS 4). More frequently they spoke of their action on behalf of justice in terms that the scriptures and Catholic social teaching associate with the work of the Spirit. For example, some spoke of a call to do justice, to be identified with the poor, to make the world better (22 percent).

Others recognized that human activities, especially collective efforts, transform injustice into a more just social order (12 percent). These ministers expect that God hears the cry of the poor and raises up prophets who respond to their needs. They spoke of their works of justice as a participation in completing the city of God (12 percent) or in God's own ongoing creation (8 percent). Fifty-one percent spontaneously described their work as participating in or carrying on God's own transforming activities.[11]

More often, however, justice practitioners linked their transformative activities to the actions of Jesus and not the Spirit.[12] They spoke of participating in Jesus' transformation, healing, liberation, or historical project as described in the gospels (10 percent).

In addition to the indwelling Spirit who guides and motivates transforming action, over one-third of the justice practitioners spoke about a vision or a dream of a better world that inspires and motivates their action on behalf of justice.[13] Most frequently (25 percent), this dream was identified with images drawn from the scriptures: the city or reign of God (12 percent), the vision of the prophets and gospels, and the worldview of the Beatitudes. Although the content of the scriptural vision or the better world was not often specified, the following characteristics were specifically mentioned: love, justice/fairness, equality, solidarity, unity, mutuality, hospitality, and non-violence.

Based on the above survey, the Spirit has a minimal explicit role in the lives of these justice ministers and practitioners.[14] However, the meanings that they associate with their activities on behalf of justice (liberation, transformation, responding to the cry of the poor), the motivations behind their justice action (vision of the city of God or a dream for better world), and their spiritual foundations (indwelling Spirit) suggest a congruency with the understanding of the Spirit in both the Scriptures and Catholic social teaching. Consequently, I contend that a more explicit recognition of the Spirit within justice ministry as well as a development of a theology of the Spirit rooted in the experience of justice practitioners would enrich both the practice of justice and pneumatology.

Building Blocks toward a Theology of the Spirit

The images and functions of the Spirit articulated in the Vatican II-era documents as well as in scripture and in the lives of justice practitioners provide the materials out of which to build a theology of the Spirit that supports action on behalf of justice and the formation of just communities.[15] Three things are necessary for this to take place. First, the Spirit must be unfettered from its role as the one who confirms institutional continuity with the past. Second, the Spirit must become a co-equal and unique person within trinitarian relationships, rather than a repetition of the Creator and Redeemer. Third, multiple metaphors for the Spirit must point to an expansive identity that cannot be hemmed in by the finite understandings of humans or institutions.

Holding these three caveats in hand, I will explore four dimensions of the Spirit that I believe can provide adequate foundations for the practice of justice, namely 1) the indwelling Spirit, 2) the eschatological horizon, 3) inclusive community, and 4) abundance. Each of these dimensions will be linked to the scriptures, Catholic social teaching, and the theological reflection of practitioners of justice. Finally, I will sketch the significance of this dimension as well as how the dimension undergirds the life and practices of the just community.

The Indwelling Spirit

The indwelling Spirit functions as an image for a persistent and intimate relationship with God. This relationship is connected with creation in the image and likeness of God as well as in the covenant traditions around Noah, Abraham/Sarah, Moses, and Jesus of Nazareth.

This Spirit dwells in human hearts as desires and longings for justice. The indwelling Spirit leads, pulls, and attracts human communities toward a better world. The Spirit breaks into this world from the messianic city of God to cajole and draw human communities toward that city. The indwelling Spirit provides a theological grounding to the human ache for a just world and engages the whole person on emotional and relational levels. Justice practitioners spoke of such dreams and dissatisfactions, but did not recognize the Spirit in these dreams and aches. However, they explicitly named the Spirit within as a guide and source of courage. The embrace of such Spirit-longings as the call to act with justice fosters the creation of the just community. A just community recognizes passionate anger as a Spirit source for a vocation to transformation.

The indwelling Spirit also arouses, energizes, and activates for action, which is the incarnation or embodiment of the Spirit in the new body of Christ. In this way, the Spirit invites human participation in building up the city of God.[16] The indwelling Spirit requires concrete bodies to make peace, justice, and community. Hence the Spirit empowers transformative activities that interpenetrate divine and human efforts, personal and structural changes, and ecclesial and civic movements, as well as the skills and passions for change. The just community enkindles the Spirit-ignited fires that arouse action on behalf of justice and provide opportunities to build skills for structural change.

Because this indwelling Spirit abides with the believing community, its persistent presence over time provides an inner source of perseverance for the justice activist. The Spirit of God hovered over the chaotic waters of creation and brought dry bones together into new life. The Spirit of God drove Jesus of Nazareth to the desert and hovered over the grief-stricken and frightened disciples on Pentecost. Surely this same Spirit will not leave those who long for the city of God and seek to build that city in their neighborhood.

The Eschatological Spirit

A second dimension of the Spirit that can provide an adequate foundation for the practice of justice is the divine eschatological presence. The eschatological Spirit reaches into the present from the already established but not yet fully realized city of God. The scriptures associate the Spirit with the inbreaking new creation.[17] The documents of the Vatican II era describe the Spirit as renewal, newness, and a fresh breeze entering opened windows and hearts. Justice ministers spoke of participation in completing what Jesus had begun and in building up the city of God, even though they did not link their participation explicitly to the Spirit.

This understanding of the Spirit differs from strategic planning that sees hidden or ignored possibilities for the future in present realities. Instead, the Spirit breaks into the present from the future, attracting and drawing believers to build up the end-times city of God in the here and now. Such a Spirit challenges the just community to become deeply rooted in a spirituality that expresses comfort with newness, surprises, and the letting go of personal ideologies so that the city of God may be established.

The already and not yet attracting future provides content under images such as a new heaven and new earth. Recurring characteristics in these eschatological images include justice, community, peace, dignity, intimate relationship with God, delight, absence of oppression, security, health, and provision of basic human needs. Wherever these characteristics are present, the attracting future is already breaking in and the eschatological Spirit has taken on a body. Such a Spirit challenges the just community to recognize and to embody the Spirit in peace, justice, and community.

Hence this Spirit provides eschatological criteria for judging and discerning any current social, political, religious or economic structure.[18] Ethical thinking today relies on norms from the past (deontology) or from the present (situation ethics), or in light of the goal (teleology), but the eschatological Spirit provides a normativity of the future,[19] which reminds us that the transcendent Spirit is always more and other than any social, political, religious or economic structure, and theory. Normativity derived from this eschatological horizon provides a standard for measuring the institutions, projects, and activities of this age. Such a Spirit challenges the just community to develop its ethical norms from the eschatological city of God, in other words, the future of humanity (JW 38) or cosmic flourishing.

The Spirit Who Builds Up Inclusive Community

A third dimension acknowledges the Spirit as the one who gathers people into the kind of inclusive community that learns and relearns how diverse people can live together well. The Spirit's role in community building is attested to in the scriptures (Rom 12, 1 Cor 12) and in Catholic social teaching. In Catholic social teaching, the intimate relationships of the trinitarian God provide a primary model for the human communities, with an accent on the unity of the Trinity. Practitioners of justice noted community and solidarity as characteristics of the better world they sought to establish, although community building was not explicitly linked to the Spirit.

For the trinitarian Spirit to provide an adequate foundation for the practice of justice in the current era, however, the accent needs to fall on the fundamental equality of diverse persons constituted by their relationships.[20] The Father, Son, and Spirit become diverse persons only through their relationships with each other. The Creator, Liberator, and Spirit become diverse persons only through their relationships with the created, the liberated, and the en-spirited. Although constituted as distinct and diverse persons through relationships, they remain fundamentally equal.

Such an understanding of trinitarian relationality provides a foundation for practitioners of justice who build inclusive communities of diverse persons. This trinitarian model points to the fundamental equality of diverse persons and to relationships (not roles or status) as constitutive of community. As a result, the tasks of community building take on theological meaning: enhancing diversity reflects divine activity; concrete protection of equality in originality echoes trinitarian life; relationality constitutes inclusive community. This community-building Spirit challenges and enables practitioners of justice to live out the central divine activity of simultaneously affirming diversity, fundamental equality in originality, and the primacy of relationships.

The Spirit that builds up the inclusive community of the Trinity manifests itself in our world wherever solidarity[21] with those marginalized and participation of disposable persons is practiced. Since the trinitarian God is creator of all, redeemer of all, and dwells in all, membership in believing communities must be available to all. Solidarity and participation are clearly hallmarks of end times; however, the embodiment of these virtues now will hasten the city of God and give flesh to Spirit. The community-building Spirit challenges practitioners of justice to listen to, to learn from, and to develop the leadership of persons who are evaluated as disposable or marginal, instead of imposing the activists' sense of what is really needed by or best for persons marginalized by social patterns.

The Spirit of Abundance

The Spirit of abundance is a final dimension that, I believe, can provide an adequate foundation for the practice of justice. The Spirit has been traditionally associated with abundance, as in the "seven gifts" or the "twelve fruits" of the Spirit. We recall also the abundance of languages at Pentecost and the rich food and choice wine at the messianic feast. In Isaiah 11 the Spirit of God gives abundant gifts to the messianic shoot of Jesse. In Luke 4 (cf. Is 61) the Spirit of God anoints the messianic figure for mission to a long list of persons typically ignored in social systems. The image of the Spirit as wind that "blows where it will" (Jn 3:8) accents an abundant universality that reaches a breadth of persons, gifts, and basic human needs.

The Spirit of abundance invites the practitioner of justice to work from a model of abundance instead of scarcity. The mere provision of basic human needs is not the goal of the works of justice; the goal rather is human and cosmic flourishing. Similarly justice is less about equality under the law, but more about each and every person having access to what is necessary for full human development. The Spirit of abundance then urges ministers of justice to circumscribe their activities within the lavishness of beauty, goodness, and celebration.

Conclusion

The above research notes a limited explicit awareness of the Spirit in the spirituality of justice ministers and practitioners. The documents of Catholic social teaching contribute an awareness of an eschatological Spirit who animates transformative action in this world through longings for a better world and discernment for action. The indwelling Spirit, the eschatological horizon, inclusive community, and abundance provide building blocks for a theology of the Spirit adequate to the practice of justice. These building blocks supply traditional and transformational vocabulary for Spirit-based action through which practitioners of justice may name the presence of the Spirit in their practices of justice. These same building blocks challenge justice educators both to highlight the work of the Spirit in justice activities and to reflect back the theological significance of Spirit-based transformation in the practices of justice.

Notes

[1]It is beyond the scope of this paper to address adequately the Spirit in the scriptures. Current scholars treating the Spirit include: Kilian McDonnell, "Theological Presuppositions in Our Preaching about the Spirit," *Theological Studies* 59 (1998): 219-35, who notes that the political Spirit and the Spirit's action throughout history have "ramifications for the sociopolitical life" although these ramifications are not developed; George T. Montague, "The Fire in the Word: The Holy Spirit in Scripture," in *Advents of the Spirit: An Introduction to the Current Study of Pneumatology,* Marquette Studies in Theology, vol. 30, ed. Bradford E. Hinze and D. Lyle Dabney (Milwaukee, Wis.: Marquette University Press, 2001), 35-65, links the Spirit and justice with justification of the believer and with the image of water, but neither of these is developed in this chapter. In an earlier work, *The Holy Spirit: Growth of a Biblical Tradition* (New York: Paulist Press, 1976), George T. Montague comments on the principal biblical texts on the Spirit, of which five

link Spirit and justice. The systematic theologian Michael Welker in *God the Spirit,* trans. John F. Hoffmeyer (Minneapolis: Fortress, 1994) describes the role of the promised Spirit of justice, with emphasis on the Spirit's universality, which extends beyond moral codes, political loyalties, these worldly realities, socio-cultural norms, and nature (108-82).

[2]Yves M. J. Congar, in *I Believe in the Holy Spirit, I: The Holy Spirit in the 'Economy': Revelation and Experience of the Spirit* (New York: Seabury Press, 1983), 167-73, describes Vatican II pneumatology as emphasizing the Spirit of Christ as active in history, animating the church, offering charisms to church and world, particularly unity, and blowing where it will. This understanding of the Spirit in the documents of Vatican Council II is reiterated in *Commentary on the Documents of Vatican II, I-V,* ed. Herbert Vorgrimler (New York: Herder and Herder, 1967), especially the commentaries by Yves Congar on *Gaudium et Spes,* nos. 41-45 in volume V, 205-20 and by Aloys Grillmeier on *Lumen Gentium* nos. 4-13 in vol. III, 142-67; Charles Moeller, in "History of *Lumen Gentium's* Structure and Ideas," *Vatican II: An Interfaith Appraisal,* ed. John H. Miller (Notre Dame: University of Notre Dame Press, 1966), 123-52; and Adrian Hastings, *A Concise Guide to the Documents of the Second Vatican Council, I-II* (London: Darton, Longman and Todd, 1968). Hastings, *Concise Guide to the Documents of the Second Vatican Council, I*, 172, notes that mention of Spirit came in documents drafted or amended after the second session.

[3]See David J. O'Brien and Thomas A. Shannon, eds., *Catholic Social Thought: The Documentary Heritage* (Maryknoll, N.Y.: Orbis Books, 1997), for the English texts of the social documents mentioned in this section. The numbers refer to the section or paragraph numbers in the texts in this collection.

[4]See also Gavin D'Costa, "Christ, the Trinity, and Religious Plurality," *Christian Uniqueness Reconsidered: The Myth of Pluralistic Theology of Religions* (Maryknoll, N.Y.: Orbis Books, 1990), for a description of the Spirit as the universality of God in contrast to the concrete and historical particularity of God in Jesus of Nazareth (18-19).

[5]In *God Breathes the Spirit in the World* (Wilmington, Del.: Michael Glazier, 1988), 78-97, Donald L. Gelpi addresses transformation and the Spirit in *Gaudium et Spes* and *Ad Gentes.*

[6]Congar (*I Believe in the Holy Spirit, I,* 170-72) and Gelpi (*God Breathes the Spirit in the World,* 79-96) address the action of the Spirit in history and the charisms of the Spirit for the world as well as for the church.

[7]See Congar, *I Believe in the Holy Spirit, I,* 167-72; Vorgrimler, *Commentary on the Documents of the Vatican II, III,* 142-67; Moeller, "History of *Lumen Gentium's* Structure and Ideas," 139; Hastings, *Concise Guide to the Documents of the Second Vatican Council, I,* 93-95. See also James B. Anderson, *A Vatican II Pneumatology of the Paschal Mystery: The Historical-Doctrinal Genesis of* Ad Gentes *I, 2-5, Analecta Gregoriana 250* (Rome: Editrice Pontificia Universita Gregoriana, 1988), 293-94. This approach to the Spirit is confirmed in John Paul II's encyclical *Dominum et Vivificantem,* "The Holy Spirit in the Church and the World," *Origins* 16 (June 12, 1986): 77-102.

[8]See also Nicholas Sagivsky, "The Eucharist and the Practice of Justice," *Studies in Christian Ethics* 15 (2002): 75-96, especially 96, where he describes the assembled community as "transformed by the Spirit to become active agents of the will of God." This community is then called to justice, for "The practice of justice by Christians in the public domain is nothing other than the public enactment of the prayer of Jesus. . . ."

[9]The survey was comprised of five open-ended questions about the respondents' practice of justice, six descriptive statements about God, five descriptive statements about the human person, and six descriptive statements about justice. The respondents specifically mentioned the Spirit in response to either 1) "Describe the connection between God and your activities on behalf of justice"; or 2) "Briefly describe an image or a personal name for God or recount a story about God which gives meaning to your activities on behalf of justice."

[10]Although this sample is small and demographically similar, it does represent the face of ministers and practitioners of justice in the Roman Catholic Church in the greater Chicago area. For complete survey results, see Mary Elsbernd and Reimund Bieringer, *When Love Is Not Enough: A Theo-Ethic of Justice* (Collegeville, Minn.: Liturgical Press/Michael Glazier, 2002), 20-22 and 25-33.

[11]They also rated on a scale of 1-5 the following description of God as transforming action as highly compatible (4.36) with the God they knew and loved: "Some ministers and practitioners of justice experience their own work on behalf of justice as participation in God's own creating, liberating, and transforming activities. They speak of their justice activities as doing what Jesus would have done, as making God present, or as God's gracious intervention in the lives of others. They recognize that human activities can be transformative."

[12]For example, Jesus' proclamation at Nazareth (Lk 4) and the Sermon on the Mount (Mt 5) turned upside down the dominant religious expectations; the miracle at Cana (Jn 2) altered the distribution of resources.

[13]They also rated the following description of God as longing for the dream as highly compatible (4.18) with the God they know and follow: "Some ministers and practitioners of justice may name their dream the reign of God or a better world. The names convey the sense that the longing for this dream is fundamental, sustaining in the dark days and somehow stretches beyond their own creation. The longing emerges from outrage at injustices or from an abiding hope that remains in spite of frustrated efforts or bone-deep tiredness. Their longing for the dream keeps them and their lives open to a future which changes how they live today." The remaining descriptions of God focused on reciprocal relationality (3.92), gracious resistance (3.8), call to conversion (3.76), and performative ritual (3.5).

[14]See Yves M. J. Congar, *I Believe in the Holy Spirit, II: "He Is the Lord and Giver of Life"* (New York: Seabury Press, 1983), 168-69, for a discussion of a lessening of social commitment among persons involved in charismatic renewal. His thoughtful argument calls for relationships with both the transcendent God and with the concrete people of this world.

[15]Although many excellent works have appeared on the Spirit over the last thirty years, my research in this area suggests that limited work has been done to

explore the Spirit and justice or the Spirit in Catholic social teachings. See, for example, the recent excellent collection of twenty-four papers and responses, *Advents of the Spirit*, ed. Hinze and Dabney, which indexes fewer than twenty references to justice.

[16]When the term *paraklesis* is seen against the backdrop of Isaiah 40-66, the work of the Spirit includes the tasks of building up, strengthening, leading like a shepherd, feeding and nourishing as well as encouraging and comforting.

[17]See the messianic reign, the true Israel, Pentecost, city of God, new life, wedding feast, and New Jerusalem.

[18]Kathryn Tanner, *The Politics of God: Christian Theologies and Social Justice* (Minneapolis, Minn.: Fortress Press, 1992), 1-30.

[19]Reimund Bieringer, "The Normativity of the Future: The Authority of the Bible for Theology," *Bulletin of European Theology: Zeitschrift Fuer Theologie in Europa* 8 (1997): 52-67.

[20]In "God in Communion with Us," *Freeing Theology: The Essentials of Theology in Feminist Perspective*, ed. Catherine Mowry LaCugna (San Francisco: HarperSanFrancisco, 1993), 83-114, here 85-88, Catherine Mowry LaCugna describes the trinitarian understanding of the early Christian Greek writers, which emphasized person, relationship, fecundity, and dynamism.

[21]See Anselm Kyongsuk Min, "Solidarity of Others in the Power of the Holy Spirit: Pneumatology in a Divided World," in *Advents of the Spirit*, 414-43, for a more ontological approach to the personhood of the Spirit in the Trinity.

The Ecological Spirit and Cosmic Mutuality: Engaging the Work of Denis Edwards

Dawn M. Nothwehr

The recent efforts of Australian theologian Denis Edwards to "re-think the theology of the Holy Spirit" has given rise to some provocative ideas that challenge the impudent abuse and destruction of the earth by human beings.[1] My discussion here draws on his ecological theology of the Holy Spirit and the four proposals he offers in support of the thesis that "it is possible to hold that there is a proper role for the Holy Spirit in the one divine work of creation."[2]

Now, within any theology lies a nascent and implicit ethics. I believe that Edwards's understanding of the role of the Holy Spirit in creation, perhaps more so than any other recent ecotheology, opens up a view of a relational community. His work moves beyond the ecofeminist treatment of the Holy Spirit as one in relationship in the life of the Trinity *ad intra* by attending to the trinitarian life *ad extra*, focusing on the proper role of the Holy Spirit in particular. Edwards thus deepens our understanding of the significance of the Holy Spirit for developing an adequate ecological theology and ethics. In what follows, I will show that Edwards's ecotheology of the Holy Spirit provides a warrant for mutuality as a central norm for Catholic environmental ethics.

Denis Edwards's Ecological Theology of the Holy Spirit

The Distinctive Role of the Holy Spirit in Creation

Edwards posits that it is not unorthodox to maintain that there is a distinct role for the Holy Spirit in creation. Beginning with John

Zizioulas's "two types of Spirit theology in the New Testament"—the power for mission (*dunamus*) and the eschatological gift of communion (*koinonia*)—Edwards suggests that "the distinctive work of the Spirit in the ongoing creation of all things can be understood in terms of the power of becoming and the gift of divine communion with each creature."[3]

The Life-Giving Spirit as the Power of Becoming

Edwards asserts that while it is the task of science to explain the emersion of the universe and all life forms (Big Bang Theory and evolution), "it is congruent with the Christian Tradition to see the Spirit as the power of becoming who enables the emergence of a life-bearing universe."[4] He points to a wide variety of sources, especially to the work of Basil of Caesarea, in support of this understanding of the Holy Spirit as the "Giver of Life" (First Council of Constantinople 381). Edwards stresses that though the Christian Testament texts focus on the role of the Spirit in the salvation of humans and their participation in the life of the Risen One, those same texts rely on the First Testament passages that point to biological life for their meaning (Gn 1:2-3; Job 33:4; or Ps 104:29-30).

Another resource Edwards utilizes in this line of development is Karl Rahner's evolutionary christology. He agrees with Rahner that the truly new in evolution needs to be accounted for by "theological reflection on God's ongoing creative action" (not only by science).[5] Further, Edwards thinks Rahner's notion of "active self-transcendence," and the idea that Jesus Christ is both the self-transcendence of the universe to God, and God's absolute self-communication to all of creation, can be developed "with the idea that the process of self-transcendence can be seen as the distinctive work of the life-giving Spirit."[6] Here Edwards reaches back to Athanasius who said, "the Father creates and renews everything through the Word and in the Spirit."[7] Moreover, following Walter Kasper, Hildegard of Bingen, and Elizabeth A. Johnson, Edwards claims it is in line with the Christian tradition to argue that God is immanent in all things through the Spirit. In short, "it is the Spirit of God who, always in profound communion with the other divine Persons, is the divine creative power of the being and becoming of the universe."[8]

The Life-Giving Spirit as Ecstatic Gift of Communion

According to Edwards, the Spirit's role is relational and "as a *personal presence* interior to each creature."[9] Just as humans have the capacity to relate to all creatures in distinct ways, so too is the relationship of the Spirit distinct in and with each being. It is through these varied relationships or presences with each being that the Spirit creates the bond of communion and empowers the being and becoming of each. Significantly, the two dimensions of *dunamus* and *koinonia* "are interrelated with each other in the *one* presence of the Spirit in each creature. . . . The Spirit is the one who *empowers* and *creates* precisely as the one who *relates* to each creature, bringing each into communion with the Trinity."[10]

Edwards cites yet another array of theological resources to bolster his point.[11] In his *Confessions* III, 6.11, Augustine spoke of God's presence as "closer to me than I am to myself." Indeed, orthodox Christianity has long understood God, who is radically transcendent, to also be present in every creature. In his Trinitarian theology, Richard of St. Victor showed that the Spirit is the *ekstatic* one. Christian Duquoc held that "the Holy Spirit is God's *ecstasy* directed toward what is God's *other*, the creature."[12] Yves Congar understood the Holy Spirit as absolute Gift, and like Duquoc, he saw the Spirit as "outside God's self, God in creatures, God in us."[13] Edwards reasons that if all of this is true, then what Paul calls "the *koinonia* of the Holy Spirit" (2 Cor 13:13) can also refer to the Spirit's presence to all creation. There is, in fact, evidence that this understanding is on Paul's horizon when he writes in Romans 8:2, "The creation itself will be set free from its bondage to decay and will obtain the freedom of the glory of the children of God."

Next, Edwards employs the thought of Jürgen Moltmann to advance these notions. Moltmann's insights are significant for Edwards's project in that he asserts that the redeeming Spirit of Christ and the creative life-giving Spirit of God are one and the same, *and* that the Holy Spirit "leads of itself beyond the limits of the Church to the rediscovery of the same Spirit in nature, in plants, and in the ecosystems of the earth."[14] Edwards explains further that Moltmann posits a "community of creation in which all created things exist with one another, for one another, and in one another, [as] a fellowship of the Holy Spirit."[15] With Moltmann, Edwards stresses that this "community of creation" "is meant to lead through evolutionary history, not to simple diversity or simple unity, but to 'differentiated community that liberates the individual members belonging to it.' "[16]

Thus, Edwards proposes that it is faithful to the Christian tradition to understand the Holy Spirit as acting in a distinctive role in ongoing creation. He summarizes his position thus:

> [T]he Spirit is the one who *empowers* the evolutionary unfolding of creation precisely as the one who relates to each creature, bringing each into *communion* with the Trinity, and thus undergirding and enabling the communion among the creatures themselves. This is a differentiated communion, because each creature is loved and respected precisely for what it is and for its own precise participation in the ecological whole. . . . Where the Spirit is, there also are the other Persons in the divine communion that is the being of God.[17]

A Proper Role of the Spirit of God in Creation

Edwards claims there is a proper role of the Holy Spirit in the one divine work of creation. He develops his thought around four proposals:

> Proposal 1: In creation and redemption, the Trinitarian Persons act only in profound communion and in undivided unity with one another; but this one undivided action does not exclude a proper role for each person.[18]

With Athanasius, Edwards holds that the divine action of creation is one, though the role of each of the divine Persons is distinct. Similarly, with Gregory of Nyssa he asserts that the Trinity acts as one, yet there is a distinctive pattern to the acts of each Person. Edwards finds in Augustine the notion that what can be said of one person of the Trinity can be said of all. Anything that is said distinctively of one Person is said as an appropriation, not as a proper distinction.

Here Edwards utilizes Aquinas's definition of appropriation, namely, to connect a thing that is common to something particular. According to Aquinas's theology of appropriation, it is legitimate to claim a particular role for the Holy Spirit in creation "on the basis of a resemblance between the particular Trinitarian Person and the work, as long as it is acknowledged that it is *only an appropriation and not proper to the Person.*[19] However, Edwards considers this an unduly limited view of trinitarian action: "But when the theology of appropriation is used at the second level, to deny that there is anything distinctive about, for example, the Spirit's work in creation, then I believe that it is being misused."[20] Edwards then moves to his second proposal.

Proposal 2: A foundation for a theology of the proper role of the Spirit in creation can be found in the work of contemporary theologians who discuss the proper roles of the Trinitarian Persons in the incarnation and Pentecost event.[21]

Edwards uses Rahner, Mühlen, Coffey, and Congar to demonstrate the inadequacy of the theology of appropriation when used in such an exclusionary manner. Certainly, as Rahner has asserted, the incarnation is not "merely *appropriated* to one Person but is *proper to the Person of the Word.*"[22] Further, both Heribert Mühlen and David Coffey understand the outpouring of the Spirit at Pentecost and the work of sanctification as the proper role of the Holy Spirit.[23] Yves Congar and Karl Rahner agree that in the process of sanctification "we each have a real and proper relationship with *each* of the divine Persons."[24] In any case, neither Rahner, Mühlen, Coffey, nor Congar deny the participation of the other divine Persons with the Spirit or the Son.[25] Edwards asserts that a similar line of thought is fitting for understanding a proper role of the Holy Spirit in creation. Strong biblical evidence for this is found in texts (Gn 1:1-2 and 2:7, where the Spirit is Life-Giver; and Jn 1:1-5 and Col 1:15-20) that "suggest an exemplary theology of Jesus Christ as the Word and Wisdom through and in whom all things are created."[26]

Having shown how acknowledging the unity of the three divine Persons in creation does not necessarily exclude the proper role of each distinct Person, and having examined the claims of several contemporary theologians that illustrate how there are distinct and proper roles for the trinitarian Persons in the incarnation and the Pentecost event, Edwards proceeds to articulate two arguments for the proper role of the Holy Spirit in creation.

Proposal 3: A first argument for a proper role of the Spirit in creation is that ongoing creation is best understood as a dynamic

relationship between each creature and the Trinity; such a relationship approach would involve distinct Trinitarian Persons.[27]

It is quite plain to Edwards that "the kind of causality involved in
creation is a relational causality" rather than the abstract system of
cause and effect that operates between one empirical reality and another.[28] There is a unique and personal relationship between God and
each creature. The trinitarian God is a radically relational being who,
in turn, creates "a world that is relational to its core."[29] Indeed, Edwards
asserts that evidence from cosmology, quantum physics, evolutionary
biology, and ecology supports such a worldview.[30] Creation, itself relational, is witness to the divine self-expression in what is not divine.
Edwards concludes:

> If God is Persons-in-communion, and if ongoing creation is a
> relational act whereby each creature is enabled to be and to
> become in a community of creatures, then this suggests that each
> divine Person is to be understood as distinctly and properly
> engaged in the one act of creating. If creation is, from the side of
> God, a personal self-giving, a personal relationship, this would
> involve what is distinctive and proper to the divine persons.[31]

Edwards then makes his fourth and final proposal:

> Proposal 4: A second argument for a proper role of the Trinitarian
> Persons in creation is that what are distinctive about the Trinitarian
> Persons (their relations of origin) come into play in the one work
> of divine creation.[32]

First, the Spirit is the "power of becoming and the ecstatic gift of communion in creation."[33] Second, following Bonaventure, the Word and
Wisdom of God is the exemplar in whom all things were made.[34] Finally, it is Bonaventure's *fontalis plenitudo*, the Fountain Fullness who
is the source of all being and the font of all goodness.[35] It is the Spirit
who unites creatures in communion with God, saves and sustains them,
and points them to fulfillment "precisely as the ecstatic gift of divine
communion with all that exists."[36] This is the proper empowering and
communion-making role of the Spirit.

The Spirit of God as Ecological Spirit

Ecology is the science concerned with the interrelationship of the various systems that support life on Earth. It is appropriate to view the Holy Spirit as ecological Spirit because it is the role of the Spirit to "enable each creature to be and to become, bringing each into relationship with other creatures in both local and global systems, and in this process of ongoing creation, relating each creature in communion within the life of the divine Persons-in-communion."[37] The entire world, then, is sacramental because it and all aspects of its history are "inspirited." Thus, it is possible to understand how encounters with the wonder of the various life forms can bring humans into communion with the fully relational trinitarian God. Edwards's understanding of the proper role of the Spirit in all of this even makes possible a renewed understanding of the violence *in* nature and *of* nature. The Spirit is also present "in the *suffering* with suffering creation," "groaning in labor pains" (Rom 8:22) with creation until all is transformed in Christ.[38] This same Spirit is known "at the heart of mutual friendship . . ." and in many other ways.[39] Indeed, as Edwards concludes, the Earth reveals a profound relationship between and among God and creatures, and all with all, through the Spirit.[40] This ecological theology of the Holy Spirit points to a morality governed by an ethics of mutuality. It is to this discussion that we now turn.

The Holy Spirit and the Formal Norm of Mutuality

The Contribution of Edwards

Denis Edwards's contribution supports the ontological status of mutuality. In fact, I think that his ecological theology of the Holy Spirit can serve as a warrant for mutuality as a central norm for Catholic environmental ethics. Edwards persuasively contends that a radically relational God has created "a world that is relational to the core."[41] He also substantiates his claim that it is the Holy Spirit who "gives life" and "creates communion" in the universe. Further, it is widely agreed throughout the academy that the interdependence of all particular elements of the cosmos is an ontological reality. Significantly, as Edwards reminds us, "Theology and science can meet in a view of reality as relational—in a relational ontology."[42]

Recent advances across numerous academic fields can be viewed as recognizing the facticity of mutuality, and even its ontological status.[43] For our purposes, it is important to recognize that facts are not value-free nor morally neutral. Indeed, Jean Porter's claim is significant: "far from there being a gap between fact and value, there can be no real understanding of the facts that is not simultaneously a knowledge of values."[44] Knowledge of what a being really is, is the same as knowledge of what is good for that thing. In this sense, reality is morality.

When we seek a central norm for a Catholic environmental ethics, what we seek is a standard of measure for what maximizes the flourishing of all, or what has been traditionally called "the common good."[45] However, in considerations of the common good in times past, an ecological understanding of the created world, especially the human person, was not addressed. The result was an anthropocentric (often androcentric) ethics that still left an opening for abusive human exploitation of women, otherkind, and the Earth itself. I suggest that if we follow the lead of Edwards and begin with an understanding of the Spirit as the " 'unspeakable closeness of God,' the one we encounter in the experience of deep connection with a place, in delight in trees, flowers, birds, and animals,"[46] then we can uncover the value that is normative in ontological relations. In fact, the norm of mutuality names the power that is at the heart of the Spirit's work as life giver and communion builder. If our ontological reality *is*, that all that exists is related to everything else, then this impacts what we understand as "the good," who we ought to be, and what we ought to do—that is, this reality impacts our ethics. In part, this renewed understanding of reality prompted feminists to reconsider the ethics of power in recent years. This renewed ethics of power reclaims mutuality as a formal norm for Christian social and ecological ethics.

Traditional Christian ethics centered on only two fundamental principles, love and justice. However, from an ecofeminist viewpoint, the classical theology that undergirded these norms was inadequate because it was patriarchal, dualistic, and never considered women and women's experience as normative standards of measure. Women represented "matter" and only things of the "spirit" were considered normative.[47] Thus, it is was possible, for example, to call an idea or action "just" or "loving" while thoroughly disregarding the perspective of women, the poor, non-humans, or those most affected by it. However, it is not only *that* one practices love and justice but *how* one does so that distinguishes the thriving of women specifically, and the cosmos, generally.

Edwards's ecotheology of the Holy Spirit challenges and corrects this spirit/matter dualism by showing that the life-giving Spirit is in all things. If all of creation is "inspirited," certainly this includes women, and that inclusion presses for the recognition of women as fully human and capable of full moral agency. Thus, from an ecofeminist perspective, any exchange of power must be based on the common recognition of the full agency of the other, the concomitant valuing of the other, and a common regard marked by trust, respect, and affection.[48] In other words, the practice of genuine love and justice requires mutuality. The notion of mutuality must be considered normative and as formative of the foundational moral experience of reverence for human persons and their environment.

Mutuality Defined

Mutuality Reclaimed

Rosemary Radford Ruether, Elizabeth A. Johnson, Carter Heyward, and Beverly Wildung Harrison situate mutuality as a formal norm for Christian social and ecological ethics, and as a corrective and a complement to the traditional construal of the norms of love and justice.[49] These thinkers are the primary pioneers in breaking through traditional theology and ethics that discounted women and women's perspectives. Their wider project of Christian feminist theology was to formulate an immediate corrective to classical theologies that stressed transcendent, patriarchal, male aspects of God to the near exclusion of immanent, egalitarian, female images. Thus, the incarnation, the linkage of creation and redemption themes, as well as historicity and embodiment became the predominant focus of early feminist theology because these foci more immediately addressed the problematic of the exclusion of women.

The development of feminist Christian ethics has paralleled the evolution of this theology. The fact that spirit/matter dualism was the occasion of grave harm to women militated against any particular discussion of pneumatology and its ethical implications.[50] Nonetheless, as feminist theologies of the Holy Spirit were advanced, they demonstrated that classical notions of love and justice are not adequate to accommodate the kinds and degrees of relationship with women and the nonhuman world that emerge as imperative if Christians are to be faithful to the immanent, egalitarian, and transcendent realities that characterize the Divine.[51]

Certainly Denis Edwards's ecological theology of the Holy Spirit, which advances a particular role for the Spirit, bolsters these theologies by illustrating that the Holy Spirit's power is that of relatedness. Prior to Edwards, Elizabeth A. Johnson's book, *Woman, Earth, Creator Spirit*, was the single work that gave sustained attention to the role of the Holy Spirit and the ethical implications of the relationality the Spirit creates and sustains.[52] Further, as Edwards suggests, the deep relatedness of all creation presses for a more concrete qualification of what constitutes adequate notions of love and justice.[53] Certainly, mutuality is a necessary condition for genuine love and/or justice. When mutuality accompanies love and justice, a vast qualitative difference in each virtue is determined, namely, the dynamic of power becomes limited to "power-with."[54] There is evidence of the normative status of mutuality. I now turn to that discussion.

What Is Mutuality?

Mutuality is a formal norm that can be conceptualized in a manner similar to our understanding of justice, and it is similarly complex. Analogous to those theories of justice that ascribe to it a tripartite nature—contractual, distributive, and social—we find four forms of mutuality, namely: cosmic, gender, generative, and social.[55]

The basic definition of mutuality is a sharing of "power-with" by and among all parties in a relationship in a way that recognizes the wholeness and particular experience of each participant toward the end of the optimum flourishing of all.

The first form of mutuality is cosmic mutuality, that is, the sharing of "power-with" by and among the Creator, human beings, all earth elements, and the entire cosmos in a way that recognizes their interdependence and reverences all.

Evidence for cosmic mutuality is advanced by astrophysics, ecology, and quantum physics, in particular, and it demonstrates a foundational kinship of everything in the entire cosmos. This is the radical relatedness that Edwards refers to as "relational ontology."[56] Edwards's singular contribution is that he places the activity of inspiring and creating this relationality as the proper role of the Holy Spirit. Beyond that, ecofeminist theory holds that the natural environment asserts itself as a living aspect of "our bodies, our selves"—it "answers back" when humans defile nature.[57] Humans violate the ecosystem to their own detriment.

Cosmic mutuality is also grounded in the fact that, from a Christian perspective, the most effective social analysis takes into account how any form of power impacts the most disadvantaged, not forgetting all elements of the ecosystem. The interest of attaining the well-being of all is best served by a social analysis informed by the biblical covenant. The biblical notion of covenant includes human well-being, social justice, and care for the earth.[58] The understanding of "right relationships," which "evokes a shared passion for justice" and a "common longing for a world where there are no excluded ones," further specifies covenant relationships.[59] The biblical covenant and ecological science both reveal the reciprocal nature of the relationship between the ecosystem and human beings, including all of their activities. Consideration of the biblical covenant renders inadequate any analysis of power that "takes account of power in an institutional matrix" and "groups already in ascendancy" while excluding an analysis of the effect of power on "those already disadvantaged in society."[60] Thus, traditional Christian cosmology is retrievable to the extent that the relatedness of the created order and the social order is stressed in light of the biblical witnesses.

The deep relatedness between God and creation, known as panentheism,[61] has been recognized for centuries as orthodox. The fact that God *is* Creator, Vivifier, and Redeemer only in relation to creation shows, in a certain analogous sense, need on God's part for relationship to the cosmos. Edwards's ecological theology adds clarity to all of this by highlighting the proper role of the Holy Spirit as the giver of life and the creator of communion. Thus, acknowledging the kinship of all creation through the Spirit's activity requires us to count non-humans as our neighbors as well. This all points to *cosmic mutuality*.

Gender mutuality is a second form of mutuality. It is defined as the sharing of "power-with" by and among women and men in a way that recognizes the full participation of each in the *imago Dei*, embodied in daily life and through egalitarian relationships.

Gender mutuality is grounded in the fact that both women and men are bearers of the full *imago Dei* (Gn 1:27) and they are both capable of full mature moral agency. For the baptized, the Holy Spirit inspires life *en Christō*, meaning they are part of a discipleship of equals (Gal 3:28) that foreshadows the eschatological "new heavens and the new earth." It was the Holy Spirit who prompted Jesus' *"kenosis* of patriarchy" that significantly precludes sexism in any form.[62] This Spirit-inspired action is important because Jesus' life, ministry, and teachings are normative for the Christian life. The four feminist pioneers mentioned above (Ruether, Johnson, Heyward, and Harrison) also advance biogenic and sociocultural evidence supporting gender equality to challenge classical dualisms and physicalist interpretations of natural law. The social sciences also show that social, political, or economic structures can be organized to purposefully empower or disempower women. Finally, all erotic, sensual, embodied knowledge (including sexuality) is a means of God's revelation of Self to us through one another.

The third form of mutuality is generative mutuality. It is the sharing of "power-with" by and among the Divine, human persons, and all creation in the on-going co-creation and redemption of the world.

Insofar as each human person bears God's image and likeness within her/his own flesh, each enjoys mutuality with God as co-creator and co-redeemer. The paradigm of the incarnation itself, Christ Jesus as both human and divine, part of the material world, also lends support to that notion. Indeed, insofar as each creature images God, each participates in the co-creation and redemption of the world. As Edwards suggests, "the Spirit can be thought of as God present in countless ways that are beyond the human."[63] In fact, the non-human, but particularly animals such as our pets or farm animals have a great capacity to teach us the meaning of cogenerativity. Edwards's life-giving Spirit brings communion among humans and all of creation, initiates human friendship with God (Aquinas, *ST* I-II, 1-5 and II-II, 23-27), and is present in the *koinonia* of the baptized—all of which are conduits of the co-creative and co-redemptive processes. As Edwards points out, humans, empowered and inspired by the Holy Spirit, participate in completing the redemption of the world begun by Jesus by struggling in daily life to "transcend themselves and . . . become what is new."[64] All of this signals that generative mutuality exists among the Divine, human persons, and all creation.

The final form of mutuality is social mutuality. This I define as the sharing of "power-with" by and among members of society in a way that recognizes the fundamental dignity of each and the obligation to attain and maintain for each what is necessary to sustain that dignity.

Perhaps Beverly Wildung Harrison explains social mutuality best when she states:

> Jesus was radical not in his lust for sacrifice, *but in his power of mutuality*. . . . His death was the price he paid for refusing to abandon the *radical activity* of love—of expressing solidarity and reciprocity with the excluded ones of his community. . . . Radical acts of love—expressing solidarity and bringing mutual relationships to life—are the central virtues of the Christian moral life.[65]

As Edwards has shown, Jesus is the bearer of the liberating Spirit who led him to heal, dine with the outcasts, form a community, and preach the reign of God.[66] Living as Jesus lived, with a commitment to mutuality, enables us to bear God into the world. As the Pentecost sequence proclaims, the Holy Spirit is the "Father of the poor" who inspires acts of justice and orchestrates liberation through the release and the taking up of power in relationships. That fidelity to mutuality requires making sacrifices for the cause of radical love, creating and sustaining relationships, or righting wrong relationships, and is exemplified by countless persons, both named and nameless, who have suffered for the sake of mutuality.[67]

The Holy Spirit animates and empowers people, enabling them to choose to share in a common power with those less powerful or oppressed, not forgetting the earth and otherkind. But, the role of the less powerful must also be stressed. Given the constitutive sociality of the human person, the less powerful are obliged to assert their claim to "power-with" in order to maintain their human dignity. This evidence suggests *social mutuality* is needed between the powerful and the powerless of our world.

Mutuality: What a Difference It Makes!

The work of Edwards demonstrates the proper role of the Holy Spirit in establishing an ontological relationality in the world, but he does not give sustained attention to the implications of that reality for ethics. We do find important indications about such matters, however. It is fair to say that he would agree that mutuality makes a great deal of difference in ethics and the outcome of moral discernment.[68] Living in mutuality is a process animated by the Life-Giving and Communion-Building Spirit, and not a static situation.

Set within a dynamic worldview, a feminist ethic of mutuality has implications, first of all, for our appreciation of truth and truth claims. According to Edwards, truth seeking is part of the ongoing "becoming" of all creation. "It is the Spirit who is the immanent principle that empowers the self transcendence of the universe towards Christ. . . . The Spirit is at work in the evolutionary emergence whenever something radically new occurs in the unfolding of the universe and in the story of life."[69]

Parties in mutual relation are oriented to the needs of the other and maintain an intentionality directed to the well-being of the other(s).[70] Mutuality thus requires a praxis view of truth in which the truth is conditioned by the intentions of the relationship.[71] What is true is related to the action-oriented intention of the speaker.[72]

Mutuality is a relationship in which each party has a distinctive particularity and history. Sustaining various kinds of relationships—cosmic, gender, generative, social—requires a *perspectival view of truth* in which all standpoints determined by culture, gender, history, economics, or politics are taken into account. Indeed, this view presses humans to also consider nonhuman perspectives when determining truths about issues such as endangered species or polluted rivers.[73] If only human perspectives are considered, then only a partial truth will be known. By contrast, if all perspectives are considered, a more complete truth will be known.

From the human perspective, creating and sustaining mutual relationships requires one to recognize that language is limited in the meaning it can bear. As Wittgenstein has argued, human language can bear only one or two perspectives at once.[74] What is true needs to be understood in a context. It is therefore necessary for humans to intentionally consider a variety of perspectives in turn, and to allow each additional perspective to enhance the original insight gained from the first perspective considered.

From Gadamer and Ricoeur, there is evidence that knowledge of any text is also an interpretation of the text. In sustaining a mutual relation this *interpretive view of the truth* needs to be acknowledged lest there be false absolutizing of unintended information or action.[75] How do we attend to the texts of the nonhuman world? What truths do we miss if we ignore them?

A final kind of truth to consider is dialogic truth. As one acts, speaks, and interprets with another there are moments when the "I" and the "Thou" combine to form the "We." It is in those moments that mutuality reaches its apex. Are we, like Martin Buber, attentive to the dialogue invited by trees, horses, cats, or rocks?[76] Edwards shows that the Spirit has a differentiated personal presence to each creature, "a presence that creates a bond of communion with each."[77] If we are not open and ready for these kinds of truth and the moment of true mutuality that happens in the "between" of dialogue, we live in a false reality, assuming that what are indeed only elements of truth are the full truth.[78]

A second set of implications mutuality holds for ethics is that mutuality shifts ethics' *understanding* of the moral subject by focusing on the sociality of the human person. Edwards shows that "human beings have their own unique relationship to the indwelling of the Holy Spirit. In the communion of the one Spirit they are kin to all of the creatures" and to one another.[79] No action can be evaluated as if a person acted in isolation. Moral actions are considered in light of the context of the situation. We are always in a situation of response to others.[80] Our actions make sense only in relationship to others, including nonhuman others.

Mutuality also *expands the idea of the moral subject.* Viewed through the lens of mutuality, the moral subject is no longer understood merely as one bearing an abstract status, a human nature. Rather, the moral subject is known as a whole person who develops, experiences, and transforms value and who is, in turn, developed and transformed by valuing. The moral capacity of the self, the individual's motivation for sacrifice and justice, is understood in terms of mutuality in relationships.

Furthermore, mutuality focuses on reciprocity in moral agency. In the situations of mutuality, the moral subject constantly exchanges valuing and being valued. We are enabled "to grasp our dependence on each other and our social institutions and relations for our moral self-regard and moral power."[81]

A third set of implications mutuality holds for ethics is that mutuality modifies what is understood as the "good." Normative mutuality moves the starting point for ethical reflection to a radically inclusive place, where literally everyone and everything is included. Edwards maintains that God companions each creature with love that respects the identity of each, its possibilities, and its proper autonomy. Thus the Spirit is grieved (Eph 4:30) when humans destroy, abuse, and disregard the experience or needs of any part of the web of life.[82] The moral horizon is the vision of the "new heavens/new earth." The present history and the future shape the two-fold context for the vision. "Goods" based on atomistic individualism and patterns of competition, adversarial relations, exploitation, authoritarianism, or paternalism are ruled out because they diminish or deny the fundamental mutual relation that exists between God and humans and that needs to exist between humans, and with all of creation.

Human good needs to fit in with all other "goods" in the cosmos with an eye toward the maximum flourishing of all—not just human thriving. This means mutuality requires an integration of independent and responsible acts as well as interdependent and relational activities. It means that in achieving the "good" what must be overcome is whatever isolates, completely separates, or arouses disinterest and atomistic individualism. There is one good that permeates both private and public spheres; mutuality empowers by including everything and everyone in the social/political/economic equation.[83]

Every human is born in need of relationships. When needs and rights are not met and honored, injustice accompanied by self-doubt, mistrust, or resentment occurs. The practice of justice in society therefore also needs to include mutual practices of reconciliation.[84] When mutuality is not recognized by both parties and an impasse in relation results, an ethics of care does not abandon the effort. Rather, it moves to confront the deeper (social-psychological) blockages and tries again and again. An ethic of mutuality may then knowingly choose to love sacrificially in order to act-the-other-into-life, moving toward greater mutuality. The Spirit is most certainly present in such an encounter. As Edwards has shown, "the Spirit is the mid-wife that groans with creation in its labor pains (Rom 8:22) as it transforms and gives birth to all things new."[85]

Conclusion

Given the facticity of the life-giving Spirit as the power of becoming and the ecstatic power of communion in the world, what are the implications for understanding mutuality as a central norm for a Catholic environmental ethics? We can see that mutuality does make a difference in our perception of truth, the moral subject, and the moral good. As Edwards reminds us, "theology and science can meet in a view of reality as relational—in a relational ontology."[86] The verity of mutuality, and even its ontological status, is widely recognized in all academic disciplines. Together these understandings affect our ecological vision of who we ought to be and what we ought to do in relationship with self, God, others, and the cosmos.

The U.S. Catholic bishops, in their 1991 pastoral, *Renewing the Earth*, challenged us "to explore links between concern for the person and for the earth, between natural ecology and social ecology."[87] If we are to address these challenges, we must engage the norm of mutuality and its probative value for uncovering the role of power in the moral life and for social and ecological ethics. In fact, mutuality (in all of its forms) stands at the heart of the positive manifestation of the eight themes from Catholic social teaching cited by the bishops as the integral dimensions of ecological responsibility, namely, a God-centered and sacramental view of the universe (cosmic); respect for human life and of all creation (cosmic, gender, generative); affirmation of global interdependence and the common good (generative, social); an ethics of solidarity (cosmic, social); understanding the universal purpose of created things (social generative); an option for the poor (social); and a conception of authentic development (social, generative).[88]

Shortly after ecology was first defined by Ernest Haeckle in 1866 as "the interrelationships of living beings among themselves and with their environment,"[89] the science became conceptualized in three forms: environmental, social, and mental ecology.[90] It is worth citing Leonardo Boff's explanation of these forms of ecology at length:

> *Environmental* ecology is concerned with the environment and relations that various societies have with it in history . . . whether they integrate human beings into or distance them from nature. *Social* ecology is primarily concerned with social relations as belonging to ecological relations; that is, because human beings (who are personal and social) are part of the natural world their relationship with nature passes through the social relationship of exploitation, collaboration, or respect and reverence. Hence social justice—the right relationship between persons, roles, and

institutions—implies some achievement of ecological justice, which is the right relationship with nature, easy access to its resources, and assurance of quality of life. Finally *mental* ecology starts from the recognition that nature is not outside human beings but within them, in their minds, in the form of psychic energies, symbols, archetypes, and behavior patterns that embody attitudes of aggression or of respect and acceptance of nature.[91]

This understanding of ecology includes the eight themes of the U.S. bishops and also the four kinds of relationship addressed in the consideration of mutuality as a formal norm. As the author of Wisdom proclaimed so long ago, "Your immortal spirit is in all things" (Wis 12:1) giving life and creating communion. Indeed, Denis Edwards's ecological theology of the Holy Spirit illustrates how this life and communion comes to be and that these kinds of relationships are exemplary for all relationship—between humans, the divine, otherkind, and all of creation. Edwards's ecotheology of the Holy Spirit thus stands as a warrant for mutuality as a central norm for Catholic environmental ethics.

Notes

[1]See these works by Denis Edwards: "The Integrity of Creation: Catholic Social Teaching for an Ecological Age," *Pacifica* 5 (1992): 182-203; "Evolution and the God of Mutual Friendship," *Pacifica* 10 (1997): 187-200; "The Ecological Significance of God-Language," *Theological Studies* 60 (1999): 708-22; "Theological Foundations for Ecological Praxis," *Ecotheology* 5/6 (July 1998/January 1999): 126-41; "Ecology and the Holy Spirit: The 'Already' and the 'Not Yet' of the Spirit of Creation," *Pacifica* 13 (2000): 142-59; "For Your Immortal Spirit Is in All Things: The Role of the Spirit in Creation," in Denis Edwards, ed., *Earth Revealing, Earth Healing: Ecology and Christian Theology* (Collegeville, Minn.: The Liturgical Press, 2001), 45-66; "Making All Things New: An Ecological Theology of the Holy Spirit," unpublished paper, presented at the Catholic Theological Society of America, New Orleans, Louisiana, June 8, 2002.

[2]This exposé of Denis Edwards's ecotheology of the Holy Spirit draws on "For Your Immortal Spirit Is in All Things: The Role of the Spirit in Creation." Quotation, 57.

[3]Ibid., 47.
[4]Ibid., 48.
[5]Ibid., 50-51.
[6]Ibid., 51.

[7]Ibid.

[8]Ibid., 52.

[9]Ibid., 53. Emphasis is that of Edwards.

[10]Ibid.

[11]Ibid., 55.

[12]Ibid.

[13]Ibid.

[14]Jürgen Moltmann, *The Life of the Spirit: A Universal Affirmation* (Minneapolis: Fortress Press, 1992), 10.

[15]Ibid.

[16]Edwards, "For Your Immortal Spirit Is in All Things," 56.

[17]Ibid.

[18]Ibid., 57. See the Council of Constantinople II of 553 and the Council of Florence in 1442.

[19]Edwards, "For Your Immortal Spirit Is in All Things," 58. Edwards cites *De veritate*, q.7, a.3. See also *Summa Theologiae*, 1a, q.37, a.2, ad 3; q.38, a.1, ad4; q.39, a.7; q.45, a.6.

[20]Edwards, "For Your Immortal Spirit Is in All Things," 59.

[21]Ibid.

[22]Ibid.

[23]Ibid.

[24]Ibid.

[25]Ibid., 60.

[26]Ibid., 61.

[27]Ibid.

[28]Ibid.

[29]Ibid.

[30]Ibid. Feminist theologians agree that these sciences provide evidence for a relational ontology. See Dawn M. Nothwehr, *Mutuality: A Formal Norm For Christian Social Ethics* (San Francisco: Catholic Scholars Press, 1998), 1. I specify this ontological relationship as mutuality.

[31]Edwards, "For Your Immortal Spirit Is in All Things," 62.

[32]Ibid.

[33]Ibid.

[34]Ibid. Edwards cites Bonaventure, *Hexaemeron* 12 and *Itinerarium,* 2:12.

[35]See Zachary Hayes's translation of Bonaventure, *The Journey of the Soul into God*, 6.2 in *Bonaventure: Mystical Writings* (New York: Crossroad, 1999), 110-11.

[36]Edwards, "For Your Immortal Spirit Is in All Things," 63.

[37]Ibid., 64.

[38]Ibid. See also Denis Edwards, "Ecology and the Holy Spirit," 142-59.

[39]Ibid.

[40]See Nothwehr, *Mutuality: A Formal Norm*, especially 233 and the definition of cosmic mutuality in particular.

[41]Edwards, "For Your Immortal Spirit Is in All Things," 61.

[42]Ibid.

[43]A small sample of this huge literature includes: in the natural sciences, Thomas Berry, *Dream of the Earth* (San Francisco: Sierra Club Books, 1988); in law, Roderick F. Nash, *The Rights of Nature: A History of Environmental Ethics* (Madison: University of Wisconsin Press, 1989); in psychology, James Serpell, *In the Company of Animals: A Study of Human-Animal Relationships* (London: Basil Blackwell, 1986); in philosophy, Erazim Kohak, *The Embers and the Stars: A Philosophical Inquiry into the Moral Sense of Nature* (Chicago: The University of Chicago Press, 1984); in political science, Jeremy Rifkin, *Biosphere Politics: A New Consciousness for a New Century* (New York: Crown Publishing, 1991); in agriculture, Wes Jackson, *New Roots for Agriculture* (Lincoln: University of Nebraska, 1987).

[44]Jean Porter, *The Recovery of Virtue: The Relevance of Aquinas for Christian Ethics* (Louisville: Westminster/John Knox Press, 1990), 44.

[45]See Daniel C. Maguire, *A New American Justice* (New York: Doubleday, 1980), 85-98.

[46]Edwards, "For Your Immortal Spirit Is in All Things," 65. See Jürgen Moltmann, *The Spirit of Life*, 12.

[47]See Rosemary Radford Ruether, *New Woman/New Earth: Sexist Ideologies and Liberation* (New York: Seabury, 1983), 186-214.

[48]See Elizabeth A. Johnson, *She Who Is: The Mystery of God in Feminist Theological Discourse* (New York: Crossroad, 1992), 14-18, 68, and 139-41. Also see Margaret A. Farley, "New Patterns of Relationships: Beginnings of a Moral Revolution," in Ronald P. Hamel and Kenneth R. Himes, eds., *Introduction to Christian Ethics: A Reader* (Mahwah, N.J.: Paulist Press, 1989), 63-79.

[49]This reclamation of mutuality is grounded in biblical tradition and in the work of their intellectual ancestors—Irenaeus, Hugh of St. Victor, Thomas Aquinas, John Duns Scotus, H. Richard Niebuhr, and Martin Buber. Here the treatment and use of formal norms is situated within the context of post-Vatican II revisionist Roman Catholic moral theology.

[50]See Catherine Mowry LaCugna, "God in Communion with Us," in Catherine Mowry LaCugna, ed., *Freeing Theology: Essentials of Theology in Feminist Perspective* (New York: Harper San Francisco, 1993), 104-8.

[51]See Elizabeth A. Johnson, *She Who Is*, 124-49, especially 148.

[52]Mahwah, N.J.: Paulist Press, 1993.

[53]Edwards, "The Integrity of Creation," 182-203.

[54]See Mary Parker Follett, *Creative Experience* (New York: Longman, Green & Company, 1924) and *Dynamic Administration* (New York: Harper and Brothers, 1942). Also Carter Heyward, *Touching Our Strength: The Erotic Love of God* (San Francisco: Harper and Row, 1989), 191: "Power is the ability to move, effect, make a difference; the energy to create or destroy, call forth or put down. Outside of a particular context, power bears neither positive or negative connotations. Power can be used for good or for ill. Using power-with others is good. Using power-over others is evil."

[55]See Nothwehr, *Mutuality: A Formal Norm*, especially 233. There I define

cosmic, gender, generative, and social mutuality in detail. This discussion of mutuality relies on that text.

[56]Edwards, "For Your Immortal Spirit Is in All Things," 61.

[57]Rosemary Radford Ruether, *Gaia and God: An Ecofeminist Theology of Earth Healing* (San Francisco: Harper, 1992), 2-3: "Ecofeminism brings together . . . ecology and feminism, in their full, or deep forms and explores how male domination of women and domination of nature are interconnected, both in cultural ideology and in social structures." See Beverly Wildung Harrison, "Politics of Energy Policy," in *Energy Ethics*, ed. Dieter Hessel (New York: Friendship Press, 1979), 56.

[58]Harrison, "Politics of Energy Policy," 58-59. See also Beverly Wildung Harrison, "Agendas for a New Theological Ethics," in *Church in Struggle: Liberation Theologies and Social Change in North America*, ed. William K. Tabb (New York: Monthly Review Press, 1986), 90-92.

[59]Harrison, "Agendas for a New Theological Ethics," 90.

[60]Harrison, "Politics of Energy Policy," 58-59.

[61]The belief that all things are imbued with God's being in the same way that all things are *in* God. God is more than all that is and is a consciousness and the highest unity possible.

[62]Rosemary Radford Reuther, *Sexism and God-Talk: Toward a Feminist Theology* (Boston: Beacon Press, 1993), 137.

[63]Edwards, "Your Immortal Spirit Is in All Things," 65.

[64]Ibid., 50-51.

[65]Beverly Wildung Harrison, "The Power of Anger in the Works of Love: Christian Ethics for Women and Other Strangers," *Union Seminary Quarterly Review* 36 (1981 Supplement): 52. Emphasis is that of Harrison.

[66]Edwards, "Making All Things New," 3-4. Basil of Caesarea held that every event of Jesus' life and every event in the history of salvation was a Spirit event and in reciprocal relation with the events of salvation.

[67]Harrison, "The Power of Anger in the Works of Love," 53. See also Carter Heyward, *Our Passion for Justice: Images of Power Sexuality and Liberation* (Cleveland: Pilgrim Press, 1984), 167.

[68]See Denis Edwards, "The Integrity of Creation," 182-203.

[69]Edwards, "Making All Things New," 5.

[70]See Leonard Swidler, "Mutuality: The Matrix for Mature Living—Some Philosophical and Christian Theological Reflections," *Religion and Intellectual Life* 3 (1985): 105-19.

[71]Ibid., 108.

[72]Ibid. Swidler cites the epistemological theories of Max Scheler and Karl Mannheim.

[73]See the reference to Laguna Pueblo/Sioux scholar Paula Gunn Allen in Johnson, *She Who Is*, 132-33.

[74]Swidler, "Mutuality: The Matrix for Mature Living," 109.

[75]Ibid., 110.

[76]See Martin Buber, *Between Man and Man*, trans. Ronald Gregor Smith (New

York: Macmillan, 1965), 22-23; Martin Buber, *I and Thou*, trans. Ronald Gregor Smith (New York: Charles Scribner, 1958), 96, 126; Robert E. Wood, *Martin Buber's Ontology*, Northwestern University Studies in Phenomenology and Existential Philosophy, ed. John Wild (Evanston, Ill.: Northwestern University Press, 1969), 70-71; and Martin Buber, "Interrogation of Martin Buber," by Maurice Friedman, in *Philosophical Investigations*, ed. Sydney Rome and Beatrice Rome (New York: Harper Torchbooks, 1970), 47.

[77]Edwards, "Your Immortal Spirit Is in All Things," 53.

[78]Swidler, "Mutuality: The Matrix For Mature Living," 111. The danger of relativism can be cared for by identifying presuppositions, acknowledging biases, purposefully seeking out other voices and opinions and probing them for the ways they challenge us, and holding modesty as the highest virtue. In the Christian community the focal coherence of scripture, traditions, and the *sensus fidelium* can provide additional safeguards.

[79]Edwards, "Making All Things New," 6.

[80]H. R. Niebuhr, *Responsible Self: An Essay in Christian Moral Philosophy* (New York: Harper and Row Publishers, 1978), 70-71.

[81]Ruth L. Smith, "Morality and Perceptions of Society: The Limits of Self-Interest," *Journal for the Scientific Study of Religion* 26 (1987): 289.

[82]Edwards, "Making All Things New," 6.

[83]Smith, "Morality and Perceptions of Society," 288-91. It could be argued that mutuality actually disempowers one because human finitude prevents any person from *always* dealing with *everything* and *everyone*. But, like the formal norms of love and justice, mutuality provides a standard and source of motivation, inspiration, vision, and instruction. To not consider mutuality, however, is to neglect a whole realm of moral responsibility and possibility.

[84]Margaret Catroneo, "A Contextual Catholic Ethics," Ph.D. diss. (Temple University, Philadelphia, Pa., 1983), 248.

[85]Edwards, "Making All Things New," 6-7.

[86]Edwards, "Your Immortal Spirit Is in All Things," 61.

[87]United States Catholic Bishops, *Renewing the Earth,* in Drew Christiansen and Walter Glazier, eds., *"And God Saw That It Was Good": Catholic Theology and the Environment* (Washington, D.C.: United States Catholic Conference, 1996), 223-43.

[88]Christine Firer Hinze, "Catholic Social Teaching and Ecological Ethics," in Drew Christiansen and Walter Glazier, eds., *"And God Saw That It Was Good,"* 167.

[89]Leonardo Boff, *Cry of the Earth, Cry of the Poor*, trans. Phillip Berryman (Maryknoll, N.Y.: Orbis Books, 1997), 104-5.

[90]Ibid., 105.

[91]Ibid.

Evangelization and Social Justice in Poland after 1989

Gerald J. Beyer

A little more than a decade has elapsed since the fall of communism in Poland. While positive changes have certainly taken place, many observers, including John Paul II, have noted the detrimental effects of the Polish socioeconomic transformations. Rising poverty, massive unemployment, sharp declines in real wages in some sectors, bungled health care reform, and growing disparities in access to education cause many Poles to wonder if things were better prior to 1989.[1] This essay analyzes the response of the Roman Catholic Church to the turbulent times in Poland since 1989. It advances the claim that Paul VI appropriately challenged local churches to apply the church's social teaching to their specific contexts, and that this requires proposing policies that embody the values espoused by Catholic social teaching.[2] With this in mind, this essay argues that the institutional church, more specifically the Polish bishops' conference,[3] has not yet fully recognized the promotion of concrete structures and policies necessary for social justice as a constitutive dimension of the preaching of the gospel (see 1971 Synod of Bishops, *Justitia in Mundo*). Moreover, the church in Poland must do so in order to be faithful to its mission of evangelization.

The argument of this paper unfolds in three stages. The initial section discusses two key themes: 1) the universal church's understanding of the relationship between evangelization, which is guided by "the gentle action of the Spirit"[4] and social justice, and 2) the specificity of the church's social teaching. By no means does it treat these issues exhaustively. However, raising them sets the stage for evaluating the Polish bishops' response to the signs of the times in post-1989

Poland. This initial section succinctly demonstrates that while the magisterium has often purported it should not propose concrete social and economic policies, it has quite appropriately done so.[5] The second section, which contains the bulk of the analysis, critically assesses some of the official positions of the Polish bishops' conference in order to discern how they have responded to the Polish "signs of the times" after 1989. Finally, the last segment of this essay indicates some normative directions for the church in order that it may faithfully respond to the signs of the times during Poland's "era of freedom."[6] It sketches a vision of solidarity, freedom, and participation that the church could appeal to in order to be faithful to its evangelical mission.

Before turning to the primary subject of this essay, a word is in order on why this topic should interest readers beyond Poland's borders. The Polish philosopher and chaplain of the Solidarity movement Józef Tischner has said that Christians on both sides of the former "iron curtain" have much to learn from one another. Furthermore, they must do so in order to restore faith in humanity after Auschwitz and Kołyma.[7] More than a decade after the fall of communism, little remains known in the United States about the churches in Poland and other countries in Central and Eastern Europe after 1989. Knowledge of theological and philosophical thought from this region is extremely scant.

While liberation theology is often viewed skeptically and misunderstood in Poland,[8] interesting parallels can be drawn between liberation theology in Latin America and the ethics of solidarity in Poland. As Fr. Józef Tischner maintained in a lecture given in Caracas in 1989, "The differences should not overshadow the similarities. . . . [T]he movement from individualistic religion towards [publicly] engaged religion is the essential achievement of both movements. We realize, of course, this is only the beginning . . . all the more reason that working together and exchanging experiences is necessary."[9] In the recent history of both places, the church has decried the deleterious consequences of neoliberalism, which assumes that economic growth (most often measured as GDP) alone fosters human and ecological well-being, that the state should continually shed its responsibilities in favor of privatization, and that the unfettered market always leads to the best outcomes.[10] The Latin American Jesuit provincials, for example, characterized neoliberalism as "a radical conception of capitalism that tends toward an absolutist view of the market, transforming it into the means, the method and the end of all rational and intelligent behavior."[11] This essay highlights the Polish bishops' increasing awareness of the pernicious effects of neoliberalism in Poland.

In addition to revealing shared values in the struggle for social justice, Catholicism in Poland intriguingly illustrates the ambiguity of the so-called "secularization thesis." Unlike most societies in Western Europe, more than 90 percent of Poles profess belief in God and 63 percent attend Sunday mass. This defies negative predictions made in the early nineties.[12] More than 35,000,000 Poles (roughly 90 percent of all Poles) are Roman Catholic. One can readily find the influence of religious values in Polish poetry, philosophy, art, and politics. In fact, the Polish government, in accordance with the wishes of John Paul II, is currently pressing for the explicit mention of "Christian values" in the European Constitution. However, almost half of all Poland's Roman Catholics believe the church should play little if any role in the public sphere.[13] The reputation of the church has been tarnished since 1989. While virtually everyone acknowledges the church's merits in the struggle with communism, its "triumphalism" after the victory generated harsh criticism.[14] Nonetheless, the institutional church continues to occupy an extremely important place in contemporary Poland. As Adam Michnik, a vocal critic of the church after 1989, states, "Polish democracy needs the church; it needs the voice of conscience. It needs a church that speaks the language of the Gospel."[15] For the outside observer, the rapid socioeconomic transformations, with events such as "Solidarity" strikes and major policy shifts taking place almost daily in Poland, provide a "living laboratory" in which the postulates of Catholic social thought can be analyzed "in real time."

Solidarity with all members of God's people must extend to this region of the world, as well as Latin America, Africa, Asia, and the rest of the globe. This often forgotten "heart of Europe," to use historian Norman Davies's phrase, continues to suffer from injustices stemming in part from American hegemony and programs forced upon it by international agencies.[16] Thus, Christians and all people of good will should take serious interest in what is going on today in Poland. Some of these negative trends have roots in the post-Yalta Soviet domination from 1945 to 1989; current global political and economic systems have caused others. Complicity in this state of affairs, which all

Westerners should acknowledge to some degree, demands attention and responsible action.

Evangelization, Social Justice, and the Specificity of Roman Catholic Social Teaching

Prior to Vatican II, the magisterium considered the pursuit of social justice, called the "social apostolate," to be "pre-evangelization." It was not seen as a part of the church's mission in the same way as, for example, celebrating the sacraments.[17] Vatican II's *Gaudium et Spes* initiated a reconceptualization of the meaning of evangelization and its relationship to social justice.[18] The 1971 Synod of Bishops went further in *Justitia in Mundo*. They argued that "[a]ction on behalf of justice and participation in the transformation of the world fully appear to us as a constitutive dimension of the preaching of the Gospel. . . . "[19] This text, in particular the word "constitutive," generated concerns about excessive "horizontalism." As a result, Paul VI clarified the issue in *Evangelii Nuntiandi* (1975), proclaiming that evangelization would be incomplete without concern for human rights and social justice. In other words, evangelization must include the pursuit of social justice as a necessary component, albeit a secondary one.[20] Announcing that God offers salvation to all in Jesus Christ constitutes the "foundation" and "center" of evangelization.[21] However, Paul VI located the primary means of evangelization in "the witness of an authentically Christian life, given over to God . . . and at the same time given over to one's neighbor with limitless zeal."[22]

Succinctly stated, the church must take some stance regarding socioeconomic issues and this constitutes an indispensable dimension of evangelization. However, disagreement arises concerning the level of specificity appropriate to the magisterium's teaching on such matters. On the one hand, Paul VI challenged local churches to "discern the options and commitments which are called for in order to bring about the social, political and economic changes . . . urgently needed."[23] Yet, *Justitia in Mundo* stated that the church's mission does not entail offering "concrete solutions in the social, economic and political spheres for justice in the world."[24] John Paul II advanced the same position in *Laborem Exercens*.[25] However, he, along with the previous popes, has not hesitated to offer specific policy proposals. For example, John Paul II offered concrete proposals concerning wages and joint ownership of the means of production in *Laborem Exercens*.[26] In an earlier case, John XXIII recommended agricultural subsidies.[27]

The U.S. Catholic Conference of Bishops clearly responded to Paul VI's challenge in *Octogesima Adveniens* (1971) with its pastoral *Economic Justice for All*. The bishops claimed that while their "prudential judgments" do not have the same level of authority as their moral principles, they "feel obliged to teach by example how Christians can undertake concrete analysis and make specific judgments on economic issues." They contended that the church's teaching cannot remain on the level of "appealing generalities."[28] The Bishops' Conference of England and Wales wrote likewise. In its view, remaining on the level of broad generalities to avoid controversy would be a "failure in moral courage."[29] The bishops recommended such policies as a statutory minimum wage, suggesting it should equal a living wage.[30]

In my judgment, these bishops' conferences appropriately heeded Paul VI for several reasons. As the French economist Jacques Drèze has said in regard to Catholic social teaching, "the concern for the poorest needs to be translated into more specific programs and effective policies; otherwise, the principle remains vague and sterile."[31] Policy proposals must consider the empirical realities of a given society. Therefore, local bishops' conferences cannot simply reiterate universal social teaching.[32] Of course, the more specific church teaching becomes the less certitude it can claim; complex policy issues may require technical expertise, and outcomes are often hard to predict. Thus, differences of opinion regarding concrete courses of action must be accepted.[33] Nonetheless, while recognizing this fact, bishops have an obligation to attempt to propose the concrete means to protect the dignity of the human person. Lay experts can and should lend their knowledge to this task.

Practically speaking, the bishops' collective voice carries much more weight than individual Catholics or Catholic organizations. Theologically speaking, if the bishops possess a special duty to proclaim the gospel,[34] and this involves the effective pursuit of social justice, they must be willing to propose policies that embody the church's social teaching. While much more could be said concerning these issues,[35] the Polish bishops' work constitutes the central concern of this essay. Turning to this, however, will facilitate exploring the "specificity question" more deeply.

The Polish Bishops' Response to the Signs of the Times
after the Revolution of 1989

The Polish bishops seldom spoke out on economic issues for most of the first decade after the fall of communism. When they did, their remarks were general and uncritically supportive of the government's reforms.[36] This was the case in spite of John Paul II's numerous pleas to read the signs of the times and respond to them. For example, during his 1997 pilgrimage the pontiff stated:

> We stand before the great challenges of the present day. I have drawn attention to this before, in my speech to the Bishops' Conference of Poland during my pilgrimage in 1991. At that time, I said "the human person is the way of the Church. . . . The task of the Episcopate and the Church in Poland is to somehow translate that into the language of concrete problems and tasks, utilizing the conciliar vision of the Church as the People of God and the related analogy of the 'signs of the times. ' "[37]

Exploring how the Polish bishops perceive the relationship between evangelization and social justice and their understanding of the specificity question will illuminate the bishops' shortcomings and more recent strides since 1989.

Evangelization and Social Justice

When asked in 2000 why the church had not issued a separate document on poverty in Poland, Bishop Chrapek of Radom responded: "Up until this point, action has been more important. I fear that we speak too uninterestingly about the Lord Jesus; social issues cannot dominate the basic mission of the Church, namely evangelization."[38] He also maintained that solidarity with the poor is a "consequence of faith." It does not belong to the most important task of the church. Yet, he also argued that the church is not faithful to its mission if it does not "stand unequivocally on the side of the poor and the marginalized."[39] There is a tension in what the bishop stated. On the one hand, he seems to view action on behalf of social justice as secondary to the church's mission. However, he also sees it as an intrinsic part of the mission. It is simply not part of what he calls "evangelization." He appears to be thinking in the pre-Vatican II terminology of "pre-evangelization." In my estimation, this confused notion of evangelization helps to explain the bishops' inertia in the face of the deleterious socioeconomic trends after 1989 in Poland.

Several important episcopal documents directly address the relationship between evangelization and social justice. Rather than making rash judgments based on one interview, an examination of these documents must be undertaken here. In a document published by the 309th Plenary Assembly of the Bishops' Conference, the bishops justified their concerns regarding poverty, unemployment, corruption, and rising crime by appealing to John Paul II's notion of "new evangelization."[40] According to the pope, "[t]he 'new evangelization' which the modern world urgently needs . . . must include among its essential elements a proclamation of the church's social doctrine."[41] An assessment of the bishops' treatment of concrete issues will follow in due course. For the moment, it suffices to note that they claimed to view concern for social problems under the rubric of "new evangelization." However, to what degree do they really accept the promotion of social justice as a constitutive element of preaching the gospel?

The Polish bishops devoted the first document ("The Need and Task of New Evangelization at the Dawn of the Third Century of Christianity") of the Second Plenary Synod, which lasted from 1991-1999, to the topic of "new evangelization" at the end of the millennium. The accent on the social justice dimension of evangelization is unmistakable here:

> The Church's mission of evangelization also concerns temporal realities. Making the world more human belongs to the essence of the economy of salvation, first, because the divine plan of making everything anew in Christ touches all of creation, and next because the inhuman dimensions of earthly realities hinders, and sometimes even precludes accepting the gift of salvation.[42]

The bishops acknowledged that evangelization entails witnessing to Christ's Gospel "by word," in addition to deed (no. 11; see also no. 13). However, they stressed the following among the "priorities of new evangelization" in Poland: propagating the principles of Catholic

social teaching (no. 52), the formation of consciences and the building of the moral order, which includes promoting the common good,
care for the needy (no. 54), and special concern for the poor, which
stems from the church's preferential option for the poor (no. 55). The
parish should facilitate attaining these goals. For example, the parish
community should teach and act in order to aid families, children, the
sick, the unemployed, and various professional groups (no. 48). Hence,
the bishops clearly highlighted concern for social justice as an aspect
of evangelization in this document. In this connection, they cited the
pope's exhortation to analyze the signs of the times (no. 15), which
was cited above.

   In the synodal document on the role of the laity ("Salt of the Earth:
The Vocation and Mission of the Laity"), which has been traditionally
neglected in the church in Poland, the bishops also described "proclaiming the Kingdom of God" through word and deed. In their view,
the laity "in their own way" participate in evangelization, which takes
place, as *Lumen Gentium* puts it, "in the ordinary surroundings of the
world."[43] Pondering this phrase, one wonders if and how the laity and
the ordained evangelize differently. This question will return later in
this essay. For the moment, the discussion of evangelization in the document on the missionary activity of the church is of immediate interest.

   In this document, the bishops appear to have qualified some of
their ideas from the document on evangelization. They chastised "excessive horizontalism," which they also referred to as the "secularization of salvation."[44] Citing John Paul II's admonitions in *Redemptoris
Missio*,[45] the bishops insisted that "Christians first and foremost should
'clearly affirm our faith in Christ, the one Savior of mankind, a faith
we have received as a gift from on high, not as a result of any merit of
our own.' "[46] Furthermore, "bearing witness to and proclaiming salvation in Jesus Christ and creating local churches" comprise the primary missionary activities of the church. Helping the poor, contributing to the liberation of the oppressed, aiding development, and
defending human rights represent legitimate missionary enterprises,
but must rightfully be seen as secondary.[47]

   Does a tension or even contradiction exist in the bishops' statements from various documents? Claiming that professing salvation in
Jesus Christ *ad gentes* constitutes the primary goal of evangelization
does not preclude viewing concern for social justice as part of its essence. This seems to be the position of the Polish bishops, which is

entirely consistent with Paul VI's position as it was described earlier. However, Paul VI also maintained, as was noted, that the primary means of evangelization, or proclaiming Christ to be our savior, comes in the form of an authentically Christian life given over to God and one's neighbor.

John Paul II and the Polish bishops have rightfully confronted religious indifferentism.[48] Giving "an account of one's hope" (1 Peter 3:15) must, of course, remain a perennial task of the church.[49] However, this goal becomes problematic if it hinders or omits striving for social justice.[50] Paul VI's formulation of "an authentically Christian life" as the primary means of evangelization precludes truncating evangelization is this manner. While the admonitions of John Paul II and the Polish bishops may be judicious, they could lead to an improper relativization or prioritization among the goals of evangelization. A dangerous lapse into seeing social justice as merely an addendum to the gospel, important but not necessary, lurks around the corner. In this case, the emphasis of *Justitia in Mundo* on "constitutive" is completely eradicated.[51]

Perhaps this type of prioritization among the goals of evangelization, whether conscious or not, partially explains the Polish bishops' scant attention to socioeconomic issues. Bishop Chrapek's statement seems to attest to this. If this is the case, the bishops have misconstrued the message of John Paul II, who told them that bishops especially must "lead the People of God . . . in announcing the Gospel of love, in calling attention to those whom no one mentions." In his words, the "enduring and selfless witness of active love has an inextricable link with evangelization because it witnesses to God's love."[52] Perhaps dissent exists among the bishops themselves regarding the weight they should accord social issues. The differences in the documents on "new evangelization" and "mission" are not irreconcilable. However, they may manifest disagreement. In fairness, one must mention a host of other factors that inhibited the bishops from speaking out. Reviewing them will demonstrate that the bishops did not sufficiently grapple with the "signs of the times" throughout most of Poland's era of freedom.[53]

Catholic social ethicist Aniela Dylus attributes the bishops' reticence during the first several years of the transformations to their fear of being perceived and portrayed as biased toward a political party. She also contends that the Polish bishops understandably wrote relatively little about the highly complex socioeconomic reforms. In her opinion, appealing to abstract principles and values such as the common good, social justice, or the primacy of labor over capital does not suffice. Evaluating socioeconomic issues, such as privatization, requires expertise beyond a general knowledge of Catholic social thought. In this sense, she justifies the "moderation" of the bishops concerning the socioeconomic realities of the nineties in Poland.[54] Jarosław Gowin blames the lack of serious and sustained reflection in this area, despite the existence of a theoretical basis for such reflection in *Centesimus Annus*, on several factors.[55] First, the bishops were not prepared for this "unexpected meeting with capitalism." In other words, the bishops lack the kind of training needed to undertake serious reflection on economics. Unfortunately, the distrust of laypersons that existed under communism continues to hinder fruitful consultation with lay experts.[56] Second, Gowin maintains that the anti-abortion theme dominated the speeches and statements of the episcopate.[57] While this may have changed in the latter part of the decade, abortion certainly absorbed the bishops' attention until 1997. Finally, the church feared that if it criticized the reforms, it would be attacked and deemed "anti-Polish" or "anti-national." In fact, the left and the right criticized the church. For example, the head of Prime Minister Hanna Suchocka's cabinet claimed that the church's hierarchy still acted as though it were in a battle with communism by not supporting the government's (neoliberal) reforms. On the other hand, Catholic intellectuals such as church historian Bohdan Cywiński criticized the hierarchy's blind acceptance of neoliberal economic proposals that invariably hurt the weakest members of society the most, thus violating the church's preferential option for the poor.[58]

This onslaught of criticism, coupled with the general decline of the church's authority in Poland, led many bishops to believe that the church should withdraw from the political arena.[59] Bishop Tadeusz Pieronek, the secretary general of the Polish episcopate from 1993 to 1998, proposed this course of action on many occasions.[60] However, like John Paul II, he has called for a church that is politically neutral but socially engaged. Bishop Pieronek offered an apologetic for and an indictment of the church's stance toward the socioeconomic trends and policies instituted in Poland in the last decade:

> Has the Church in Poland sufficiently called attention to the fate of the weakest? It was difficult to protest against appropriate

reforms. It was difficult to demand of bishops that they knew and proposed to the economists better solutions, especially because they assured us that the economic recovery would benefit all. The Church was still accused of not supported the reforms strongly enough. However, the Church can never give up calling attention to the most needy. . . . Enough of that voice did not exist in recent years, or at least it was not heard enough.[61]

Bishop Pieronek's observations, along with those of Aniela Dylus, point us in the direction of the related specificity question. In dealing with this issue, we will be able to examine more closely just what the bishops did or did not say.

The Specificity of Catholic Social Teaching

Should the bishops say nothing at all if they cannot adeptly handle complex socioeconomic policy questions, as Dylus seems to imply? Many Polish Catholics believe that the church should never publicly advocate a position on social issues, regardless of the bishops' knowledge of the subject.[62] Fr. Franciszek Kampka, an advisor to the bishops' conference on social issues, contended that when "it seems that the economic system does not respect the dignity of the human person, the Church cannot be silent and must take a strong stance." Yet, he maintained that the church's teaching on economic life must remain at a certain level of generality. The church should not analyze the technical, economic changes that economists handle. For example, the church might speak in favor of private property, but it should not propose a concrete model of privatization.[63]

As I have alluded, the bishops did write about the socioeconomic transformations of the early nineties, but only sporadically throughout most of the decade. They did delve into some specific policy areas in a few of the more recent synodal documents and in the 2001 pastoral *W trosce o nową kulturę życia i pracy* ("In Concern for a New Culture of Life and Work"). On these occasions, they have taken positive steps. However, they still have not gone far enough.

Prior to the synodal documents, the bishops' conference touched in a few places upon privatization and re-privatization,[64] poverty, unemployment, and the "wealth gap" in Poland.[65] Appealing to *Centesimus Annus*, the bishops mentioned that those plagued by unemployment and poverty deserve protection by "political organizations, unions and greater interest and aid from society."[66] They failed, however, to recommend concrete ways in which these various agents can and should aid those who suffer. The documents lack analysis of the causes of poverty and unemployment, and no relationship is shown between low wages and poverty.[67] To their credit, the bishops note that "blameless poverty" (a term the World Bank has used in contradistinction to "deserved poverty") often precludes educational opportunities for advancement. Yet, there is no mention of policies to remedy this injustice (such as targeted scholarship aid, raises in salaries for teachers in villages, and so on). In short, these documents, along with others similar in nature and tone, represent necessary attempts to speak out on social ills in Poland. However, they do not respond to Paul VI's call to "discern the options and commitments" necessary for social, economic, and political change that would make Polish society more just.

In the synodal document entitled "The Church on Socioeconomic Life," the bishops stated that although the church does not provide specific policy recommendations, it must denounce all forms of social injustice and formulate general principles that should govern socioeconomic life.[68] The bishops reiterated this stance in several other documents.[69] They also pointed out that some politicians mistakenly expected the hierarchy to designate "the Catholic position" in cases where the church leaves room for debate and disagreement on concrete applications of its teaching.[70] Appealing to *Gaudium et Spes*, they argued that the laity themselves should look for their own answers, and that it is wrong to expect concrete solutions to every problem from the bishops.[71] It is important to note that they excluded a significant qualification from the same paragraph of *Gaudium et Spes*: Bishops must endeavor in "unremitting study" in order to engage in greater dialogue with the world and ensure that "all earthly activities . . . will be bathed in the light of the Gospel."[72]

Many Poles had great expectations for the documents of the Second Polish Plenary Synod of Bishops. Committees headed by esteemed theologians such as Fr. Józef Tischner and Fr. Andrzej Zuberier created the preparatory documents. Lay experts also contributed to them. According to Gowin, however, many Polish bishops did not want to analyze problems seriously. They treated the synod as another celebratory, perfunctory event. They eventually limited the role of the laity, with the head of the conference, Archbishop Glemp, spearheading the way.[73] The preparatory documents, published in a collection, did not stimulate discussion among the hierarchy and eventually were tabled. Bishop Pieronek expressed his disappointment by saying that "we must openly admit that the bishops neglected the pastoral opportunity created by the Synod."[74]

Much of the synod's output amounted to "nice generalities," as Gowin opines.[75] For example, the document on evangelization spoke of all subjects taking on their responsibilities in the church and in society (no. 39) and concern for the poor (no. 55). The bishops did not discuss what this would look like concretely. The document on political life ("The Church on Political Reality") failed to go beyond prioritizing "effective education, a just distribution of goods, and conditions that foster creating jobs" (no. 17). It also tended to be much less critical than other documents of the obvious failures of the last decade, thanking "Mary, Mother of God, Queen of Poland" for the "decade of miraculous transformations in solidarity" (no. 54).[76] The document on education ("The School and University in the Life of the Church and Nation"), a worthy topic given Poland's sweeping educational reforms, did not describe discriminatory patterns regarding the right to education, which the Polish constitution of 1997 enshrines.[77] However, in spite of their claims to provide only norms, in some places the bishops moved to the level of concrete realities and policies. If one reads the first document as merely attempting to provide the theological basis for social concern by linking evangelization and social justice, then remaining on the level of generalities seems justified. As such a foundation, it is quite successful. However, the less than apparent links between the documents, along with outright tensions, cause the reader to wonder if the various committees responsible for each document view the specificity question differently.

The document on socioeconomic life is the most promising, along with some noteworthy portions of other documents. First, this document provides a philosophical framework that emphasizes solidarity while critiquing neoliberal economic policies and understandings of freedom that value profits over people (see nos. 8, 12, 26, 31, 45). To my knowledge, here for the first time the bishops explicitly echo John Paul II's criticisms of neoliberalism and its "false notion of freedom" in Poland.[78] Furthermore, the bishops attempt to demonstrate what an ethic of solidarity looks like in socioeconomic life. For example, they urge politicians and corporate boards to remember that "demanding and earning incommensurably high salaries is an expression of a lack of solidarity with millions of poor and it extinguishes the hope for a justly managed country" (no. 32). This is a timely exhortation, as politicians in Poland earn disproportionately high salaries[79] in the face of profound distrust toward them.[80] In a manner reminiscent of Józef Tischner's *Etyka Solidarnosci*[81] and John Paul II's *Laborem Exercens* from 1981, the bishops called on employers to "humanize" work by respecting the rights of workers and for workers to do their jobs diligently and honestly. This will forge healthy relations between labor and capital, which will be built on a "foundation of the virtue of solidarity" (no. 42). The bishops also exhorted all citizens to be in solidarity with the decision-makers who undertake often painful, but necessary reforms. This does not preclude real dialogue and the ability to raise doubts about specific policies. However, citizens should not berate public figures; this does not contribute to genuine public debate (no. 31).

The bishops discussed many other public policy issues in this document. For example, they opposed high taxes, which, in their conviction, hinder economic growth (no. 21). They proposed a system that would "equally distribute burdens and foster the creation of new jobs." It should also be "stable, just and take into consideration the taxpayer's number of dependents" (no. 33). The bishops repeated this last plea, which is part of the call for "pro-family politics" in several of the other documents.

The document on family life ("The Vocation to Life in Marriage and the Family"), placed immediately after the document on evangelization, pointed to specific rights of the family, which include the rights to having a family, residence, to work, medical services, and family benefits.[82] It deemed the current tax system "anti-family" for not securing these rights and denying children of large families the possibility of education and access to other cultural goods (no. 20). As the document on socioeconomic life mentioned, especially children from poorer families in villages complete higher education much less frequently than children of other backgrounds (no. 27). The document on socioeconomic life also described the various aspects of poverty and proposed concrete ways of combating it. For example, it pointed to the rising mortality rate of young men in Poland. It attributed this to the poor health of Poles, which is a consequence of environmental degradation, the organization of work, harmful technologies, and the stress caused by deprivation (no. 24). It also encouraged low-interest, long-term loans in order to ease the housing crisis (no. 36). In addition, the document on charitable work showed sensitivity to the many dimensions of poverty: the material, the social (in other words, marginalization), the psychological (helplessness), the intellectual, and the spiritual. As the bishops maintained, poverty can be measured objectively, according to empirical criteria and subjectively, considering the individual's determination of his or her own social status. According to the bishops, "the scope of human poverty, seen on various levels, has widened" (no. 21).

For the sake of brevity, this essay cannot examine every policy proposal in the synodal documents. It has merely attempted to demonstrate that the document on socioeconomic life, to a much greater degree than the others, exemplifies the direction in which the bishops should move. This is not to say that it is without flaws. Some of the concrete analysis lacks sophistication. For example, the discussion of taxes, which generates much debate among ethicists and economists, fails to cite from the ample research on the subject.[83] When do high taxes become inefficient and unacceptable? Are burdens shared equally by a "flat tax," which some economists in Poland have suggested? Rawls, for example, argues that progressive tax schemes are necessary in order to prevent excessive concentrations of wealth, which vitiate fair equality of opportunity.[84] Should there be a tax on dividends? How will the expensive social programs involved in their "pro-family politics" be funded? The discussion of poverty points to the rise in poverty in Poland without citing any sources. This may appear unnecessary. However, given that some dispute whether poverty has risen in Poland, the bishops should provide empirical verification.[85] Furthermore, the bishops would do well to point out that children suffer the most from poverty, not the elderly, as many mistakenly believe.[86] Certainly agriculture also merits attention. Approximately 30 percent of Polish society works in this sector and farmers suffer disproportionately from poverty. However, simply reiterating John XXIII's support for small family-owned farms appears naïve, given the contemporary challenges facing Polish agriculture.[87]

Despite any shortcomings, the document on socioeconomic life represents the best effort of the Polish bishops to take more seriously *Octogesima Adveniens*, no. 4, along with John Paul II's exhortations to them. In this vein, the Polish bishops noted that while charitable endeavors remain important, the church must "first and foremost shape the structures of social life, so that they will more effectively protect the weak and guarantee all people equal access to the common good."[88] The bishops even recommended the creation of a permanent institute dedicated to the study of socioeconomic affairs (no. 49). These are significant steps, given the historical neglect of Catholic social teaching and previous lethargy in the face of the crippling socioeconomic transformations.[89]

After the synod, the bishops published a pastoral letter on socioeconomic issues to commemorate the 110th anniversary of *Rerum Novarum,* along with several other shorter statements. Space precludes extensive treatment of these documents here. Only a few of the strengths and weaknesses of the pastoral letter may be noted.[90] Importantly, the bishops again stressed the relevance of an ethic of solidarity today. They intensified their critique of a "radical ideology of capitalism" and a distorted version of liberalism in Poland today. They also underlined an understanding of development that encompasses more than economic growth. The letter also situated concern about unemployment—its focus—within the framework of evangelization.

The treatment of unemployment itself largely recapitulated John Paul II's teaching on the dignity of labor from *Laborem Exercens.* It provided a helpful statistical overview of unemployment according to sectors, regions and age groups. However, the scant policy proposals were taken largely from *Centesimus Annus,* such as the bishops' mention of the role of the government in creating jobs. In doing so, they cited the pope's balancing of solidarity and subsidiarity and his recommendation of unemployment benefits and job retraining in order to facilitate workers' transition from faltering industries (see *CA* 15). They rightfully disapproved of the fact that 80 percent of the unemployed in Poland cannot obtain unemployment benefits. The bishops did assert that education must change with the times, in order to prepare young people for the new conditions of the labor market, which require the lifelong acquisition of skills. However, one searches for more specificity concerning unemployment in Poland. In this pastoral letter, the bishops repeatedly stated, "proposing technical solutions to the problem of unemployment exceeds our competence and our mission." Yet, as I have demonstrated, they have offered some concrete policies in their synodal document on socioeconomic life. In fact, their discussion of unemployment in that document accomplished more than the pastoral letter.[91]

Thus, one continues to encounter several tensions in the bishops' writing. On the one hand, they often reiterated that their teaching must remain on a certain level of generality. On the other hand, they moved at times to the level of policy. Hence, it appears obvious that the bishops continue to struggle with the specificity question. As we have seen, they posited a close relationship between evangelization and social justice in their writing in recent years. The effort put forth in the synodal document on socioeconomic life attests to this. However, the pastoral letter on unemployment, while containing much of value, does not accomplish enough. It is difficult, perhaps impossible, to discern why this is the case. Do the bishops not wholeheartedly see social justice as a constitutive element of preaching the gospel? Perhaps the real issue resides in the specificity question and the bishops' interpretation of *Octogesima Adveniens*, no. 4.

The Polish bishops seem to believe that Paul VI's challenge imposes the duty of creating policy options on the laity. In their pastoral letter, they cite *Octogesima Adveniens*, no. 48, which states that "it belongs to the laity, without waiting passively for orders and directives, to take the initiative freely and to infuse a Christian spirit into the mentality, customs, laws and structures of the communities in which they live." This essay has argued that the U.S. bishops appropriately taught by example how Catholic social teaching should be applied to the particulars of a given society. As Archbishop Weakland said upon the tenth anniversary of *Economic Justice for All*, "the teaching has grown and become more refined precisely because there were attempts to apply it to different problems at different periods of time."[92] Bishops must be a part of the task of translating Catholic social teaching into "the language of concrete problems and tasks," as John Paul II told the Polish bishops.[93] Certainly, the church teaches that the laity and clergy have different roles in the world; laypersons can and should hold political office, while priests should not. However, Paul VI did say that discerning the options necessary for social change belonged to "Christian communities, with the help of the Holy Spirit, in communion with the bishops who hold responsibility" and in dialogue with other Christians and persons of good will (*OA* 4). Ultimately, only the bishops can put forth an authoritative reading of the signs of the times in local churches. As I mentioned earlier, the unified voice of a bishops' conference will be able to project its ideas onto decision makers in politics and business more effectively than lay groups. Having said that, the role of the laity is indispensable, for the laity often possesses expertise that the bishops do not. Second, they can and should affect politics "on the inside" by holding office and by lobbying. If the Polish bishops truly want to shape socioeconomic realities in the way they intimated, then employing lay lobbyists as the U.S. bishops do seems appropriate.

This, of course, is but one means of "infusing the world with light of the Gospel," as is official social teaching. To their credit, the Polish bishops have acted by creating a foundation that awards one thousand scholarships annually to children of poor families from villages and small towns.[94] This essay has focused on the "educational-cultural" and "legislative-policy" functions of the Polish bishops' conference.[95] In other words, it has dealt with the church's role as a teacher through its social teaching, and it has hinted at its role as a political actor through direct policy advocacy. The conclusion offers some directions in which the Polish bishops may go in order to utilize these roles better to fulfill its mission of evangelization.

Conclusion: Toward the Church as Witness of Solidarity, Freedom, and Participation in Poland after 1989

In order to be faithful to its mission of evangelization, which must include striving for social justice, the church must promote solidarity, freedom, and participation. It must do so in the educational-cultural, legislative-policy, and prophetic-witness modes. In other words, the church must function as a teacher through its social teaching, a political actor through direct policy advocacy, and a witness by creating "within the church a clear counterpoint to existing societal vision and policies."[96] As this essay has intimated, John Paul II has continually stressed the need for the bishops to take on this responsibility. In his most recent pilgrimage to Poland, he implored the Polish bishops to "create and realize a pastoral program of mercy." This program, according to the pope, should shape the internal life of the church and "when right and necessary" should give rise to involvement in national, European, and global sociopolitical issues.[97]

The bishops have already begun their task by urging the return to an ethic of solidarity. After the successful bout with communism, many Poles did not see the relevance of solidarity to their new reality. The Polish bishops have begun to teach how solidarity relates to the concrete realities of contemporary Poland. They should continue to do so. Following John Paul's cues, they have also rebuked any understanding of freedom that puts economic growth above all else and that evades responsibility for others. This element of their teaching is extremely important, given that Poles continue to struggle to understand their newly found freedom.[98] Freedom is often confused with license or is reduced to economic freedom. It is often perceived to be hopelessly in conflict with solidarity. This notion of freedom has had, and will continue to have, pernicious consequences as policy makers craft courses that are influenced by it.

The bishops must also underscore the need for all members of Polish society to see themselves as active contributors to the common good. The marginalization of many groups, sometimes real, sometimes perceived, has deeply disenchanted many Poles since 1989. The bishops mention the principle of participation in their synodal document on political life (no. 7). They should also more vigorously emphasize that the denial of the right to participation, namely marginalization, can be a result of a denial of economic rights.[99] Their 2001 pastoral letter on unemployment contains this notion, as it portrays work as one's contribution to the divine plan and to one's society.

To reiterate, the key to an effective witnessing of solidarity, freedom, and participation will be applying these norms to concrete areas of life. The bishops did this admirably in their example of inordinately high wages among politicians and corporate managers. The next step should be applying Catholic social teaching on wages by advocating a living wage in Poland. The details of the Polish minimum wage statute cannot be described here.[100] In short, the minimum wage in Poland does not meet the "social minimum" category; in other words, it does not guarantee the basic necessities. In addition, the Federation of Private Employers has attacked legally mandating a minimum wage in its "Capitalist Manifesto." Thus, it is imperative that the Polish bishops defend the traditional Catholic living wage, as bishops in the United States and England have. Advocating a living wage has been one of the church's best expressions of solidarity with workers in the United States. Finally, a witness of solidarity, freedom, and participation must also draw attention to the particular obstacles experienced by women,[101] children, and minorities in Poland. While the bishops have begun to evangelize in the new Poland, much work remains to be done in order to protect the weakest members of society. This must entail greater and continued consultation with lay experts and the willingness to show how Catholic social teaching should apply to concrete realities in Poland today. In other words, they must achieve greater specificity in their social teaching.

While it is understandable that the bishops were not prepared to deal with complex social questions in a capitalist, democratic society, as Dylus and Gowin have pointed out, one must consider the extent to which the bishops have attempted to equip themselves with the necessary skills and knowledge. As Aquinas maintained, ignorance is culpable if the attempt is not made to gain as much knowledge as possible about a given situation. This essay suggests that the bishops have only begun to meet the new challenges of Polish society. Some of the Polish bishops clearly embrace the task more than others. Bishop Gołębiewski, for example, has created a committee for socioeconomic affairs in his diocese that addresses pressing concrete issues. He views this as an important component of the church's option for the poor.[102] He also has given his salary to families who were devastated by the massive floods in Poland in the nineties. Clearly, however, other bishops do not prioritize such attempts at promoting social justice and do not demonstrate solidarity in such ways.

One may ask to what extent the bishops, their advisors, and clergy truly live in solidarity with the poor. Bishop Pieronek believes that Catholics in Poland have a tendency to distance themselves from "others" and to listen to Christ's call "when it is convenient for them." Popular religiosity in Poland has not facilitated "a conversion of the heart" that leads to looking at "the other" through the eyes of Jesus.[103] While the bishops have initiated programs such as the scholarship aid mentioned above, many of them do not have routine, direct contact with the women, children, and men who experience suffering, prejudice, and marginalization. Most of them remain silent regarding intolerance toward immigrants, minorities, and those with AIDS.[104]

There are some positive examples. Bishop Zimoń from Śląsk, which suffers extraordinarily high unemployment, does attempt to defend and engage in dialogue with the blighted working class.[105] Yet, one still wonders if the option for the poor has been fully embraced by the bishops and the clergy in Poland today. Many lead a privileged lifestyle[106] and have little contact with the laity. Very few live like Sr. Małgorzata Chmielewska, who recently received an award from the bishops for creating communities for the homeless. She has made a conscious decision to live among the poor and share life with them, not just to sporadically reach out to them. Recognizing the many charitable works undertaken by the church, Jesuit Stanisław Musiał bemoans the fact that hundreds of people freeze to death in Poland each year, while church doors remain under lock and key every night. Maybe the bishops, or even the primate of Poland, should attend their funerals, he claims, in order to raise awareness. Moreover, he maintains that if bishops such as St. Basil and St. John Chrysostom lived in Poland today, much more money would be spent on scholarships, housing for the poor and elderly and free catechesis and Bible study rather than on massive basilicas and statues of John Paul II.[107]

As Christ taught, we should not judge our neighbors before truly repenting ourselves (Mt 7:1-5). Very few Christians can claim to be in solidarity with the poor always and in every possible way. One hopes, however, that today bishops in Poland and everywhere will lead the church in striving to fulfill the option for the poor. To a large extent, the witness of the church's leaders will determine whether or not Catholicism in Poland will remain strong and truly preach the gospel. This must entail, as Johann-Baptist Metz points out, demanding less "doctrinal rigorism" and more "radicalism" in the struggle for justice. He believes that people yearn for such a church. Poland needs a demanding church that eschews what Metz calls "bourgeoisie religion," which legitimates the prosperity of the "haves" by adopting an eschatology that projects God's reign of justice beyond this world.[108] The church in Poland must proclaim the good news with the poor and marginalized by awakening believers from their moral complacency. As the church in Poland struggles to find its place in a pluralistic, democratic, capitalist society, it must accept this role. It must, as Jarosław Gowin puts it, become "a church of more freedom and more demands."[109] For certain, many will resist this call and find solace elsewhere. The "haves" in Poland can now numb the emptiness of life without God and *communio* by turning to a life of materialistic pursuit, as many in Western countries have done for a long time. However, as Stefan Swieżawski argues, it is not the number of churchgoers that counts. Rather, it is more important to have even just a few believers who witness to the gospel with their whole lives.[110] It is most important that the church becomes a church of evangelization and social justice.

Notes

[1] In one survey, 56 percent of those polled declared that they lived a better life under the regime of Party First Secretary Edward Gierek from 1970 to 1980. Artur Wróblewski, "Place, placze," *Polityka*, 8 January 2000, 9. I have analyzed some of these socioeconomic phenomena in Gerald J. Beyer, "Towards an Ethical Evaluation of Poland's Transition to a Free-Market Economy and the Roman Catholic Church's Response," *Religion in Eastern Europe* XXI, no. 4 (2001): 12-42. The current essay uses some of the same information in order to explore a different issue.

[2] Paul VI, *Octogesima Adveniens*, no. 4, in *Catholic Social Thought: The Documentary Heritage*, ed. David J. O'Brien and Thomas A. Shannon (Maryknoll, N.Y.: Orbis Books, 1992), 266.

[3] Given my present limitations, I have chosen to focus on the bishops, rather than local Catholic organizations and individual members of the church. The rationale for this choice will become apparent in what follows.

[4] Paul VI, *Evangelii Nuntiandi*, no. 75, in *Catholic Social Thought: The Documentary Heritage*, ed. David J. O'Brien and Thomas A. Shannon (Maryknoll, N.Y.: Orbis Books, 1992), 335.

[5] I refer here to both the ordinary universal and ordinary nonuniversal magisterium (individual bishops, groups of bishops, and the bishop of Rome). See Richard R. Gaillardetz, *Teaching with Authority: A Theology of the Magisterium in the Church* (Collegeville, Minn.: Liturgical Press, 1997), 162ff.

[6] I have borrowed this phrase from the title of Jarosław Gowin's comprehensive study of the Roman Catholic Church in Poland after 1989. Jarosław Gowin, *Kosciol w czasach wolnosci 1989-1999* (Krakow: Znak, 1999).

[7] Józef Tischner, *W krainie schorowanej wyobrazni* (Krakow: Znak, 1997), 87. Kołyma is the Polish term for the largest of the Soviet "work camps," in which tens of millions of people died. Millions of Poles were deported to these camps, never to return to their homeland.

[8] See, for example, Tadeusz Dzidek, "Dokad zmierza wspolczesna teologia?," *Znak* 577 (2003): 16-18. The author accuses liberation theology of horizontalism. Gowin maintains that a similar perception of liberation theology prevented Poland's Primate Archbishop Glemp from fully supporting the Solidarity movement in the 1980s. Jarosław Gowin, "Kosciol a 'Solidarnosc,' " in *Leckja Sierpnia: Dziedzictwo "Solidarnosci" po dwudziestu latach,* ed. Dariusz Gawin (Warszawa: IFiS PAN, 2002), 21.

[9] This lecture was published as "Teologia wyzwolenia a etyka solidarnosci," in Józef Tischner, *Etyka solidarnosci oraz homo sovieticus* (Krakow: Znak, 1992), 200-201. According to Tischner, both movements link social liberation and religious salvation. Among the differences, Tischner highlights different perspectives on Marxism. He implies that liberation theologians might learn from the tragic results of the "Marxist revolution" in Poland.

[10]Neoliberalism in Latin America has also been described in William Greider, *One World, Ready or Not: The Manic Logic of Global Capitalism* (New York: Simon & Schuster, 1997), 263-284. For a useful comparison of what the author refers to as "Neo-Americanism" (i.e., neoliberalism) and the Rhine model of capitalism, see Michel Albert, *Capitalism vs. Capitalism: How America's Obsession with Individual Achievement and Short-Term Profit Has Led It to the Brink of Collapse* (New York: Four Walls Eight Windows, 1993).

[11]Jesuit Provincials of Latin America, "A Letter on Neoliberalism in Latin America," *Promotio Justitiae* 67 (1997): 43-49.

[12]Roman Andrzejewski, et al., *Katolicyzm polski dzis i jutro* (Krakow: Wydawnictwo M, 2001), 9-20.

[13]Ibid., 75-88.

[14]According to the Polish polling agency CBOS (1994), from 1987 to 1993 the approval of the Roman Catholic Church's role in public life fell from approximately 80 percent to 54 percent. Gowin describes this phenomenon and its reasons in *Kosciol po komunizmie*. He chronicles the events that caused the church to lose its popularity: the hierarchy's repeated uncompromising stance on abortion (including its prohibition when a mother's life is in jeopardy); the demand to return Roman Catholic religion classes to public schools; and the demand to regain church property that the Communists appropriated, even when this meant the closing of schools, hospitals, and shelters. See Jarosław Gowin, *Kosciol po komunizmie* (Krakow: Znak, 1995), 7. See also Piotr Mazurkiewicz, *Kosciol i demokracja* (Warszawa: Pax, 2001), 286-291. Mazurkiewicz also points to the fear of the church's desire to create a theocratic state and a post-communist ploy that actively sought to denigrate the church's reputation.

[15]Adam Michnik, *Kosciol, lewica, dialog* (Warszawa: Swiat ksiazek, 1998), 306. See also Roman Graczyk, *Polski Kosciol, Polska Demokracja* (Krakow: Uniwersytas, 1999), esp. 37-45.

[16]For example, the U.S. government recently provided a $3.8 billion loan to Poland for the purchase of 48 F-16 jet fighters, built by Lockheed Martin in Texas. Critics have called the deal a prime example of U.S. corporate welfare. Fighter planes manufactured by France and Sweden were said to have been more technologically advanced and offered at a lower price. See Charles M. Sennott, "Arms Deal Criticized as Corporate US Welfare," *The Boston Globe*, 14 January 2003, A1.

[17]Richard P. McBrien, "The Future Role of the Church in American Society," in *Religion and Politics in the American Milieu*, ed. L. Griffin (South Bend, Ind.: University of Notre Dame Press, 1986), 92.

[18]See, for example, *Gaudium et Spes*, nos. 34, 39, 40, 4, in Walter M. Abbott, *The Documents of Vatican II* (New York: Guild Press, 1966).

[19]World Synod of Bishops, "Justice in the World (*Justitia in Mundo*)," in *Catholic Social Thought: The Documentary Heritage*, ed. David J. O'Brien and Thomas A. Shannon (Maryknoll, N.Y.: Orbis Books, 1992), 289.

[20]Charles M. Murphy, "Action for Justice as Constitutive of the Preaching of

the Gospel: What Did the 1971 Synod Mean?," *Theological Studies* 44 (1983): 305. I rely here on Murphy's illuminating discussion of the drafting of *Justitia in Mundo* and its subsequent interpretation. Paul VI states: "evangelization would not be complete if it did not take account of the unceasing interplay between the Gospel and of man's concrete life, both personal and social. This is why evangelization involves an explicit message, adapted to the different situations constantly being realized, about the rights and duties of every human being, about family life without which personal growth and development is hardly possible, about life in society, about international life, peace, justice and development. . . ." Paul VI, *Evangelii Nuntiandi*, no. 30. See also nos. 29 and 31.

²¹Paul VI, *Evangelii Nuntiandi*, no. 27.

²²Ibid., no. 41.

²³Pope Paul VI, *Octogesima Adveniens*, no. 4.

²⁴World Synod of Bishops, *Justitia in Mundo*, 294.

²⁵See John Paul II, *Laborem Exercens*, no. 1, in *Catholic Social Thought: The Documentary Heritage*, ed. David J. O'Brien and Thomas A. Shannon (Maryknoll, N.Y.: Orbis, 1992), 352.

²⁶John Paul II, *Laborem Exercens*, nos. 19, 14. In regard to wages, John Paul II states that proper remuneration for a worker responsible for a family can and should be achieved by one of two means: a family wage or grants to mothers who devote themselves "exclusively to their families." Generally speaking, J. Bryan Hehir refers to the "moral and political specificity" of John Paul II's social teaching. See J. Bryan Hehir, "The Right and Competence of the Church in the American Case," in *One Hundred Years of Catholic Social Thought: Celebration and Challenge*, ed. John A. Coleman (Maryknoll, N.Y.: Orbis Books, 1991), 62.

²⁷Pope John XXIII, *Mater et Magistra*, no. 137, in *Catholic Social Thought: The Documentary Heritage*, ed. David J. O' Brien and Thomas A. Shannon (Maryknoll, N.Y.: Orbis Books, 1992), 106.

²⁸National Conference of Catholic Bishops, *Economic Justice for All: A Catholic Framework for Economic Life*, no. 20; see also nos. 134 and 135 in *Catholic Social Thought: The Documentary Heritage*, ed. David J. O'Brien and Thomas A. Shannon (Maryknoll, N.Y.: Orbis Books, 1992).

²⁹Catholic Bishops' Conference of England and Wales, *The Common Good and the Catholic Church's Social Teaching* (1996, accessed 1 May 2003), no. 54; available from http://www.osjspm.org/cst/britbish.htm.

³⁰Ibid., no. 97. A lengthier analysis would examine the work of other bishops' conferences as well.

³¹Jacques H. Drèze, "Ethics, Efficiency and the Social Doctrine of the Church," in *Social and Ethical Aspects of Economics: A Colloquium in the Vatican*, ed. Pontificium Consilium de Iustitia et Pace (Vatican City: Pontifical Council for Justice and Peace, 1992), 45.

³²See McBrien, "The Future Role of the Church in American Society," 92.

³³Charles Curran, *Catholic Social Teaching 1891-Present: A Historical, Theological and Ethical Analysis* (Washington, D.C.: Georgetown University Press, 2002), 113.

[34]See Paul VI, *Evangelii Nuntiandi*, no. 68.

[35]I recognize that many would disagree with my arguments here. J. Bryan Hehir discusses the criticisms of the "legislative-policy" function of the church in Hehir, "The Right and Competence of the Church in the American Case."

[36]See Gowin, *Kosciol po Komunizmie*, 273-278.

[37]John Paul II, *Jan Pawel II w Polsce, 31 maja 1997–10 czerwca 1997: przemowienia i homilie* (Krakow: Znak, 1997), 176. See also John Paul II, *Program dla Kosciola w Polsce: Jan Pawel II do polskich biskupow* (Krakow: Znak, 1998), 27, 37, 48; John Paul II, *Jan Pawel II: Polska 1999: przemowienia i homilie* (Marki: Michalineum, 1999), 76-77.

[38]See the interview with the bishop in Tomasz Goąb, "Kosciol ubogich" (*Gosc Niedzielny*, 21 January 2001, accessed 1 February 2001); available from http://www.opoka.org.pl/ biblioteka/T/TA/ TAC /kosciol_ubogich.html.

[39]Ibid.

[40]Konferencja Episkopatu Polski, *Szukajac swiatla na nowe tysiaclecie: slowo biskupow polskich na temat niektorych problemow spolecznych* (Opoka, 2000, accessed 12 January 2001); available from http://www.opoka.org.pl/biblioteka/ W/WE/kep/problemy_spoleczne_17122000.html. See also Konferencja Episkopatu Polski, *Komunikat z 322. zebrania plenarnego* (Konferencja Episkopatu Polski, 2003, accessed 23 May 2003); available from http://www.episkopat.pl/dokumenty/ komunikat322.html. In the latter document, the bishops deem care for the unemployed a part of the "mission of the Church."

[41]John Paul II, *Centesimus Annus*, no. 5, in *Catholic Social Thought: The Documentary Heritage*, ed. David J. O'Brien and Thomas A. Shannon (Maryknoll, N.Y.: Orbis Books, 1992), 443.

[42]Konferencja Episkopatu Polski, *Potrzeba i zadania nowej ewangelizacji na przelomie II i III tysiaclecia chrzescijanskiego* (Konferencja Episkopatu Polski, 2001, accessed 24 January 2003), no. 14; available from http://www.episkopat.pl/ dokumenty/synoddokumenty.pdf.

[43]Konferencja Episkopatu Polski, *Sol ziemi: powolanie i poslannictwo swieckich* (Konferencja Episkopatu Polski, 2001, accessed 24 January 2003); available from http://www.episkopat.pl/dokumenty/synoddokumenty.pdf. See also *Lumen Gentium*, no. 35.

[44]Konferencja Episkopatu Polski, *Misyjny adwent nowego tysiaclecia* (Konferencja Episkopatu Polski, 2001, accessed 24 January 2003); available from http://www.episkopat.pl/dokumenty/synoddokumenty.pdf.

[45]See John Paul II, *Redemptoris Missio,* nos. 9-11.

[46]The citation of John Paul II is taken from the English translation of *Redemptoris Missio*, no. 11.

[47]John Paul II, *Redemptoris Missio*, no. 83. Cited in Konferencja Episkopatu Polski, *Misyjny Advent Nowego Tysiaclecia*, no. 70. See also nos. 59, 63, 73 of the bishops' document, which stress charitable activities as a part of evangelization.

[48]John Paul II recently reminded the Roman Catholic bishops of Brazil that "it is not an act of charity to feed the poor or visit the suffering by taking human resources to them but not communicating to them the Word that saves." See

"Church's Social Work Is Not Political, John Paul II Says: Gospel Message Must Accompany Aid, He Tells Brazilian Bishops" (Zenit News Agency, October 21, 2002, accessed 7 November 2002); available from http://www.zenit.org.

[49]See Karl Rahner, "Anonymous Christianity and the Missionary Task of the Church," *Theological Investigations XII* (New York: Seabury Press, 1974), 177. For Rahner, missionary activity constitutes a form of love for God and the neighbor.

[50]One could adduce myriad biblical texts to support this claim. Amos 5:21 and Jeremiah 22:13-16 are among the well-known examples. John R. Donahue contends that knowing Yahweh is to take the cause of the needy and poor. In his view, doing justice is the "substance, not the application of religious faith." See John R. Donahue, "Biblical Perspectives on Justice," in *The Faith That Does Justice: Examining the Christian Sources for Social Change*, ed. John C. Haughey (Mahwah, N.J.: Paulist Press, 1977), 76.

[51]Murphy describes the effort to change "constitutive" by Bishop Torrella and later by John Paul II. See Murphy, "Action for Justice as Constitutive of the Preaching of the Gospel," 301-303.

[52]See John Paul II, *Program dla Kosciola w Polsce*, 36-37. The pope goes on to say, "let the voice of the Church be clear and audible everywhere where the fate and the rights of the homeless, deserted, hungry, disabled, and the marginalized needs to be recalled."

[53]I have discussed some of the following material in Beyer, "Towards an Ethical Evaluation of Poland's Transition to a Free-Market Economy and the Roman Catholic Church's Response." The article closely analyzes empirical trends in wages and poverty, which I cannot undertake here given the differences in nature and scope of the present paper.

[54]Aniela Dylus, *Zmiennosc i ciaglosc: polskie transformacje ustrojowe w horyzoncie etycznym* (Warszawa: Centrum im. Adama Smitha, 1997), 27-28.

[55]Gowin, *Kosciol w czasach wolnosci 1989-1999*, 274.

[56]This phenomenon is fairly widely recognized and criticized in Poland. Stanisława Grabska describes it in "Obywatele Kosciola" in *Dzieci Soboru zadaja pytanie: rozmowy o Soborze Watykanskim II*, ed. Zbigniew Nosowski (Warszawa: Biblioteka Wiez, 1996), 308. The bishops themselves criticize the lack of cooperation between the laity and clergy in the parish. See Konferencja Episkopatu Polski, *Sol ziemi: powolanie i poslannictwo swieckich*.

[57]Jarosław Gowin, *Kosciol po komunizmie* (Krakow: Znak, 1995), 107.

[58]Gowin, *Kosciol w czasach wolnosci 1989-1999*, 273.

[59]The controversy over "Radio Maryja," a "Catholic" radio station that tells its listeners whom to vote for and which parties to support also contributed to the problem. Its anti-European Union and anti-liberalism campaigns, along with the anti-Semitic comments of its listeners, generated much consternation. See also Jarosław Gowin, "Katolicy i polityka," *Rzeczpospolita*, 4 October 2003, A5.

[60]Gowin, *Kosciol w czasach wolnosci 1989-1999*, 278.

[61]Tadeusz Pieronek, "Zatroskanie o czlowieka," *Wiez* 488, no. 2 (1999): 47.

[62]See Mirosława Marody, "Polak-katolik w Europie," *Odra* 2 (1994): 696. Only

46 percent said that the church should advocate a public position on unemployment. Marody points out that in Ireland 76 percent said the church should take a position on unemployment.

[63]Franciszek Kampka, *Antropologiczne i spoleczne podstawy ladu gospodarczego w swietle nauczania kosciola* (Lublin: Redakcja Wydawnictw KUL, 1995), 26.

[64]Re-privatization refers to property appropriated by the Communists and its subsequent return to its prior owner.

[65]See, for example, Konferencja Episkopatu Polski, *"Spoleczny wymiar jubileuszu odkupienia: list na luty"* (Konferencja Episkopatu Polski, 2000, accessed 12 January 2001); available from http://www.episkopat.pl/dokumenty/d-17c.htm. Konferencja Episkopatu Polski, *Komunikat z 303. zebrania plenarnego* (Konferencja Episkopatu Polski, 2000, accessed 12 Jan. 2001); available from http://www.episkopat.pl/dokumenty/komunikat303.htm. The latter document contains a slightly higher degree of specificity than the other cited documents. It cites *Centesimus Annus* in regard to the primary duty of the state (see John Paul II, *Centesimus Annus*, no. 48). Yet, concrete directives as to how to fulfill that duty are absent.

[66]See Konferencja Episkopatu Polski, *Szukajac swiatla na nowe tysiaclecie.*

[67]See Beyer, "Towards an Ethical Evaluation of Poland's Transition to a Free-Market Economy and the Roman Catholic Church's Response."

[68]Konferencja Episkopatu Polski, *Kosciol wobec życia spoleczno-gospodarczego* (Konferencja Episkopatu Polski, 2001, accessed 24 Jan. 2003), no. 3, cf. no. 9; available from http://www.episkopat.pl/dokumenty/synoddokumenty.pdf.

[69]See Konferencja Episkopatu Polski, *Kosciol wobec rzeczywistosci politycznej* (Konferencja Episkopatu Polski, 2001, accessed 24 Jan. 2003), nos. 3, 10; available from http://www.episkopat.pl/dokumenty/synoddokumenty.pdf.

[70]Konferencja Episkopatu Polski, *Sol ziemi: powolanie i poslannictwo swieckich,* no. 19.

[71]Konferencja Episkopatu Polski, *Kosciol wobec rzeczywistosci politycznej,* no. 15.

[72]*Gaudium et Spes*, no. 43 in Abbott, *The Documents of Vatican II,* 244-45.

[73]Gowin, *Kosciol w czasach wolnosci 1989-1999,* 458.

[74]See Bishop Pieronek's statement in "Co Sobor zmienil w Polsce?," *Znak* 524, no.1 (1999): 15. Cited in Gowin, *Kosciol w czasach wolnosci 1989-1999,* 458.

[75]Given the limitations of this paper, I cannot examine all of the synodal documents in detail. Rather, I provide a sampling of the documents, in order to portray their overall character and the differences among them.

[76]For example, the document on charitable work states the following: "The years of transformations following 1989 are marked not only by indicators of growth, but also by myriad difficulties causing the impoverishment of many social groups, while others become rich. The state and local governments are not handling the social questions in this area. As a result, a mechanism of social degradation has appeared, which envelops the unemployed, large families, the homeless, the dis-

abled, children and inhabitants of villages and small towns." Konferencja Episkopatu Polski, *Posluga charytatywna kosciola*, no. 18 (Konferencja Episkopatu Polski, 2001, accessed 24 January 2003); available from http://www.episkopat.pl/dokumenty/synoddokumenty.pdf.

[77]See Konferencja Episkopatu Polski, *Szkola i uniwersytet w zyciu Kosciola i narodu* (Konferencja Episkopatu Polski, 2001, accessed 24 January 2003); available from http://www.episkopat.pl/dokumenty/synoddokumenty.pdf. This phenomenon is described in United Nations Development Program Poland, *National Human Development Report Poland 1998: Access to Education* (Warszawa: UNDP Poland, 1998), 45. See also Piotr Legutko, "Dwie szkoly, dwie Polski," *Tygodnik Powszechny*, 5 January 2003.

[78]Most recently, see his homily in Krakow on August 18, 2002. John Paul II, "Misterium nieprawosci i wyobraznia milosierdzia," *Tygodnik Powszechny*, 25 August 2002; available from http://www.tygodnik.com.pl/pielgrzymka%2011/homilia-blonia.html.

[79]See Beyer, "Toward an Ethical Evaluation of Poland's Transition to a Free-Market Economy and the Roman Catholic Church's Response," 20.

[80]On this topic, see "Enough," *The Economist*, 17 April 2003, 44.

[81]Józef Tischner, *Etyka Solidarnosci* (Krakow: Znak, 1981). The English translation is Jozef Tischner, *The Spirit of Solidarity*, 1st ed. (San Francisco: Harper & Row, 1984). See also Gerald J. Beyer, "Fr. Jozef Tischner (1931-2000): Chaplain of *Solidarnosc* and Philosopher of Hope," *Religion in Eastern Europe* XXI, no. 1 (2001).

[82]See Konferencja Episkopatu Polski, *Powolanie do życia w malzenstwie i rodzinie*, no. 15 (Konferencja Episkopatu Polski, 2001, accessed 24 January 2003); available from http://www.episkopat.pl/dokumenty/synoddokumenty.pdf.

[83]Herman Daly and John Cobb provide an overview of many of the issues in Herman E. Daly, John B. Cobb, and Clifford W. Cobb, *For the Common Good: Redirecting the Economy Toward Community, the Environment, and a Sustainable Future*, 2nd ed. (Boston: Beacon Press, 1994), 315-331.

[84]John Rawls, *A Theory of Justice*, rev. ed. (Cambridge, Mass.: Belknap Press of Harvard University Press, 1999), 246, 63.

[85]On a personal note, an editor of one of my manuscripts refused to believe that poverty has risen in Poland since 1989. For statistics on poverty, see Beyer, "Towards an Ethical Evaluation of Poland's Transition to a Free-Market Economy and the Roman Catholic Church's Response."

[86]Sociologist Elżbieta Tarkowska states that "[p]resently poverty in Poland is to a large degree the poverty of children. . . . This fact somehow does not reach the public consciousness, which associates poverty with old age rather than childhood. However, the latest . . . research shows that children to the age of fourteen represent 1/3 of all those living in extreme poverty, in other words, lower than the minimum for existence. Almost half of that group is constituted by persons below the age of twelve." Elżbieta Tarkowska, " 'Dziecinstwa zadnego nie mialem': bieda i dzieci," *Wiez* 488, no. 6 (1999): 65. The issue has important policy implications for pensions, among other things. The bishops do not mention this in their

discussion of pensions. See Beyer, "Towards an Ethical Evaluation of Poland's Transition to a Free-Market Economy and the Roman Catholic Church's Response," 18, 26.

[87]On the problems of agriculture in Poland, see for example Matthew Valencia, "Poland: Limping Towards Normality," *The Economist*, 27 October 2001, 14-15. Professor Edward Feliksik of the Academy of Agriculture in Krakow related to me in conversation that Polish farmers must be able to attain low-interest loans in order to create larger conglomerates. This, he believes, would give them the best chance of modernizing and competing with the heavily subsidized competition from Western Europe.

[88]Konferencja Episkopatu Polski, *Posluga charytatywna kosciola*, no. 57.

[89]Fr. Franciszek Kampka articulated to me in conversation that the bishops have not undertaken an analysis of the magnitude of *Economic Justice for All* partly because it is difficult enough to convince priests in Poland of the importance of Catholic social teaching. As for the neglect of Catholic social teaching, see Stanisław Pyszka, "Zaangazowanie chrzescijanin w polityke dzisiaj," in *Katolicka nauka spoleczna wobec wybranych problemow wspolczesnego swiata*, ed. Tomasz Homa (Krakow: WAM, 1995), 92-93.

[90]See Konferencja Episkopatu Polski, *W trosce o nową kulturężycia i pracy* (Konferencja Episkopatu Polskiego, 2001, accessed 24 January 2003); available from http://www.opoka.org.pl/biblioteka/W/WE/kep/list_spoleczny_30102001.html.

[91]See pages 66-68 in Konferencja Episkopatu Polski, *Kosciol wobec życia spoleczno-gospodarczego*.

[92]United States Catholic Conference of Bishops, "Economic Justice for All: Ten Years Later," *America* 176 (1997). Cited in Terence McGoldrick, "Episcopal Conferences Worldwide on Catholic Social Teaching," *Theological Studies* 59, no. 1 (1998): 23.

[93]See above, note 25.

[94]See the website of "Dzielo nowego tysiaclecia" at http://www.dzielo.pl/program_stypendialny.html.

[95]I borrow these categories from Hehir. See Hehir, "The Right and Competence of the Church in the American Case," 66-68.

[96]Ibid., 68.

[97]John Paul II, "Misterium nieprawosci i wyobraznia milosierdzia."

[98]Hence, the title of one of Józef Tischner's books, "The Unfortunate Gift of Freedom." Józef Tischner, *Nieszczesny dar wolnosci* (Krakow: Znak, 1996).

[99]David Hollenbach, "The Growing End of an Argument," *America* 153, no. 16 (1985): 363. See also National Conference of Catholic Bishops, *Economic Justice for All*, no. 71.

[100]I take this up in detail in Beyer, "Towards an Ethical Evaluation of Poland's Transition to a Free-Market Economy and the Roman Catholic Church's Response." See also Daniel Vaughan-Whitehead, *Paying the Price: The Wage Crisis in Central and Eastern Europe* (New York: St. Martin's Press, 1998), 252-271.

[101]A UNDP Poland-sponsored report claims that the situation of women has deteriorated in many respects since 1989. See Urszula Nowakowska, *Polish Women*

in the 90's (Women's Rights Center, 2000, accessed 19 March 2003); available from http://free.ngo.pl/temida/rapcont.htm.

[102]See Bishop Gołębiewski's statement in "Co Sobor zmienil w Polsce?," *Znak* 524, no. 1 (1999): 26.

[103]See Bishop Pieronek's statement in "Co Sobor zmienil w Polsce?," 21.

[104]Roman Graczyk, *Polski kosciol, polska demokracja*, 40.

[105]Damian Zimoń, "Gornicy to nie ballast," *Gazeta Wyborcza*, 12 September 2003, 21.

[106]See the statement on church finances by Bishop Gołębiewski in "Co Sobor zmienil w Polsce?," 28.

[107]Stanisław Musiał, *Dwanascie koszy ulomkow* (Krakow: Wydawnictwo Literackie, 2002), 89-95.

[108]Johann-Baptist Metz, "Messianic or 'Bourgeois' Religion?" in *Faith and the Future: Essays on Theology, Solidarity, and Modernity*, ed. Johann-Baptist Metz and Jürgen Moltmann (Maryknoll, N.Y.: Orbis Books, 1995), 23.

[109]Andzrejewski et al., *Katolicyzm polski dzis i jutro*, 114.

[110]Ibid., 118.

Discipleship and the Logic
of Transformative Catechesis

Robert Brancatelli

In the Matthean story of the "rich young man" who queries Jesus about eternal life (Mt 19:16-30), there is a confrontation between religious certainty and the demands of discipleship.[1] The young man assures Jesus that he has fulfilled the obligations of the law by not committing perjury, adultery, theft, or murder, and by honoring his parents and loving his neighbor. He appears to be a well-formed Jew, sincere in his quest to know God and eager to learn more about his faith. " 'All of these I have observed. What do I still lack?' " he asks Jesus (Mt 19:20). Jesus answers that if he wants to be "perfect" (*teleios*), he must sell his possessions, give the money to the poor, and follow him. But upon hearing this the young man "went away sad, for he had many possessions" (Mt 19:22).[2] Being rich, he lives in a state of privilege that prevents him from meeting the challenges of the kingdom. By adhering not only to the dictates of the law but to his possessions and all that they represent—certainty, security, control—he remains fixed in his own view of righteousness. He seems to have had an answer to his question even before approaching Jesus, and proves incapable of a discipleship in which the "many who are first will be last, and the last will be first" (Mt 19:30). However, even more than his riches, his certainty prevents him from attaining perfection. In the cultural and religious context of first-century Palestine, such certainty resulted from studying the Torah and prophets and abiding by the interpretations of the law of the scribal class. Today, in the Christian church religious certainty of this kind is often the unintended effect of catechesis.

The word "catechesis" has a somewhat obscure origin. It is derived from the ancient Greek *katecheo*, meaning to echo or resound, and appears in the Christian scriptures in the sense of giving instruction or witnessing to the faith (such as in Lk 1:4; Acts 18:25; Gal 6:6). In the early church it referred to the teaching a non-Christian received as part of the process leading to acceptance into the community of believers. The word survives today mainly in Roman Catholic and Orthodox Christianity in cognate forms such as "catechism," "catechumen," and "catechist," all of which relate to efforts to help individuals develop mature faith. Contemporary catechesis tends to emphasize the formation of disciples and not merely doctrinal instruction, which was the purpose of catechisms like the Baltimore Catechism and the parish program widely known as "CCD" (Confraternity of Christian Doctrine), both of which sought to impart church teaching and theological precepts to children and youth.[3] As a means of formation, catechesis socializes members into the cultural ethos of the church with the corresponding psychological, epistemic, and sociolinguistic systems supporting that ethos. In this way, it functions as a *true school of the faith*," helping individuals become disciples in the world and strengthen their commitment to the church.[4] It attempts to move beyond the instructional model by forming disciples who are ready "to be poor, without money or knapsack; to know how to accept rejection and persecution; to place one's trust in the Father and in support of the Holy Spirit; to expect no other reward than the joy of working for the Kingdom."[5]

However, this paper will argue that the way in which catechesis tries to achieve discipleship often mitigates against the faithful developing these evangelical characteristics and attitudes. Often, it leads to the kind of discipleship associated with the rich young man rather than the perfection demanded by Jesus. Fortunately, catechesis has another side. Rather than form disciples in the cultural ethos of the church, catechesis has the potential to challenge the faithful to a radical change of their personalities and the social structures in which they live. This is catechesis not as information or formation but *transformation*, which has been the subject of debate among catechetical theorists for some time, and is mentioned throughout contemporary magisterial documents such as the *General Directory for Catechesis* (1997) and the new *National Directory for Catechesis for the United States* (2004).[6] In fact, John Paul II has written that catechesis should help Christians understand "the mystery of Christ in the light of God's word, so that the whole of a person's humanity is *impregnated* by that word."[7]

In presenting a theory of transformative catechesis, this paper will connect Rosemary Haughton's distinction between formation and trans-formation to conversion. Specifically, it will 1) explore the ways in which catechesis as formation functions in a maintenance capacity despite stated objectives to the contrary; 2) identify the existence of what Jürgen Habermas and other critical theorists referred to as a "ra-tionality deficit" within catechesis; 3) offer an alternative rationality for catechesis derived from the concept of paradox; and 4) outline the principal characteristics of a transformative catechesis. In developing these points, this paper will refer to the Matthean story of the rich young man. Finally, although the context for this paper is Roman Ca-tholicism, including church documents, ecclesial structure, and a cer-tain sacramental sensibility, it is hoped that the implications of trans-formative catechesis will be relevant and applicable to all Christian faith traditions.

Catechesis as Formation

Although numerous magisterial documents describe the nature, purpose, objectives, and tasks of catechesis, defining it with any clar-ity and consistency has proven to be difficult given the complexity of conversion and maturity in the faith. These documents describe catechesis as a ministry of the word that "matures initial conversion to make it into a living, explicit and fruitful confession of faith: *'Catechesis has its origin in the confession of faith and leads to con-fession of faith.'"*[8] It attempts to put Christians "not only in touch, but in communion and intimacy, with Jesus Christ."[9] Ministry of the word refers to the gospel mandate to preach the kingdom of God and bap-tize all those who respond to the call to repentance. Since catechesis is said to take place after initial conversion, many regard it as enhancing *a priori* faith and therefore concerned strictly with formation. This view, however, ignores the unfortunate but common pastoral problem of Christians who are catechized but not yet "converted."

Rosemary Haughton's distinction between formation and transfor-mation in the context of relationships and the church is helpful to the current discussion. She identifies formation as "the process of using all the influences of culture to help people understand themselves and each other and the world they share."[10] It helps people "form satisfy-ing and stable emotional and social relationships. This is to be done through a well-ordered community setting in which mutual responsibility and the care of the weak are taken for granted."[11] Formation provides values and standards that create order out of chaos and a law for right living—namely, a social structure or society. Haughton views transformation differently. Rather than emphasize acceptance of and conformity to social norms, transformation involves the death of the old and the birth of the new person. It results from "surrender to the command to love" and the abandonment of all that went before—all certainty, security, control.[12] She defines this jump into the unknown as faith, which is required for the birth of the authentic human being rather than someone who is religious in the conventional sense. She believes that transformation leads to the "dissolution of all that ordinary people ordinarily value in themselves or others. The result of this dissolution, this death of the natural man, is the birth of the whole human being, the perfection of man, meaning both man as an individual and man as a race, because the process is at once personal and communal."[13]

Historically, Christianity has linked transformation to conversion or *metanoia*, but conversion to the formative structures of church does not always inspire people to reject ordinary values. Often, it involves accepting established patterns of behavior that have been sanctioned as normative by hegemonic groups that are as much a part of the church as they are of society. Seen in this way, conversion legitimizes the existing social and ecclesial orders instead of transforming them for the kingdom. Rather than change in response to an encounter with "other," which is the basis of Christian experience, conversion becomes an act of acquiescence to the socially determined ideals of discipleship, tradition, morality, and the law.[14] Discipleship is reduced to saying the right things in the right situations without taking the risk of faith, which has social and political implications far beyond knowing the catechism (information) and socialization (formation). Discipleship functions, as Peter Berger noted about religion in general, as a "sheltering canopy of the nomos," providing meaning for "those experiences that may reduce the individual to howling animality."[15] However, Haughton views the discipleship demanded by Jesus as "having no hierarchies, no morality, no past, no future, and no possibility of control or even of the observation of what is happening."[16] It lacks the canopy that law and religious certainty provide. This presents obvious challenges for those working in pastoral ministry. But if conversion remains a known quantity—a controlled experience entered into by those who have a conscience about the direction of their lives but without the willingness or ability to risk losing control—then it will be incapable of bringing about the death that Haughton's transformation requires.

In what ways does contemporary catechesis support formation? The new *National Directory for Catechesis* notes two of the most serious problems the ministry faces today: the lack of attention given to adult faith formation and the "relatively high percentage of Catholic children and young people who are not enrolled in any systematic catechetical program" (*NDC*, no. 9.32). The directory estimates this figure to be as high as one-third of all eligible children, with the number of high school youth "generally much higher" (*NDC*, no. 9.32). It is not surprising that these are considered to be serious problems, since both reflect a mindset in which the purpose of catechesis is to produce church members involved in the ministerial life of the community but not necessarily the kind of Christians ready to sell their possessions and follow Christ. Here, the purpose of catechesis is maintenance of the community rather than transformation of the individual who is then reintegrated into a body of like-minded and similarly transformed individuals. This difference is particularly striking given the fact that the baptismal catechumenate, in which one enters into a "sacramental sharing in Christ's dying and rising,"[17] is held up as the "source of inspiration" for all other forms of catechesis.[18] In catechesis as formation, "the believer is united to the community of disciples and appropriates the faith of the Church. The faith of the Church 'is a gift destined to grow in the hearts of believers'" (*NDC*, no. 20.19). In this socialization model, faith is demanded not in a transformative sense to Christ but in a formative way to the church, which is the "historical realization of God's gift of communion. As such, she is the origin, *locus*, and goal of catechesis. Catechesis springs from the Church" (*NDC*, no. 22.44).[19]

However, building the church and building the kingdom of God are not identical tasks, since the church has a purpose beyond its own survival.[20] By transmitting the *fidei depositum* in order to immerse youth "more deeply" in the church (*NDC*, no. 22.54), formative catechesis often legitimizes the status quo and fails to translate the symbolic language of Christianity into the language of everyday life.[21] This failure is evident in the inability of many parish programs to convey the implications of the faith in an age characterized by economic globalization, genetic engineering, suicide bombers, and "weapons of mass destruction."[22] Instead, catechists continue to teach the content of faith by employing traditional pedagogical models.[23] Priority is given to the church's faith (*fides quae*) over adult acceptance and exercise of that faith (*fides qua*) in the context of their lived experience. This leads to disillusionment on the part of parents and the "graduation effect" among youth who, once confirmed, move on to other concerns that have little or nothing to do with church.

Recent studies reflect this formative understanding of catechesis by measuring levels of participation in and satisfaction with religious education or CCD programs, but not analyzing the significance of these levels for conversion.[24] Such studies point to a growing concern over Catholic identity but continue to measure church vitality in terms of mass attendance, program enrollment, adherence to church teaching, and satisfaction with church leadership.[25] However, these are all measures of formative structures that do not take into account the prophetic or transformative dimension of church. The fact that many parishes continue to treat catechesis as if it were a subject taught in school with its own texts, lesson plans, discussion guides, and even holidays (Catechetical Sunday), undermines if not destroys its role in leading "people to enter the mystery of Christ and to uncover its meaning" (*NDC*, no. 22.42). Despite its popularity among diocesan and parish leaders, this school approach weakens the relationship between catechesis and the paschal mystery, which, as Haughton notes, must involve death in an existential sense or it is meaningless.

In many parishes, catechesis consists of preparing the "class" for a sacrament instead of offering participants an experience of dying-death-resurrection.[26] And although not exclusively an adult phenomenon, entering the mystery of Christ requires a radical change of the person, which is beyond the capacity of many young people trying to forge an identity during the difficult times of adolescence and early adulthood. This is the reason that "a fully Christian community can exist only when a systematic catechesis of all its members takes place and when an effective and well-developed catechesis of adults is regarded as the *central task* in the catechetical enterprise."[27] Unfortunately, not only is this ignored in many settings, but when adult formation does occur, it is often done through children's programs, as if this were the best way of capturing wayward parents. "Catechetical leaders identify children's sacramental preparation as one of the best underutilized opportunities in parishes for catechizing adults."[28]

Interestingly, although catechesis tends to function in this formative role in actual ministerial settings, some theorists have argued for its transformative dimension. For instance, Thomas Groome has identified a "conative pedagogy" based on "the wisdom of lived Christian faith and human freedom"[29] that educates people to "realize their own identity and agency in the world."[30] The philosophical mooring of this pedagogy is an "epistemic ontology" that regards those being catechized as "agent-subjects-in-relationship" and not merely *tabulae rasae* to be written upon for the purpose of instruction, or formed for a particular confessional identity.[31] His rejection of socialization as a model for catechesis, his emphasis on the need for individuals and communities to develop a historical-critical consciousness, and his creation of a process of "shared Christian praxis" demonstrate a lifelong commitment to the transformative aspects of catechesis.[32] Other theorists include Jane Regan, who advocates adult faith formation as well as the importance of transformative learning theory for catechesis, and Anne Marie Mongoven, who has elaborated a theory of "symbolic catechesis" whose purpose is personal and social transformation.[33] However, while these theorists approach catechesis as transformation, some differences exist between their articulation of transformation and transformative catechesis as presented here.[34]

The Rationality Deficit in Catechesis

If the neglect of adult catechesis and the inability of parish programs to transform people result from a preoccupation with formation, what are the reasons for this? There can be little doubt that this preoccupation exists, influencing the creation of catechetical theory as well as strategic plans, budgets, and resources on nearly every level.[35] Formation as the purpose of catechesis is such an established part of the ministry that to question it seems absurd. But the answer lies in the absurdity of such an act, for it is the *rationality* of catechesis that confines it to a formative role. This means that as long as catechesis remains grounded in the rationality of formation, it will fail to transform individuals and faith communities. What, then, is the rationality supporting formative catechesis?

In attempting to explain the relationship between human thought and action, critical theorist Jürgen Habermas described rationality as having "less to do with the possession of knowledge than with how speaking and acting subjects *acquire and use knowledge*."[36] In his work on rationality, he identified three "knowledge-constitutive interests" or areas of human activity related to knowledge:

> The human species has three cognitive interests: the technical, the practical and the emancipatory. These develop in three social media: labour, interaction and power (relations of domination and constraint). They are the conditions for the possibility of three sciences: the empirical-analytical, the hermeneutic and the critical. The role of the three sciences is to systematise and formalise the procedures required for basic human activities (controlling external conditions, communicating and reflecting) necessary for the functioning of the human species.[37]

For Habermas, technical interests are based on an instrumental rationality that refers to physical being: that which can be seen, scanned, weighed, measured, probed, or analyzed by its physical properties, including motion, time, and space. Instrumental rationality forms the basis of most scientific and technical experimentation in which observation, prediction, and verifiability are the distinguishing characteristics. This rationality is inappropriate, however, when applied to interests that are not characterized by the invariant laws of causality. For example, an instrumental interpretation of the Matthean story might regard discipleship as a way to earn "eternal life" and thus measurable by length of service, number of duties, and adherence to the Deuteronomic code (" 'All of these I have observed' " [Mt 19:20]).[38] As a result, Jesus' demand for sacrifice and perfection makes no sense. But this rationality fails to account for the changes that can occur during discipleship, when individuals and the group must grapple with substantive critical issues, questions of identity, and paradoxical situations.

Practical interests, on the other hand, involve a search for meaning through dialogue. The dialogue consists of inquiry and analysis to arrive at shared meanings and interpretations of events, rather than task-oriented solutions to problems. Along with practical interests, thought and behavior are judged to be rational when they conform to agreed-upon norms, with individuals determining rationality through interaction and consensus. The rationality underlying this interest is interpretative and hermeneutic, achieved through a distillation of the views expressed in the dialogue. Discipleship in this sense might involve the young man and other disciples interpreting Jesus' enigmatic sayings in a variety of ways, from a form of pedagogy to encoded messages concerning the anticipated revolt against the Romans. Ultimately, this rationality depends on the process of the dialogue and the background of the participants. What they think about Jesus and his demand to sell everything might change considerably over the course of the dialogue. There is a need, however, to reach agreement by the end of the process.

Habermas's final area of knowledge moves beyond the causality of instrumental logic and the subjectivity of hermeneutics to a critical theory of human existence. Emancipatory interests focus on power, domination, and the liberation of individuals from distorted knowledge.[39] Adults reflect critically on "reality" in order to become aware of and free from ideologies that impose social, political, economic, religious, or sexual constraints.[40] Through emancipation, they gain insight into their personal biographies in the context of the community and the community's historical development. Adults break free of ideological thinking not merely by gathering data (information), or reaching consensus with others (formation), but by dismantling and carefully reconstructing their lifeworld.[41] When viewed as an emancipatory interest, the young man's dilemma is seen as a confrontation between the widely held perception of discipleship and Jesus' demand for perfection. Jesus forces him to confront his intellectual detachment and conceptual manipulation of God, as well as his idolatry of mammon. As in all emancipatory interests, the young man is challenged to become a critical thinker capable of relating to self and others in new ways.

Which of these interests relate to contemporary catechesis? Catechesis functions as a practical interest by emphasizing conformity to a way of life (such as mass attendance, Lenten observances, sacraments, social justice activities, community building). But it also emphasizes knowledge of the faith (for example, the catechism, church teachings, magisterial documents, scripture). In this way, it uses hermeneutic rationality but holds fast to a twofold concept of discipleship as knowing the law (technical interest) and acting in accordance with that law (practical interest). Together, these create the metaphor of the people of God on a journey toward their heavenly home. Habermas defines this as *"normatively regulated action"* that orients a group to common values and an identity.[42] This regulated action provides cohesiveness and a sense of purpose that distinguish the group from all others. However, the disadvantage of catechesis as formation is its inability to reveal distortions, since it is concerned primarily with reconciling individuals to an existing reality (for example, church as people of God).[43]

In elaborating a communicative rationality common to all three interests, Habermas confronted instrumental logic and its dominance of modern consciousness. As a member of the Frankfurt School, he believed that this logic has become synonymous with reason itself so that the values of efficiency, measurability, uniformity, and a "tinkering attitude toward areas of experience that can be dealt with in terms of technological solutions" are seen as normative, while non-mechanistic thinking is treated as illogical and irrelevant.[44] Technical interests and their problem-solving logic have become the basis of Western reason. But critical theorists have argued that the "positivistic separation of fact from value, means from ends, politics from administration, and the exclusion of discourse over ends, values and purposes" have led to social crises.[45] They define a "rationality deficit" as the inappropriate application of instrumental rationality to practical and emancipatory interests. The application is inappropriate because the areas of knowledge, functions of language, and claims to validity are different for each interest. They have identified deficits in education, civil administration, and social policy, among others, due to the misapplication of "scientific solutions" to these areas. The demand for outcome-based curricula and improved standardized test scores among students in the nation's public school system are just two current examples of this misapplication.

An analogous deficit exists in contemporary catechesis, which continues to form children and youth through hermeneutic reasoning rather than concentrate on raising critical awareness among adults so that they will be capable of committing themselves to the kingdom. This deficit results from the inability of the formative processes in hermeneutic rationality to provide the encounter with the "other" needed for transformation, since these processes tend to support the assumptions of given reality rather than challenge them. Dialogue and consensus building do not guarantee emancipation from the psychological, epistemic, and sociolinguistic distortions resulting from socialization.[46] Habermas believed that hermeneutics lacks a "reference system" for moving beyond expressed values and ideals to the underlying social reality, which is often unconscious.[47] Thus, formative catechesis is incapable of transforming lives in any systematic way because of the limitations of its own rationality. In the end, it can only perpetuate existing worldviews, theories, programs, and structures, since the invitation to death it would offer the faithful represents its own demise.

The dependence on hermeneutic rationality as the basis for catechesis has far-reaching implications for the church. Ironically, by emphasizing formation over transformation, the church fosters the very apathy and alienation among youth that it seeks to eliminate. It presents an ordered reality consisting of classes, programs, social activities, and similar events that presume conversion among participants and a level of maturity in the faith that do not exist. Unfortunately, attempts to correct this style of ministry often result in even greater formative measures (such as more retreats, longer catechetical sessions, multi-year confirmation programs). For catechesis to be effective, it must work from an alternative rationality that transforms adults and liberates them from ideological structures, religious as well as secular.

Paradoxical Logic as an Alternative Rationality

A solution to the rationality deficit in catechesis may be found in Habermas's concept of an alternative rationality, which he believed could be applied to all three interests. This rationality involves

> discourse over norms and values as well as over means and facts. In such practical discourse the cultural traditions, aspirations, values and commitments of individuals would be negotiated in a form of communicative ethics which is implicit in human speech. Such discourse is essentially a practical discourse which relates to the questions of what can, might, and should be done in specific situations. . . . [S]uch discourse supports a normative order directed towards "emancipation, individuation, and the extension of communication free of domination."[48]

Ideally, an alternative rationality for catechesis will have the following characteristics. First, it will transcend instrumental and hermeneutic rationalities, since these tend to reinforce ideological thinking without challenging individuals or communities to change. And although better suited than instrumental rationality for catechesis, hermeneutic rationality does not necessarily lead to transformation.[49] Second, an alternative rationality will involve personal liberation as well as discipleship. For individuals to respond to the gift of God's grace, they must achieve a degree of awareness and freedom as human beings, for "God is fittingly honored by the person who is fully alive, and all the more so if the person is a mature adult. The Kingdom of God, like the seed in the field, grows above all through the activity of its adult members."[50] Third, the locus of reason for an alternative rationality must be situated in the community and not the individual, since solidarity is needed for free and open communication. This means that personal liberation from distortions depends on the emancipation of the group. Fourth, emancipation includes social, economic, and political systems, since building the kingdom requires eradicating oppressive structures and not merely isolated instances of injustice. Fifth, an alternative rationality must allow for ambiguity, contradiction, and conflict. It acknowledges *paradox* as a constitutive part of human and, therefore, Christian existence.

Haughton's treatment of ambiguity relates to this final characteristic. She believes that Christianity is ambiguous, because Christians must commit to "a whole series of irreconcilable assertions" that combine two perfectly acceptable concepts in a way that makes little or no sense.[51] For instance, Christians believe that through sacrifice and death one attains life, through poverty one finds riches, through the scandal of the cross one achieves salvation, and by eating bread and sharing wine one becomes part of the body of Christ. While it may seem reasonable for any religion to consider sacrifice, poverty, and death as part of its theological construct of the world, when it links these to fulfillment, riches, and life—and certainly not in a coincidental way— then the faith it offers demands acceptance of and surrender to ambiguity. Haughton believes that Christian transformation occurs precisely at this moment: "when the pathetic little spark of faith leaps between the poles of 'crucified' and 'Lord,' and the world is consumed in the transforming love of Christ."[52]

Ambiguity does not refer to the existence of opposite entities but to their combination in a seemingly irrational way. This reflects the paradoxical nature of faith, the ultimate expression of which is the Eucharist, which Haughton believes is an encounter not between the assembly and God but the assembly and ambiguity.

> The encounter is not with bread and wine as symbols of Christ's historical death even if we think of that death as a sacrifice, *nor* with Christ as a word meaning the individual's experience of salvation. It is both and both at once, and *that* is what makes the encounter a saving or a condemning one. The encounter is with the ambiguity, it is a demand for a leap not from one fact to the other but "in between," a self-giving into a blank which is *essentially* a blank to the human mind because there is no way whatever in which the two concepts, both perfectly easy to grasp separately, can be combined.[53]

The fact that the liturgy claims to be a memorial of Christ's passion (*anamnesis*) and a ritual meal shared through the invocation of the Holy Spirit (*epiclesis*)—combining past, present, and future in an eschatological *nunc aeternum* or "eternal now"—presents a problem. How can the liturgy be about Jesus' death and the community's life at the same time? This is a logical impossibility, contradicting the laws of instrumental rationality and the norms of hermeneutic rationality. But Haughton believes that acceptance of this paradox is a necessary condition of faith, and that acceptance requires personal surrender. "This surrender is senseless—you *can't* make *sense* of this link up, that is why it seems so suicidal."[54] Anything short of surrender leads to the self-deluding belief in one's ability to control other people and events. The fact that the rich young man walks away from Jesus reveals his fear not just of giving up his possessions but of relinquishing his *quid pro quo* understanding of salvation.

As part of the reality of human existence and Christian faith, paradox is anything but irrational. As a form of logic, it may be more rational than other forms because it concerns the ways in which people actually acquire and use knowledge. Paradoxical logic is also the focal point of a sacramental vision of life, revealing the reality beyond physical being through physical being. As such, it is decidedly incarnational. Thus, bread and wine become body and blood while retaining the appearance of bread and wine. The *Logos* becomes fully human while remaining fully divine. Two persons become one in marriage while remaining distinct. And the kingdom of God is fulfilled while remaining incomplete. These events of Christian faith describe a reality beyond the boundaries of instrumental and practical interests. They can be understood only in an emancipatory sense, which places the emphasis not on cause-effect or consensus but on the ability of the individual and community to undergo transformation. Paradoxical logic overturns conventional thinking because of its apparent "illogic." It is exemplified in parables, which "point not to another, supernatural world but to a new potentiality within this world of ours: to a real possibility of coming to see life and the world, and to experience them, in a way quite different from the one we are accustomed to."[55]

The concept of paradoxical logic is not new. Similar thinking has appeared throughout Christian history to further theological understanding and formulate doctrine. From Augustinian-Dionysian thought concerning the "dissimilar similarity" between creator and creatures and Thomas Aquinas's substantial presence in the Eucharist (*per modum substantiae*), to Nicholas de Cusa's "coincidence of opposites" and current sacramental theology, paradoxical logic has provided an alternative to conventional thought even if not considered a formal system of logic. Modern symbolic logic relies on deductive, tautological propositions but acknowledges the possibility of alternative forms. Ludwig Wittgenstein even imagined a "logic of contradictions" derived from human speech and communication.[56] He believed that "one needs to change one's imagery in the case of contradictions. One can change one's imagery in such a way that 'p and not-p' sounds entirely natural, as when we say, 'The negative doesn't add anything.' This is most important. We shall have to get into positions where it is necessary to have a new imagery which will make an absurd thing sound entirely natural."[57] Paradoxical logic does this by acknowledging the contradictory nature of human interaction. It defies technical and practical interests but is well suited for emancipation, because it frees people from roles and allows them to encounter each other in the disarray of authentic relationships.

How does paradoxical logic reflect the characteristics of an alternative rationality for catechesis listed earlier? To begin with, one must "accept the new 'logic of grace and of having compassion,'" or return to the purposive mentality and Weberian rationalization of religion found in modern consciousness.[58] Thus, paradoxical logic requires a rejection of instrumental and hermeneutic rationalities. Second, those who break free of ideological thinking and encounter paradox must rebuild their lifeworld according to their emancipated view of reality. Discipleship does not just accompany this act of rebuilding, but is a constitutive part of it. Third, catechesis can provide a community that welcomes these individuals and encourages others to a similar conversion. Haughton believes that transformation emerges from and returns to formation so that there is continuous movement toward deeper levels of conversion. Fourth, the commitment to free oneself from distortions is similar to that needed for social transformation, differing mainly in degree. However, since personal transformation does not guarantee social action, catechesis can help Christians understand that social, economic, and political systems are part of their faith and not secular phenomena to be acted upon through the application of credal statements or theological precepts.[59] Finally, paradoxical logic is itself paradoxical, since individuals must participate in and separate from the community at the same time. Ironically, the community that ignites "a total personal revolution, a complete change of the mode of existence, from the estrangement and muddle of sin to sharing in the life of God," may also stifle genuine efforts to change.[60] Paradoxical logic recognizes this not as hypocrisy but as a moment of grace and potential transformation.

Transformative Catechesis

The purpose of transformative catechesis is similar to that of formative catechesis: to provide opportunities for the faithful "to enter the mystery of Christ and to uncover its meaning" (*NDC*, no. 22.42). However, instead of relying on hermeneutic rationality to achieve this, transformative catechesis treats the mystery of Christ as an emancipatory interest, helping adults dismantle and reconstruct their lifeworlds in order to enter it. *Transformative catechesis helps Christians encounter the paschal mystery at the same time that they encounter their own dying-death-resurrection through a critical process of enlightenment and emancipation.* It offers an encounter with the paschal mystery in such a way that adults regard this mystery as real, relevant, and redeeming of their personal suffering and the social structures that deny their humanity. Thus, entering the mystery of Christ and uncovering its meaning are transformative only to the extent that people are able to do the same with their own lives in the faith community and wider world. Although many do not welcome transformation because it means questioning one's identity and facing one's fears, both are necessary for discipleship.

However, transformative catechesis is not another form of experiential catechesis, relating church teaching and scripture to human experience. It does not teach, mold, form, shape, or instruct through instrumental or hermeneutic rationalities. *Rather than reconcile the content of faith to a given reality, transformative catechesis creates a new reality founded on emancipation and discipleship.* It contains two basic approaches: creating opportunities for an encounter with Christ as "other," and helping individuals deal with an encounter that already has taken place. In either case, the encounter triggers emancipation and discipleship.[61] Without it, both of these may become stifled or evolve separately, with discipleship waning over time because of its perceived irrelevance to modern consciousness. Such an attitude only reinforces the formative view of catechesis and trivializes the role of religion in society. Naturally, the encounter alone may not transform, since ongoing discernment is needed to give it meaning and depth. But whether spontaneous, as in Paul's encounter on the road to Damascus, or gradual, as in Martin Luther's struggle to become a "professional monk," transformation depends on an affirmative response to the new lifeworld.[62] In other words, it must be received.

The pattern of seeking-finding-selling-buying found in many gospel narratives concerning the kingdom offers a possible critical process for transformative catechesis.[63] It is similar to processes identified by catechetical theorists as well as those found in critical theory and cognitive development.[64] The pattern resembles Bernard Lonergan's four transcendental activities, which lead people to deeper levels of consciousness. For instance, in Matthew's account the young man approaches Jesus in a seeking action that has been described as the "*sine qua non* for conversion" throughout scripture.[65] Conversion must begin with this action either in an overt form such as this, or an affirmative response to Jesus' call as in the case of Simon, Andrew, and James (Mk 1:16-20). At first, it appears that the young man has found what he had been searching for as Jesus reminds him of the law ("'If you wish to enter into life, keep the commandments'" [Mt 19:17b]). However, the young man gets more than he bargained for in the challenge to sell everything he has and follow Jesus. He cannot bring himself to cross the divide between seeking-finding and selling-buying, because he inhabits a lifeworld in which certainty and security weigh heavily upon him.[66] The fact that he "went away sad" indicates not only that Jesus' invitation does not make sense to him, but that it challenges his idea of truth. He has had an encounter of the magnitude required for transformation but has rejected its internal logic.

In this tale of "stymied conversion," the encounter required for transformation occurs between seeking-finding and selling-buying.[67] During that moment, the young man comes face to face with the reality of discipleship, which does not adhere to the conventional faith of his lifeworld.[68] But his assumptions about eternal life and his own righteousness have been shaken, since he seems to have appreciated the full import of Jesus' words: a new way of being a Jew through the loss of his socio-economic status. Having experienced seeking-finding, he discovers to his shock that he cannot accept what he has found. He proves incapable of selling his old life and buying the new one that Jesus offers, because doing so would change not only *what* he does but *who* he is. This demonstrates the fundamental difference between formative and transformative catechesis: the former does not depend on liberation from ideological thought and behavior, while the latter cannot occur without it. The young man turns away from discipleship, because he is unwilling to reconstruct his lifeworld and accept an alternative rationality. His fears of loss and ambiguity have blocked the transformative potential of the encounter.

In addition to providing a process for transformative catechesis, this seeking pattern is important for understanding the nature of transformation. At first, the pattern appears to be non-religious, since it contains no overtly religious themes or actions and presumably could be employed for a variety of ends. But closer inspection reveals that the divide between seeking-finding and selling-buying can be crossed only with faith. Instrumental knowledge induces few people to sell everything they have and buy a new way of being. Hermeneutic rationality also falls short, since the norms it establishes can actually undermine an individual's ability to challenge given reality. Attempts to cross the divide with anything other than emancipated faith will result in a rationality deficit that cannot be overcome with more factual knowledge or group sharing. Transformation is not merely a "human mechanism for conflict resolution . . . set in a religious context."[69] Rather, a transcendent "other" is a constitutive part of the process, since completion of the process requires Haughton's "jump into a void." In this way, transformation involves commitment as well as surrender, and in transformative catechesis the commitment is to Christ, who both models and effects redemption.

The *General Directory* recognizes the existential quest at the heart of transformation and connects it to the risen Christ:

> Faith and conversion arise from the *"heart,"* that is, they arise from the depth of the human person and they involve all that he is. By meeting Jesus Christ and by adhering to him the human being sees all of his deepest aspirations completely fulfilled. He finds what he had always been seeking and he finds it superabundantly. Faith responds to that *"waiting,"* often unconscious and always limited in its knowledge of the truth about God, about man himself and about the destiny that awaits him. It is like pure water which refreshes the journey of man, wandering in search of his home.[70]

There is a direct connection here between the human thirst for fulfillment and faith in Christ, who quenches that thirst as if "pure water." Through the paschal mystery, Christ shows that the way to become fully human is by giving oneself to the Father. In seeking truth and freedom in the struggle to be human, one encounters the God of creation and redemption. Thus, the seeking pattern works as a critical process for transformative catechesis, because it can be applied to emancipation and discipleship at the same time. For instance, many of the issues adults face that lead to encounter (such as job loss, divorce, mid-life crisis, retirement, death) are often paradoxical situations involving the search for meaning described above. This search is necessarily paschal, since it consists of the death of an oppressive lifeworld and the birth of a liberating one.

Instead of "teaching," transformative catechesis emphasizes the autonomy of adults as people who can bring their life experience to bear on questions of faith. This means that the catechetical process must be compelling enough to warrant their attention and commitment. The way to achieve this is not by creating artificial challenges, but by helping adults recognize the meaning of encounters they currently face. It involves reaching out to adults rather than expecting them to come to the parish or diocese to learn about their faith in a classroom setting. Transformative catechesis helps adults break free of ideological distortions and at the same time shows them that their struggle for emancipation is a faith-filled endeavor. It helps them question assumptions about reality and construct a new reality filled with the redemption of Christ.

Conclusion

This essay has argued that the way in which contemporary catechesis functions often leads to the kind of discipleship associated with the rich young man rather than the perfection demanded by Jesus. In order to counter this, this paper has presented another way of viewing catechesis and conversion based on critical theory and an alternative rationality. Rather than treat catechesis as formative, it has argued for recognition of the transformative dimension of catechesis, which requires a radical change of the person. The specifics of this change and the manner in which a Christian community balances formation and transformation—since both are needed for discipleship—require further research and reflection. But there can be little doubt that the answers to the questions raised here touch a number of disciplines, both within the catechetical world and without. For example, although the seeking pattern has been described as a faith endeavor, it remains a concern of psychologists, sociologists, and educators as well as catechists and pastoral leaders. And, as noted earlier, since the restored baptismal catechumenate is meant to inspire other forms of catechesis, what are the implications of its developmental model for transformative catechesis?

On a practical level, adult faith formation presents the most immediate opportunity and challenge. It is an opportunity, because it consists of specific goals with measurable outcomes and a direct connection to transformation theory. Thus, redirecting the emphasis from youth to adults in catechesis might not be as formidable a task as some suggest. It is a challenge because of the tremendous investment in formative catechesis that has been made historically at the parish and diocesan levels. However, the future of catechesis and evangelization rests on the ability of the church to convey not just the content of the Good News but its relevance to contemporary adult lives. It is in this sense that the United States' bishops have called for a change in the way catechesis is done and the way it is viewed by those responsible for it.

We are well aware that placing ongoing adult faith formation at the forefront of our catechetical planning and activity will mean real change in emphasis and priorities. In refocusing our catechetical priorities, we will all need to discover new ways of thinking and acting that will vigorously renew the faith and strengthen the missionary dynamism of the Church.[71]

Transformative catechesis is offered here as a possibility for thinking and acting in new ways. Its vision of transformation within the context of the human struggle for freedom may prove particularly relevant to a new age beset with age-old problems. It is a call for Christians to consider not just eternal life, but their earthly existence.

Notes

[1]All scriptural passages are taken from *The New American Bible* (Iowa Falls: World Bible Publishers, 1987). Compare Matthew's version with Mark 10:17-31 and Luke 18:18-30.

[2]In Mark's gospel in the original Greek he literally is "shocked" (*stygnasas*) by Jesus' response. See Mark 10:22.

[3]For a historical survey of the catechism, see Berard Marthaler, *The Catechism Yesterday and Today: The Evolution of a Genre* (Collegeville, Minn.: Liturgical Press, 1995). Marthaler notes that as early as "the thirteenth century the basic outline of the catechism was well established: the Creed, the Ten Commandments, the twofold precept of love of God and love of neighbor, the seven deadly sins, the seven principal virtues (faith, hope, charity, justice, prudence, temperance, fortitude), and the seven sacraments" (9). Whether intended solely *ad parochos* (*Catechismus Concilii Tridentini*), the clergy (*The Lay Folks' Catechism*), or everyone (the "Baltimore Catechism"), catechisms traditionally have attempted to provide systematic instruction to counter "confusion and ignorance regarding Catholic teachings" (110).

[4]Sacred Congregation for the Clergy, *General Directory for Catechesis* (Washington, D.C.: United States Catholic Conference, 1997), no. 91. Italics in original. Hereafter *GDC*.

[5]Ibid., no. 86, "Missionary initiation" (a).

[6]Since the publication of Horace Bushnell's *Christian Nurture* in 1847, the debate has been defined in terms of "nurture" or "conversion," although the contemporary tendency is to view it as nurture *and* conversion. See Mary C. Boys, *Educating in Faith: Maps and Visions* (Kansas City, Mo.: Sheed & Ward, 1989), 40-44. For transformation and "the new life of grace" in the *GDC*, see nos. 116-17. For the directory, see National Conference of Catholic Bishops, *National Directory for Catechesis for the United States* (Washington, D.C.: United States Catholic Conference, publication pending). Hereafter *NDC*. All citations refer to the draft version dated January 2002.

[7]John Paul II, Apostolic Exhortation, *Catechesi Tradendae* (16 October 1979): *AAS* 71 (1979), no. 20. Italics added. Hereafter *CT*.

[8]*GDC*, no. 82. Italics in original.

[9]*CT*, no. 5.

[10]Rosemary Haughton, *The Transformation of Man: A Study of Conversion and Community*, rev. ed. (Springfield, Ill.: Templegate Publishers, 1980), 7.

[11]Ibid.

[12]Ibid., 81. This surrender "is extremely painful because it means leaving behind all that seemed certain and comforting before, risking them—in fact, it means dying to them. And this is a real dying, a real leaving behind, without conditions, or it does not work. Faith is total abandonment, a jump into a void."

[13]Ibid., 7.

[14]For the importance of an encounter or *Begegnung* with "other," see Martin Buber, *I and Thou*, trans. Walter Kaufmann (New York: Charles Scribner's Sons, 1970). For Buber, "All actual life is encounter" (62). See also Donald Gelpi, "Religious Conversion: A New Way of Being," in *The Human Experience of Conversion: Persons and Structures in Transformation*, ed. Francis A. Eigo (Villanova, Pa.: Villanova University Press, 1987), 177. Echoing Bernard Lonergan, Gelpi defines initial conversion as "the decision to turn from irresponsible to responsible conduct in some realm of human experience."

[15]Peter L. Berger, *The Sacred Canopy: Elements of a Sociological Theory of Religion* (New York: Doubleday & Company, 1967), 55.

[16]Haughton, *The Transformation of Man*, 244. "It is this that creates the decision situation. The decision demanded is one involving self-surrender, a blind handing over of oneself in the face of a future which is blank." Interestingly, and contrary to the position taken in this paper, Haughton believes that "[t]here is no conscious *content* to the conversion event. Transformation is a timeless occurrence to which all previous and succeeding circumstances are totally irrelevant." Italics in original.

[17]*The Rite of Christian Initiation of Adults*, rev. ed., International Commission on English in the Liturgy (Collegeville, Minn.: Liturgical Press, 1988), no. 8.

[18]*GDC*, nos. 90-91.

[19]Italics in original. For a treatment of catechesis as socialization, see Berard Marthaler, "Socialization as a Model for Catechetics," in *Foundations of Religious Education*, ed. Padraic O'Hare (New York: Paulist Press, 1978), 64-92. The socialization model of "education in the faith has three objectives . . . (1) growth in personal faith; (2) religious affiliation; and (3) the maintenance and transmission of a religious tradition" (77).

[20]See Paul VI, Apostolic Exhortation, *Evangelii Nuntiandi* (8 December 1975): *AAS* 58 (1976), no. 14, and John Paul II, Encyclical Letter, *Redemptoris Missio* (7 December 1990): *AAS* 83 (1991), nos. 12-20.

[21]For "transmission" in catechesis, see *GDC*, nos. 78-79; *NDC*, nos. 19.14-15, 22.39-41; and *CT*, no. 6. *GDC*, no. 78 declares that the "true subject of catechesis is the Church."

[22]See the *National Profile of Catechetical Ministry: A Joint Project of the Na-*

tional Conference for Catechetical Leadership, the National Catholic Educational Association, and the United States Catholic Conference (Washington, D.C.: Center for Applied Research in the Apostolate, 2000), 3.

[23]Ibid., 4-6.

[24]Ibid., 4. Table 2 shows how parish religious education programs are "Stronger on Content of the Faith, Weaker on Its Implications."

[25]See, for example, Bryan T. Froehle and Mary L. Gautier, *The Catholic Church Today,* vol. 1, *Catholicism USA: A Portrait of the Catholic Church in the United States,* Center for Applied Research in the Apostolate (Maryknoll, N.Y.: Orbis Books, 2000), 63-86.

[26]*National Profile of Catechetical Ministry,* 5. "Sacramental preparation and a focus on children in general remains the centerpiece for parish religious education."

[27]International Council for Catechesis, *Adult Catechesis in the Christian Community: Some Principles and Guidelines* (Washington, D.C.: United States Catholic Conference, 1992), no. 25. Italics in original. Hereafter *ACCC.*

[28]*National Profile of Catechetical Ministry,* 3. Whatever might be gained in the short term by this tactic ultimately is lost by the continued neglect of substantive adult catechesis. See National Conference of Catholic Bishops, *Our Hearts Were Burning Within Us* (Washington, D.C.: United States Catholic Conference, 1995), 13, which states clearly that "adult faith formation should serve as the point of reference for catechesis for other age groups. It ought to be the 'organizing principle, which gives coherence to the various catechetical programs offered by a particular Church.'"

[29]Thomas Groome, *Sharing Faith: A Comprehensive Approach to Religious Education and Pastoral Ministry: The Way of Shared Praxis* (New York: HarperCollins, 1991), 85. Groome prefers "religious education" over "catechesis." For "conation," see 26-35; for "conative pedagogy," 85-131.

[30]Ibid., 28.

[31]Ibid., 20.

[32]Groome believes that in order to achieve "identity *and* agency in Christian faith, socialization alone is insufficient, in and of itself, to promote ongoing conversion in people's faith journey, the renewal of the faith community itself, and the ministry of the church to be a sacrament of social transformation. As the church educates, so the church needs to be educated" (ibid., 102). Italics in original. In addition to critical social theory, Groome works with Martin Heidegger's concepts of *Dasein* ("being itself") and *Seinsvergessenheit* ("forgetfulness of being") to develop his theory of epistemic ontology.

[33]See Jane Regan, *Toward an Adult Church: A Vision of Faith Formation* (Chicago, Ill: Loyola Press, 2002) and Anne Marie Mongoven, *The Prophetic Spirit of Catechesis: How We Share the Fire in Our Hearts* (Mahwah, N.J.: Paulist Press, 2000). For Mongoven, catechesis "calls both individuals and the community to conversion. This call is not just to those joining the church for the first time, but it is a lifelong continuing summons to transformation of life to every member of the community" (26).

[34]The major differences between Groome's conative pedagogy and transformative catechesis include their respective philosophical underpinnings (epistemic ontology versus paradoxical logic), the recognition in transformative catechesis of a "trigger event" in conversion, transformative catechesis's focus on discernment rather than dialogue, and the close connection of transformative catechesis to the model of catechesis presented in the RCIA. These differences will be developed elsewhere.

[35]*Our Hearts Were Burning Within Us*, 13-14. "While most Catholic parishes place a high priority on the faith formation of children and youth, far fewer treat adult faith formation as a priority. This choice is made in parish staffing decisions, job descriptions, budgets, and parishioner expectations."

[36]Jürgen Habermas, *The Theory of Communicative Action*, vol. 1, *Reason and the Rationalization of Society*, trans. Thomas McCarthy (Boston: Beacon Press, 1984), 8. Italics in original.

[37]R. Roderick, *Habermas and the Foundations of Critical Theory* (New York: St. Martin's Press, 1986), 53, quoted in Gerry D. Ewert, "Habermas and Education: A Comprehensive Overview of the Influence of Habermas in Educational Literature," *Review of Educational Research*, 61 (Fall 1991): 347.

[38]See Edward Schillebeeckx, *Jesus: An Experiment in Christology*, trans. Hubert Hoskins (New York: Crossroad, 1979), 162-63. "Jewish spirituality in those days was based on obedience to God, with the Law as a norm. It was an objective quantity . . . by which to gauge concretely the prospect of coming to salvation or to judgment. . . . An exact knowledge of the Law was naturally a proviso and the basis of any reasonable hope of salvation. The *'amè ha' ares*, the common people, who had no such knowledge of the Law, were because of that very fact badly placed as regards salvation. But anyone who knew the Law and fulfilled it exactly could be assured of salvation; for then God was obligated, by dint of his own righteousness, to give that faithful one salvation."

[39]For distortions, see Jack Mezirow, *Transformative Dimensions of Adult Learning* (New York: John Wiley & Sons, 1991), 118. A distortion is an assumption or premise that leads people "to view reality in a way that arbitrarily limits what is included, impedes differentiation, lacks permeability or openness to other ways of seeing, or does not facilitate an integration of experience." Mezirow identifies epistemic, sociolinguistic, and psychological premise distortions (123-43).

[40]Jack Mezirow, "A Critical Theory of Adult Learning and Education," *Adult Education* 32 (1981): 5-6, quoted in Ewert, "Habermas and Education," 354.

[41]Mezirow, *Transformative Dimensions of Adult Learning*, 69. This is "a vast inventory of unquestioned assumptions and shared cultural convictions, including codes, norms, roles, social practices, psychological patterns of dealing with others, and individual skills. Communicated through language, it provides learners with a basis from which to begin negotiating common definitions of situations."

[42]Habermas, *The Theory of Communicative Action*, vol. 1, 85. Italics in original.

[43]See Wilfred Carr and Stephen Kemmis, *Becoming Critical: Education, Knowledge and Action Research* (Philadelphia: Falmer Press, 1986), 98. Carr and Kemmis

conclude that "the interpretive approach encourages people to change the ways that they *think* about what they are doing, rather than suggest ways in which they should change what they *are* doing. Hence, although interpretive theories may be able to transform consciousness of social reality they can reveal no direct interest in providing methods for a crucial examination of social reality itself." They see this approach as "indifferent to the need for social theory to be critical of the *status quo*." Italics in original.

⁴⁴C. A. Bowers, "Emergent Ideological Characteristics of Educational Policy," *Teachers College Record* 79 (1): 36-37, quoted in Ewert, "Habermas and Education," 349.

⁴⁵R. J. Bates, "Towards a Critical Practice of Educational Administration" (paper presented at the annual meeting of the American Educational Research Association, New York, April 1982), 6-7, quoted in Ewert, "Habermas and Education," 368.

⁴⁶Carr and Kemmis, *Becoming Critical*, 94-99. See also Ewert, "Habermas and Education," 353. "It is entirely possible that social reality reflected in the norms, expectations, and understandings of action can be both meaningful to its members and totally false." In transformative catechesis, dialogue is seen as limited in its ability to overcome ideological distortion, and in this point it follows Habermas rather than Hans-Georg Gadamer. As stated earlier, this is different from Groome's pedagogy, which is more in line with Gadamer's hermeneutical theory. See Groome, *Sharing Faith*, 476-78.

⁴⁷Georgia Warnke, *Gadamer: Hermeneutics, Tradition and Reason* (Stanford, Calif.: Stanford University Press, 1987), 116-17. Habermas argued that a "theoretical, methodologically self-conscious approach" is needed, "for which hermeneutics is insufficient" (117).

⁴⁸Bates, "Towards a Critical Practice of Educational Administration," 7, quoted in Ewert, "Habermas and Education," 368. This "practical discourse" will be developed elsewhere as a form of discernment that plays a crucial role in the process for transformative catechesis.

⁴⁹Carr and Kemmis, *Becoming Critical*, 99. In both the instrumental and hermeneutic approaches, "the researcher stands outside the researched situation adopting a disinterested stance in which any explicit concern with critically evaluating and changing the educational realities being analyzed is rejected. Thus despite its insistence that educational realities are subjectively structured, rather than objectively given, the interpretive approach, like positivism, pursues the common methodological aim of describing social reality in a neutral, disinterested way."

⁵⁰*ACCC*, no. 24.

⁵¹Haughton, *The Transformation of Man*, 273.

⁵²Ibid., 280.

⁵³Ibid., 274. Italics in original.

⁵⁴Ibid., 275. Italics in original.

⁵⁵Schillebeeckx, *Jesus: An Experiment in Christology*, 157. "Parables open up new and different potentialities for living, often in contrast with our own conventional ways of behaving; they offer a chance to experience things in a new way. Parables can have a strong practical and critical effect that may prompt a renewal

of life and society. Although derived from familiar things and happenings in everyday life, by slipping in the scandalous, paradoxical or surprising element they cut right across our spontaneous reactions and behavior."

[56]Cora Diamond, ed., *Wittgenstein's Lectures on the Foundations of Mathematics* (Ithaca, N.Y.: Cornell University Press, 1976), 189.

[57]Ibid., 187. "I would say that anything which we give and conceive to be an explanation of *why* a contradiction does not work is always just another way of saying that we do not want it to work. . . ."

"In logic one deals with tautologies—propositions like '~(p.~p)'. But one might just as well deal with contradictions instead. So that *Principia Mathematica* would not be a collection of tautologies but a collection of contradictions" (ibid.). Italics in original. Interestingly, in *Principia Mathematica* Bertrand Russell attempted to show that mathematics is based on universal, objective truths and therefore free of contradiction. His aim, as Descartes' before him, was certainty rather than ambiguity. Russell "wanted certainty in the kind of way in which people want religious faith. I thought that certainty is more likely to be found in mathematics than elsewhere. But I discovered that many mathematical demonstrations, which my teachers expected me to accept, were full of fallacies, and that, if certainty were indeed discoverable in mathematics, it would be in a new field of mathematics, with more solid foundations than those that had hitherto been thought secure" (Bertrand Russell, *Portraits from Memory and Other Essays* (New York: Simon & Schuster, 1956), 54, quoted in Philip J. Davis, "Fidelity in Mathematical Discourse," in *New Directions in the Philosophy of Mathematics*, ed. Thomas Tymoczko (Boston: Birkhäuser, 1985), 165.

[58]Schillebeeckx, *Jesus: An Experiment in Christology*, 158.

[59]See Daniel M. Bell, *Liberation Theology after the End of History* (New York: Routledge, 2001), 72-73. Bell views "Christianity not as the apolitical custodian of abstract moral values like 'love' that have to be translated into politics, but, rather, as a social, political, economic formation (an ensemble of technologies of desire) vying with other formations (technologies of desire) on a single field of lived experience. . . . All of this is to say that the Church is a public that, short of emasculation, cannot inhabit the private, apolitical space assigned to it as a prison cell by modernity."

[60]Haughton, *The Transformation of Man*, 215-16.

[61]The need for some type of encounter appears throughout the literature on religious conversion and human transformation. See, for example, Mezirow, *Transformative Dimensions of Adult Learning*, 169-74, for "disorienting dilemma" and "trigger event"; Haughton, *The Transformation of Man*, 38, for "conflict situation"; James Loder, *The Transforming Moment: Understanding Convictional Experiences* (San Francisco: Harper & Row, 1981), 35, for "conflict" and "tension"; Frank Musgrove, *Margins of the Mind* (London: Methuen, 1977), for the experience of "marginality"; and Ross Keane, "The Doubting Journey: A Learning Process of Self-Transformation," in *Appreciating Adults Learning: From the Learners' Perspective*, ed. David Boyd and Virginia Griffin (London: Kogan Page, 1987), 90, for a "disorientation phase."

[62]Erik Erikson, *Young Man Luther* (New York: Norton, 1959), 93, quoted in V. Bailey Gillespie, *The Dynamics of Religious Conversion* (Birmingham: Religious Education Press, 1991), 166. For a brief but interesting comparison of James Loder and James Fowler on the question of spontaneous or gradual transformation in the context of Haughton's work, see Andrew Grannel, "The Paradox of Formation and Transformation," *Religious Education* 80 (1985): 384-98.

[63]Michael H. Crosby, "The Biblical Vision of Conversion," in *The Human Experience of Conversion: Persons and Structures in Transformation*, ed. Francis Eigo (Villanova, Pa.: Villanova University Press, 1987), 53. "Seeking-finding-selling-buying describe the elements within the various parables which describe the stages or process of entering in and experiencing the kingdom."

[64]See Regan, *Toward an Adult Church*, 87. Regan notes four moments in the process of transformative learning: "(1) questioning the present perspective, (2) exploring alternatives, (3) applying the transformed perspective, and (4) reintegrating and grounding of the new perspective." For Lonergan and catechesis, see Groome, *Sharing Faith*, 118.

[65]Crosby, "The Biblical Vision of Conversion," 53. In Mark's version he runs up and kneels before Jesus (Mk 10:17).

[66]Ibid., 57. His " 'finding' or experience of Jesus was not so significant as his riches. His possessions had more authority over him than Jesus' word of invitation." The idea of buying also appears in the parable of the man who finds treasure hidden in a field and then sells everything he has in order to buy the field (Mt 13:45).

[67]Ibid.

[68]Conventional faith as used here is closer to Fowler's "individuative-reflective faith" (stage four) rather than his "synthetic-conventional faith" (stage three). The "embrace of polarities," characteristic of "conjunctive faith" (stage five), approaches the paradoxical logic of transformative catechesis. See James Fowler, "The Vocation of Faith Development Theory," in *Stages of Faith and Religious Development: Implications for Church, Education, and Society*, ed. James Fowler, Karl Ernst Nipkow, Friedrich Schweitzer (New York: Crossroad Publishing, 1991), 25.

[69]Daniel O'Rourke, "The Experience of Conversion" in *The Human Experience of Conversion: Persons and Structures in Transformation*, ed. Francis Eigo (Villanova, Pa.: Villanova University Press, 1987), 13. O'Rourke contrasts the "descriptive" with the "religious" views of conversion.

[70]*GDC*, no. 55. Italics in original.

[71]*Our Hearts Were Burning Within Us*, 4.

Contributors

Gerald J. Beyer is a doctoral candidate in the Department of Theology at Boston College. He has studied at Georgetown, Yale, Jagiellonian University, the Pontifical Academy of Theology, and the Academy of Economics in Krakow.

Robert Brancatelli is an Assistant Professor in the Graduate School of Counseling Psychology, Education, and Pastoral Ministries at Santa Clara University, where he teaches courses in catechesis and liturgy. He recently published on Hispanic popular religion in *Worship* and has been awarded a Lilly grant for research on catechesis and liturgical inculturation in El Salvador.

Mary Elsbernd, O.S.F., is Director of the Institute of Pastoral Studies, Loyola University Chicago and Associate Professor in Social Ethics. She received her S.T.D. from Katholieke Universiteit Leuven. A recent publication is *When Love Is Not Enough: A Theo-ethic of Justice* (Liturgical Press, 2002).

Harold E. Ernst is a doctoral student in the Department of Theology at the University of Notre Dame. He received the College Theology Society's 2003 Graduate Student Essay Award for his article, "The Theological Notes and the Interpretation of Doctrine," which appeared in *Theological Studies* in 2002.

Elizabeth Groppe is Assistant Professor of Theology at Xavier University in Cincinnati. She is the author of *Yves Congar's Theology of the Holy Spirit*, the American Academy of Religion Academy Series (Oxford University Press, 2003).

Dennis Hamm, S.J., is Professor in the Department of Theology at Creighton University. Most of his publications have focused on Luke-Acts, including his commentary on the Acts of the Apostles forthcoming in the Collegeville Bible Commentary.

Bernd Jochen Hilberath is Professor of Dogmatic Theology and the History of Dogma and Director of the Institute for Ecumenical Research at the University of Tübingen, Germany. His many books include *Heiliger Geist—heilender Geist* (Matthias-Grünewald, 1988), *Pneumatologie* (Patmos, 1994), *Karl Rahner: Gottgeheimnis Mensch* (Matthias-Grünewald, 1995), *Zwischen Vision and Wirklichkeit: Fragen nach dem Weg der Kirche* (Echter, 1999), and co-authored with Matthias Scharer, *Kommunikative Theologie: Eine Grundlegung* (Matthias-Grünewald, 2002).

Bradford E. Hinze is Associate Professor of Theology at Marquette University. He is the author of *Narrating History, Developing Doctrine: Friedrich Schleiermacher and Johann Sebastian Drey*, the American Academy of Religion Academy Series (Oxford University Press, 1993); and co-editor with D. Lyle Dabney, *Advents of the Spirit: An Introduction to the Current Study of Pneumatology* (Marquette University Press, 2001). His current research and writing is on the shift to a dialogical and trinitarian approach to the church's identity and mission.

Jane E. Linahan is Assistant Professor of Systematic Theology at Saint Francis Seminary in Milwaukee. She completed her Ph.D. at Marquette University with a dissertation on Jürgen Moltmann's theology of kenosis.

Maria Teresa Morgan serves on the theology faculty at St. John Vianney College Seminary, Miami. She holds a D.Min. from Barry University. Her research and praxis focus on theological method involving images, symbols, and metaphors.

Dawn M. Nothwehr, O.S.F., is Assistant Professor of Ethics at the Catholic Theological Union, Chicago. Mutuality, feminist ethics of power, ecological ethics, and Franciscan theology are her major interests. Her books include: *Mutuality: A Formal Norm For Christian Social Ethics* (Catholic Scholars Press,

1998), and *Franciscan Theology of the Environment: An Introductory Reader* (Franciscan Press, 2003).

Jamie T. Phelps, O.P., is Professor of Systematic Theology and the Director of the Institute for Black Catholic Studies of Xavier University of Louisiana. She is the editor of *Black and Catholic: The Challenge and Gift of Black Folk* (Marquette University Press, 1998) and co-editor with Cyprian Davis, O.S.B., of *Stamped with the Image of God: An African American Catholic Documentary History*, the American Catholic Identities Series (Orbis Books, 2004). She is currently working on a book on communion and trinitarian theology and its significance for social transformation.

Robert J. Schreiter, C.PP.S., is the Bernardin Center Vatican Council II Chair in Theology at the Catholic Theological Union, Chicago, and Professor of Systematic Theology at the University of Nijmegen, Netherlands. His many books include *Constructing Local Theologies* (1985), *Reconciliation: Mission and Ministry in a Changing Social Order* (1992), *The New Catholicity: Theology Between the Global and the Local* (1997), and *The Ministry of Reconciliation: Spirituality and Strategies* (1998), all published by Orbis Books.